WE MAY HAVE LESS TIME THAN YOU THINK

Susan Roy
BOMBOOZLED!™

How the U.S. government misled itself
and its people into believing they could
survive a nuclear attack

Editorial Director: Suzanne Slesin

Design: Stafford Cliff

Production: Dominick J. Santise, Jr.

Managing Editor: Regan Toews

POINTED LEAF PRESS, LLC.
WWW.POINTEDLEAFPRESS.COM

PAGE 1 A drawing published in the New York State Civil Defense Commission booklet, *Survival in a Nuclear Attack*, used arrows to represent the routes that Soviet missiles carrying nuclear bombs would use to attack sites in the United States. The purpose of the sixty-six-page publication was to persuade New York residents to support the state's proposed extensive (and expensive) Civil Defense policies, which would have required every residence and business to be equipped with a fallout shelter.

PREVIOUS PAGE LEFT A terrified man reacts to an atomic bomb explosion in the Civil Defense film *Living with the Threat*.

RIGHT A vintage postcard of the Atomic Bomb exhibit at the Air Force Museum at the Wright-Patterson Air Force Base near Dayton, Ohio, depicts replicas of the first and only atomic weapons ever used in war. At right is "Fat Man," the atomic bomb the United States dropped on the city of Hiroshima, Japan, on August 6, 1945. At left is "Little Boy," the atomic bomb that was dropped three days later on Nagasaki, Japan.

OVERLEAF The nuclear paranoia that gripped the nation is evident in this posed photograph of a man who has taken every possible precaution to protect himself during an atomic attack. Wearing a gas mask and a full-body plastic jumpsuit, he is entering his underground shelter. Once inside, he will close the hatch tightly to seal it against radioactive fallout.

CONTENTS

BOB DYLAN'S NUCLEAR LAMENT

During the early years of the Cold War, when the world lived in the shadow of the atomic bomb, songwriter Bob Dylan had his own strategy for survival. He kept a Geiger counter—a device for measuring lethal radioactivity—in his New York City apartment. He explained why in his 2004 memoir, *Chronicles, Volume 1*: After a nuclear attack, the device "might become your most prized possession, telling you what's safe to eat and what's dangerous." Dylan was outraged by the government's campaign to persuade Americans they could survive nuclear war by building fallout shelters. In 1962 he wrote a song that forcefully and clearly expressed his opinions called, "Let Me Die in My Footsteps."

I will not go down under the ground
'Cause somebody tells me that death's comin' 'round
An' I will not carry myself down to die
When I go to my grave my head will be high
Let me die in my footsteps
Before I go down under the ground

There's been rumors of war and wars that have been
The meaning of life has been lost in the wind
And some people thinkin' that the end is close by
'Stead of learnin' to live they are learnin' to die
Let me die in my footsteps
Before I go down under the ground

I don't know if I'm smart but I think I can see
When someone is pullin' the wool over me
And if this war comes and death's all around
Let me die on this land 'fore I die underground
Let me die in my footsteps
Before I go down under the ground

There's always been people that have to cause fear
They've been talking of the war now for many long years
I have read all their statements and I've not said a word
But now, Lawd God, let my poor voice be heard
Let me die in my footsteps
Before I go down under the ground

If I had rubies and riches and crowns
I'd buy the whole world and change things around
I'd throw all the guns and the tanks in the sea
For they are mistakes of a past history
Let me die in my footsteps
Before I go down under the ground

Let me drink from the waters where the mountain streams flood
Let the smell of wildflowers flow free through my blood
Let me sleep in your meadows with the green grassy leaves
Let me walk down the highway with my brother in peace
Let me die in my footsteps
Before I go down under the ground

Go out in your country where the land meets the sun
See the craters and the canyons where the waterfalls run
Nevada, New Mexico, Arizona, Idaho
Let every state in this union seep down deep in your souls
And you'll die in your footsteps
Before you go down under the ground

PREVIOUS PAGES An enormous mushroom cloud was created by the Baker atomic bomb test on July 25, 1946, that was detonated over the Marshall Islands in the Pacific. The bomb vaporized one entire island.

OPPOSITE In December 1946, the cover of *Arts & Architecture* magazine visually represented atomic anxiety in a photo-illustration created by the prominent twentieth-century graphic designer Herbert Matter. He imagined a mushroom cloud inside the silhouette of a man's head facing the Earth.

DECEMBER 1946

arts & architecture

PRICE 50 CENTS

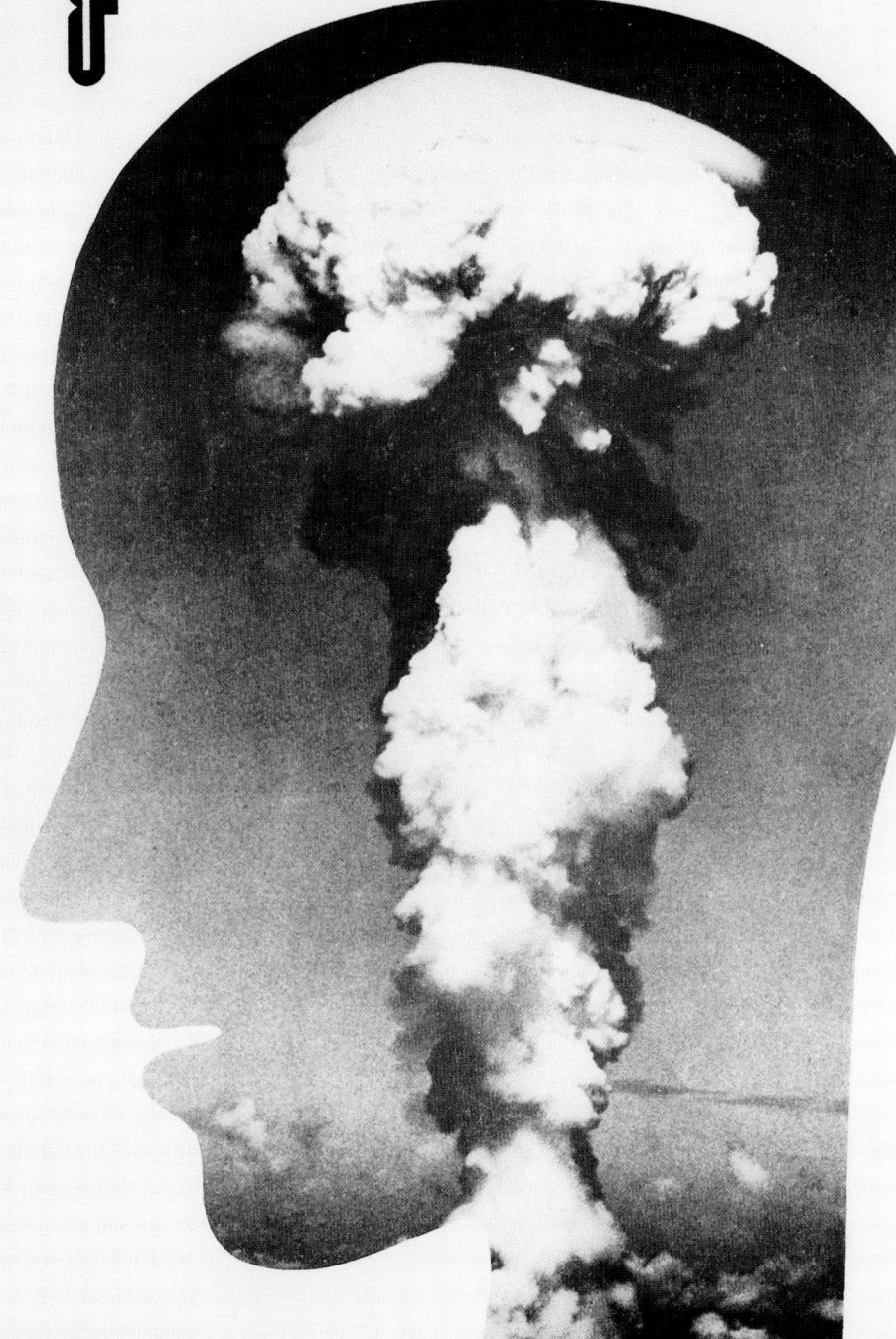

matter

SCIENTISTS WARN OF WORLD SUICIDE

Radioactive Dust of One H-Bomb Could Prove Enough to Kill Everyone, Is Experts' Opinion

NEW YORK, Feb. 26 (AP)—The hydrogen bomb, if it works, could easily be made a suicide bomb to kill everyone in the world, four top atomic scientists warned today.

At the same time they said it would be another three years before it is even known whether such a bomb can be produced.

If and when such a bomb is made, it could kill slowly by poisoning everything and everyone with radioactive dusts.

The dusts would be carried around the world by the winds.

The dust would be in the air people breathed.

It would settle onto and poison plants and trees, everything humans ate or used.

Fantastic Killer

You could intentionally rig an H-bomb to do thi~
~"

of Illinois; Dr. Leo Szilard, biophysicist, and Dr. Harrison Brown, chemist, both of the University of Chicago.

One Bomb Enough

They told of the suicide bomb in a University of Chicago Round Table broadcast, over NBC, originating here.

These are the facts, they said:

The H-bomb, as conceived in theory, would create huge amounts of atomic particles called neutrons. These neutrons can change harmless atoms, like cobalt or carbon, or almost anything, into radioactive, poisonous atom~

ATOMIC ANXIETY

On August 2, 1939, Albert Einstein wrote a letter to President Franklin D. Roosevelt informing him the Nazis were working with the nuclear element uranium to develop "extremely powerful bombs of a new type." Einstein recommended to the President that the United States do the same.

That letter started the United States on a journey that ended on July 16, 1945, in Alamogordo, New Mexico, when the physicists of the Manhattan Project prepared to detonate the world's first atomic bomb. No one knew exactly what would happen after it exploded. One scientist feared it could create a chain reaction that would blow up the entire planet.

The test was successful. The bomb went off. The scientists who created it were stunned by its destructive power. Some time later, haunted by the memory, Manhattan Project head J. Robert Oppenheimer ruefully recalled a line from

the Hindu devotional work, the Bhagavad Gita, that had leapt into his mind after the blast: "Now, I am become Death, the destroyer of worlds."

The bomb was no longer needed as a weapon to be used against Hitler. Germany had surrendered two months prior. But the war against Japan dragged on. President Harry S. Truman decided to use this new weapon. On August 6, 1945, the United States B-29 bomber, the Enola Gay, dropped the first atomic bomb ever used in war on Hiroshima, Japan. Three days later, on August 9th, the United States bombed Nagasaki, a second Japanese city. The bombs killed at least 150,000 people. Both cities were destroyed. Japan surrendered, ending World War II.

Before the invention of the atomic bomb, in order to destroy a city and kill tens of thousands of people, the military would have had to deploy hundreds of planes and drop thousands of conventional bombs, risking the lives of hundreds— perhaps thousands—of American pilots and crewmen. The atomic bomb was more

efficient. The destruction of Hiroshima was accomplished with one bomb, dropped from a single plane carrying 13 crewmen. A horrifying weapon of unprecedented power had been added to the world's arsenal. "Now, with the release of atomic energy," said Henry L. Stimson, the United States Secretary of War in 1947, "man's ability to destroy himself is nearly complete."

After the bombings, the United States government closely controlled the images that were seen by the American people. There were photographs of the ruins in the destroyed cities, but few if any photographs of the injured or dead. The full impact of the human suffering caused by the atomic bomb only hit home the following year, in 1946, when Americans read John Hersey's "Hiroshima," published first as an article in the *New Yorker,* and then later that year as a best-selling book. After interviewing many survivors of the attack, Hersey chose to tell the story of the bombing as it was described by six Japanese citizens—two Christian clergymen, a widowed mother of three, a female office worker and two physicians. No longer were the victims an anonymous and invisible mass. They were individuals.

Hersey's book made it painfully clear that the bomb did far more than destroy buildings. In the bomb's blast and the firestorms, human beings were instantly incinerated, leaving behind a ghostly shadow on the steps where they had been sitting. Others were burned to death. Still others received surface burns that ate away their skin and caused them to lose their hair and, over a period of days, weeks or years, die painfully of a disease that the United States government was reluctant to admit existed: radiation sickness. Now that Americans had a vivid picture of what the bomb did to its victims, they could imagine what it could do to them.

In 1946, Americans could be comfortable in the knowledge that the United States was the only nation on earth that possessed the atom bomb. But that security blanket of invulnerability was yanked away three years later, on August 29, 1949, when the U.S.S.R.—the nation's new Cold War enemy—detonated its first atomic bomb. America's nuclear monopoly had come to an end, and its citizens suddenly faced a frightening new reality: We could be the target of an atomic attack! This terrifying realization unleashed a national firestorm of atomic anxiety. Would the Russians attack? When? Where would they drop their bombs? On cities? On manufacturing centers? On harbors? Would we know they were coming? What would we do? Where would we go? Could we protect ourselves? And if so, how?

On April 2, 1952, an estimated thirty-five million Americans got their first look at a live detonation of an atomic bomb. Tests at the nation's nuclear test site, the Nevada Proving Grounds outside of Las Vegas, were usually top secret. This test was an exception. It was open to the press and nationally televised. Though the exact size of the bomb remained classified, observers estimated that it had

the same destructive power as the bombs dropped on Hiroshima and Nagasaki. Gene Sherman, a reporter for the *Los Angeles Times* who witnessed the blast, described what happened. First, there was "brilliance at least 50 times the sun's for a fractional instant." Thirty seconds later, "the observation point was rocked by a terrific crash, like the lash of an invisible giant whip. With the shock came...the long rumble of atomic violence. It echoed across the floor of the basin and bounced menacingly between the mountain rims. And then, ten miles away, bloomed the deadly mushroom."

In his final State of the Union address in 1953, President Truman—the man who ordered the dropping of the bombs on Japan—warned of the unimaginable ramifications of a war fought with nuclear weapons. "The war of the future would be one in which man could extinguish millions of lives at one blow, demolish the great cities of the world, wipe out the cultural achievements of the past," Truman said, "and destroy the very structure of a civilization that has been slowly and painfully built up through hundreds of generations."

As atomic paranoia raced across the nation, the media's imagination went wild. Magazines and newspapers were filled with dire scenarios of nuclear apocalypse. In 1951, the national mass magazine *Collier's* devoted an entire issue to a "Preview of the War We Do Not Want." It hired prominent journalists and writers—broadcaster Edward R. Murrow, political novelist Arthur Koestler, and historian Allan Nevins, among them—to write first-person accounts describing "The Third World War," as though it had already happened. In its February 27, 1950, issue, *Life* devoted seventeen pages to a section called "War Can Come: Will We Be Ready?"

No one was immune to atomic anxiety. The *New York Times* published an article on November 6, 1951, entitled "Young React to the Fear of Radiation." Reporter Phyllis

Ehrlich wrote, "Last week, a six-year-old boy was found busily digging a hole in the smooth lawn in front of his home. 'What are you doing?' his horrified mother asked. Without stopping, the boy answered, 'I'm digging a big hole in the ground to hide from the bomb!'"

Newspapers fanned the flames of the nation's bomb fever. On July 20, 1956, readers of the *Buffalo Evening News* were shocked to read this front-page headline: "125,000 Known Dead, Downtown in Ruins," followed by a subhead, "2 Nuclear Bombs Hit Buffalo and Northern Suburbs: Damage Heavy." In smaller type, at the top of the page, a headline said, "Warning: This Didn't Happen...But It Could!" Similar articles were published in the *Los Angeles Times*, the *Chicago Tribune*, and other newspapers.

The entertainment industry was quick to exploit America's nuclear obsession. In the 1953 film, *The Beast from 20,000 Fathoms*, a bomb explosion in the Arctic awakens a dinosaur that then attacks New York City. In the 1954 film, *Them*, radiation from atom-bomb tests transforms common ants into giant killing monsters. Man's feeling of powerlessness in the face of the nuclear threat is poignantly evoked in the 1957 film, *The Incredible Shrinking Man*. In it, after passing through a cloud of radiation from a bomb test, a man gradually, and inexorably, becomes tinier and tinier until he becomes infinitesimally small, leaving everyone and everything he knows behind.

Clearly, the U.S. government had an enormous problem. How could it reassure its terror-stricken citizens—assaulted by images and stories of apocalypse everywhere they turned—that the government could protect them in the face of the worst threat to mankind that ever existed?

OPPOSITE An illustration in the 1953 government publication *What About You and Civil Defense?* shows the threats posed to the United States by its Cold War adversary, the U.S.S.R.

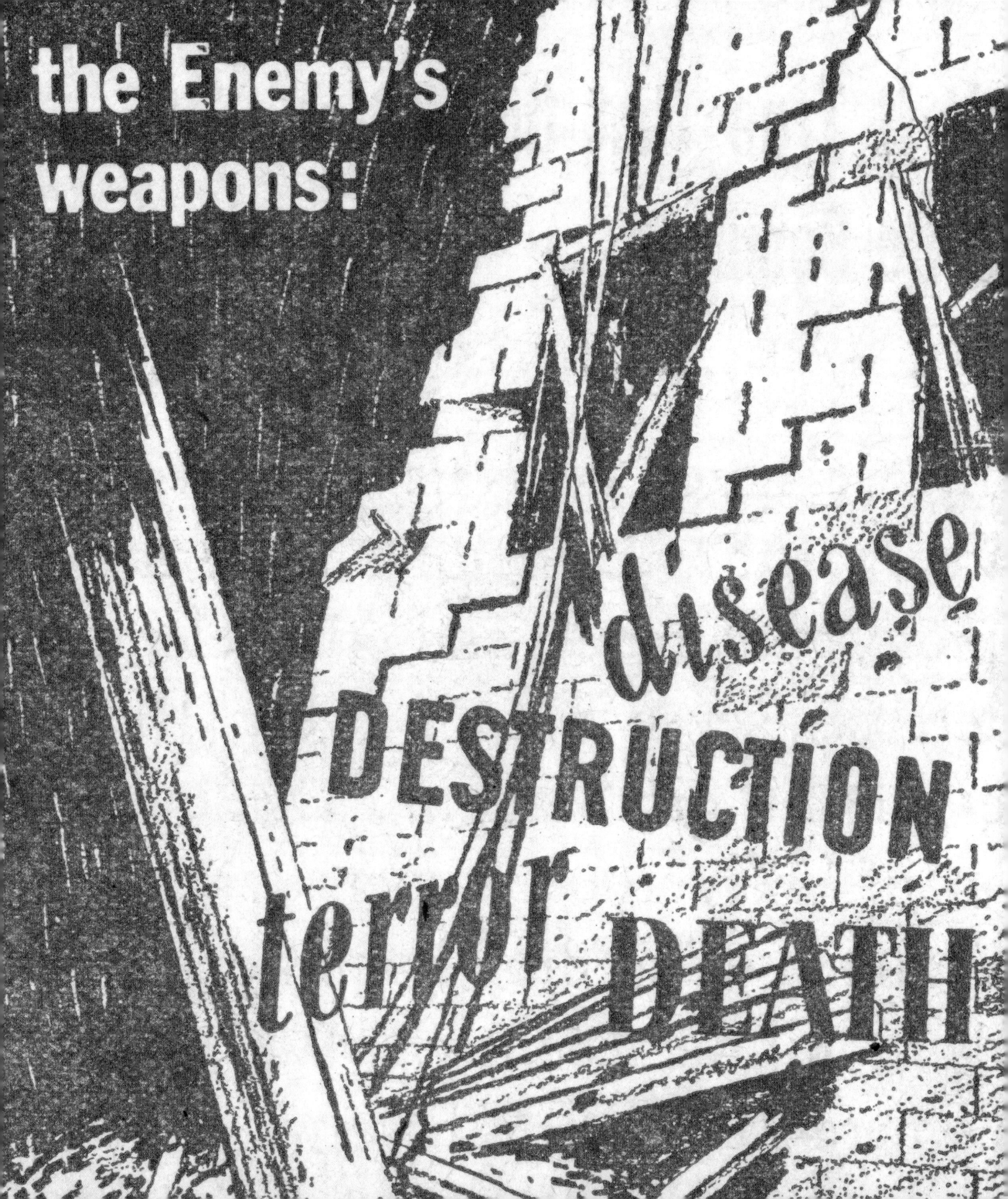

Collier's

15c

August 5, 1950

HIROSHIMA, U.S.A.

Can Anything Be Done About It?

LEFT The cover of the August 5, 1950, issue of *Collier's,* with the headline "Hiroshima, U.S.A.: Can Anything Be Done About It?" featured an illustration by Chesley Bonestell that imagined the island of Manhattan immediately following an atomic attack. An emblematic mushroom cloud of the atomic bomb rises into the sky as firestorms race across the city.

OPPOSITE An illustration in the official government report on the Operation Crossroads atomic bomb tests over the Marshall Islands in the Pacific used the New York City skyline to indicate the scale of the unexpectedly gigantic blast that was created by the Baker detonation on July 25, 1946.

OVERLEAF Flames engulf New York City in Bonestall's painting for *Collier's* article, "Hiroshima, U.S.A.: Can Anything be Done About It?" The article, by John Lear, presented an alarming fictional account of an attack on New York City and was intended to motivate readers to pressure state, local, and federal governments to develop plans for protecting its citizens. The caption described the devastation wrought by the bomb: "A cloud of black grime masked the lower city. Where 100,000 people had lived—in an area roughly fifteen blocks long and twenty blocks across—there was now an ugly brown-red scar. Beyond the rim of the scar, thousands of fires were lighted."

VISED IT WILL FILE FROM HERE SHORTLY. . . BULLETIN -- HOBOKEN N J -- DOCK WORKERS ON THE NEW JERSEY

GRIM PICTURE OF BOMB HIT IN LOOP IS GIVEN

You'd Need a Shelter 1,000 Feet Deep!

(Nuclear scientists say Chicagoans could survive a direct hit by an H-bomb—if we are prepared to pay the price. In this, the fourth of a series of articles, The Tribune examines the shelter problem.)

BY HOWARD JAMES

If a 10 megaton bomb struck at State and Madison streets, it would leave a crater 300 feet deep and a half mile wide. The crater would run as far north as Lake street, as far south as Jackson boulevard, as far east as the Illinois Central railroad tracks, and as far west as La Salle street.

Only the stubs of buildings would be left as far north as Division street, as far south as 16th street, as far east as the

How underground shelter can be constructed next to basement.

lake, and as far west as Racine avenue.

Yet people at the corner of State and Madison could survive, if they were in an adequate shelter.

What Nuclear Bomb Would Do to Chicago

12 MILE AREA: LIGHT DAMAGE TO BUILDINGS 90% SURVIVAL

SEVEN MILE AREA: CONCRETE BUILDINGS DAMAGED PERSONS IN BASEMENT SHELTERS SURVIVE; 50% OF UNSHIELDED PERSONS SURVIVE

FOUR MILE AREA: FEW BUILDINGS REMAIN, FEWER SURVIVORS

CRATER HALF MILE WIDE, 300 FT. DEEP

ALL DEAD EXCEPT PERSONS IN SHELTERS 1,000 FT. UNDER GROUND

Sketch shows how death and destruction caused by a nuclear bomb dropped at State and Madison streets would diminish at increasing distances from the blast site. Adequate shelters would save many lives.

Scientists Give Opinion

This is the opinion of three scientists of Armour Research Foundation at the Illinois Institute of Technology. The three, Dr. Eugene Sevin, Arne Wiedermann, and Kieth McKee, have taken part in the United States nuclear testing program for the last 10 years, and have studied the effects of a nuclear blast on buildings similar to those in Chicago.

To survive at ground zero, or in the crater area, they explained, a person would have to be in a tunnel approximately 1,000 feet below the surface [less if in rock]. Then he would have to be prepared to dig his way out after the blast.

tween you and the fallout will cut down the amount of radiation that reaches you," the booklet states. "Sufficient mass will make you safe.

List Protective Materials

"Concrete or bricks, earth or sand, are some of the materials heavy enough to afford protection by absorbing radiation. There is about the same amount of shielding in eight inches of concrete, for instance, as in 12 inches of earth, 16 inches of books, or 30 inches of wood. In most of the country, everywhere except in areas hit by heaviest fallout, these thicknesses would give ample protection for a basement shelter."

The booklet, entitled "The Family Fallout Shelter," is available free at the Chicago civil defense office, 140 S.

and general home protection are also available. The Chicago office will mail out a complete kit to all those who request it.

The city council passed an ordinance Friday during an emergency session to establish specifications for fallout shelters. The building department will charge a $15 fee for a construction permit, and the ordinance requires approval of shelter plans by building and fire departments.

Cost of fallout shelter materials would range from $700 to $1,500, according to Building Commissioner George L. Ramsey. Package plans at various prices also are being advanced by private contractors and construction companies, some of which would include food, bottled water, and medicine.

OPPOSITE An article headlined "Grim Picture of Bomb Hit In Loop is Given" in the August 23, 1961 issue of the *Chicago Tribune* presented predictions of what a hydrogen bomb attack would do to the city. The scenario was based on interviews with nuclear scientists at the Armour Foundation at the Illinois Institute of Technology. A hydrogen bomb that exploded in central Chicago would create a crater 300 feet deep and a half-mile wide—"as far north as Lake Street, as far south as Jackson Boulevard, as far east as the Illinois Central railroad tracks, and as far west as La Salle Street." The scientists said the only possible way to save Chicagoans would be to construct "a network of tunnels about 1,000 feet below the ground" which would cost "hundreds of thousands of billions of dollars."

RIGHT A page in the *Seattle Civil Defense Manual* published in the early 1950s graphically depicts the destruction that would result from nuclear attacks. The silhouetted drawing, top, shows damage extending two miles from the site of the detonation. A chart, left, describes the potential damage in more detail. A map, far right, shows specifically how the extent of the damage would vary depending on which area of the city a bomb hit.

ATOM BOMB EXPLOSION
BLAST DAMAGE

| GROUND ZERO | COMPLETE DESTRUCTION | ½ MILE | SEVERE DAMAGE | 1 MILE | MODERATE DAMAGE | 1⅝ MILES | PARTIAL DAMAGE | 2 MILES | LIGHT DAMAGE |

BLAST DAMAGE CHART
(Air Burst) (AEC)

Feet	Damage	(Statistics relate to Japanese explosions.)
0	Ground Zero — or directly beneath the air burst.	
1,500	Mass distortion of heavy steel frame buildings.	
2,000	Limit of severe structural damage to earthquake resistant reinforced concrete buildings.	
2,500	To this point virtually complete destruction of all buildings, other than reinforced concrete.	
3,500	18-inch brick walls completely destroyed.	
4,000	Roof tiles melted by heat.	
4,500	Light concrete buildings collapsed.	
5,000	12-inch brick walls severely cracked.	
5,500	Electrical installations and trolley cars destroyed.	
6,000	Severe damage to entire area. Severe structural damage to steel frame buildings.	
6,600	Structural damage to multistory brick buildings.	
8,000	Severe damage to homes, heavy damage to window frames and doors, foliage scorched.	
8,300	Moderate damage to area.	
9,000	Heavy plaster damage.	
10,000	Blast damage to majority of homes. Severe fire damage. Flash ignition of combustible materials.	
10,300	Partial damage to structures in area.	
11,000	Flash charring of telegraph poles.	
12,000	Light damage to window frames and doors, moderate plaster damage.	
8 MILES	Limit of light damage.	

While giant skyscrapers with reinforced concrete structures and long periods of vibration should withstand the shock very well the masonry would be stripped off, girders twisted and people literally blown out of the top floors

BLAST DAMAGE AREA

■ Total Destruction ▨ Major Damage
▨ Damage Beyond Repair ▫ Minor Damage

Hypothetical atom bombing problem as worked out in Seattle, July, 1950.

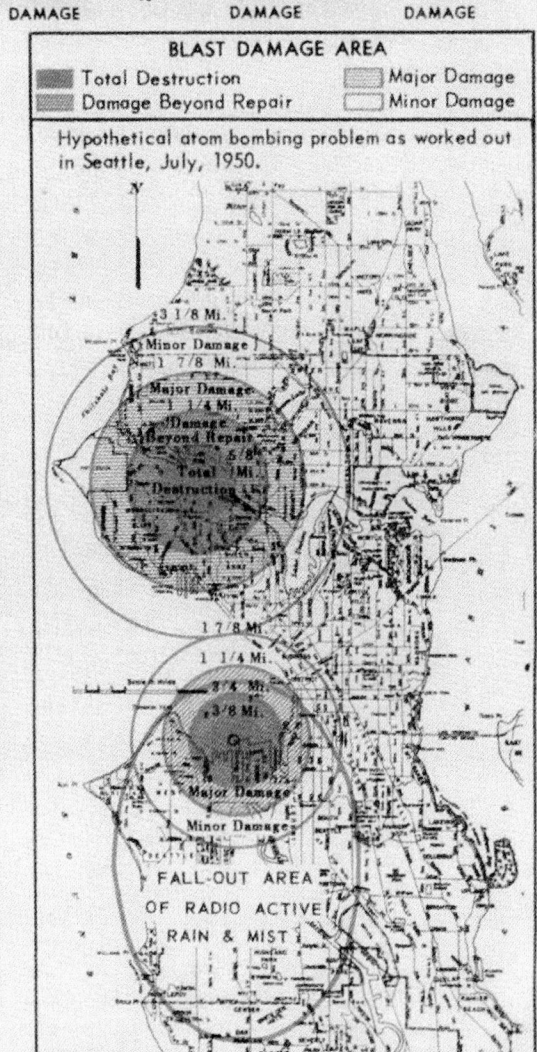

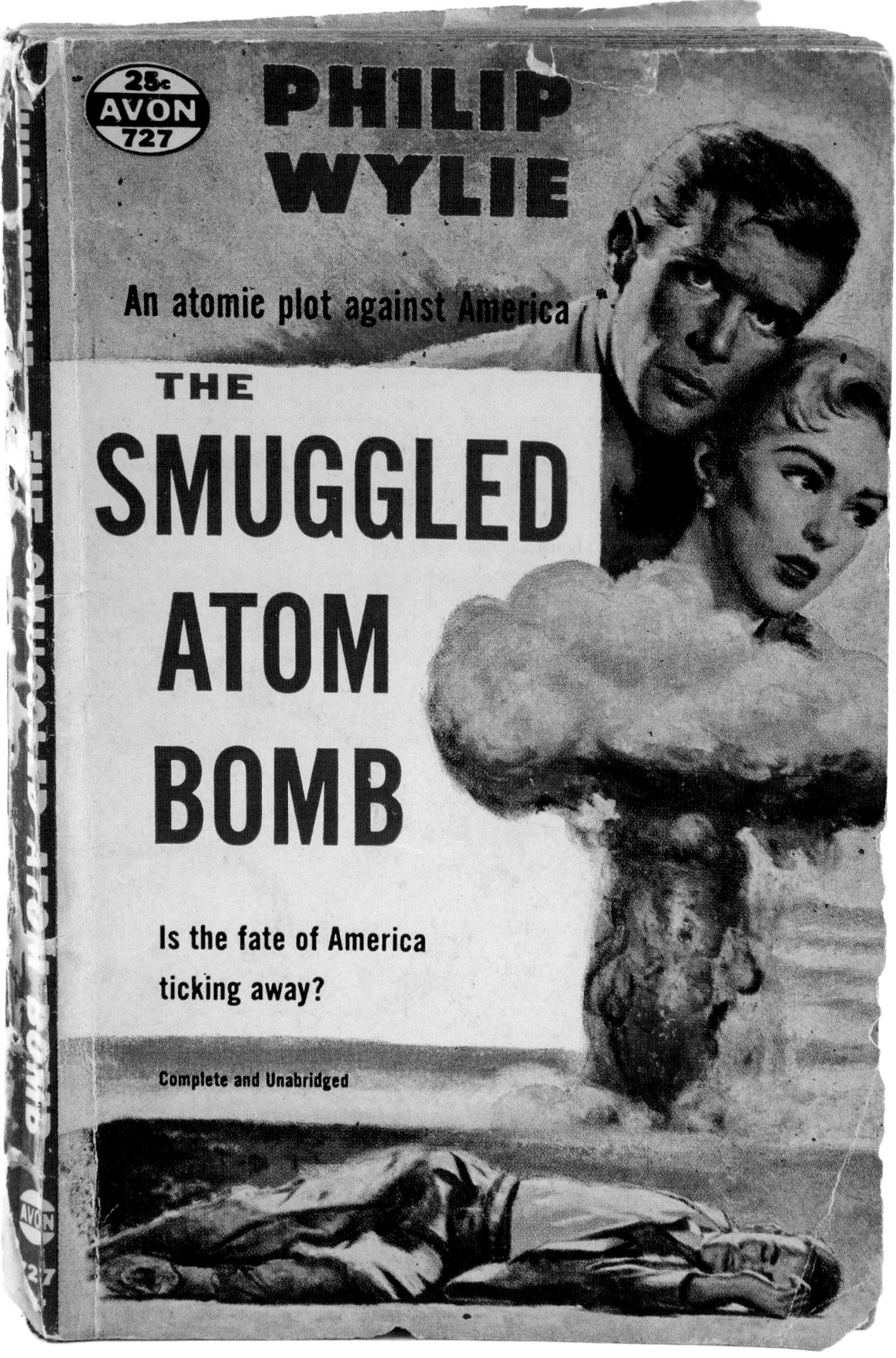

The cover illustration includes:

25¢ AVON 727

PHILIP WYLIE

An atomic plot against America

THE SMUGGLED ATOM BOMB

Is the fate of America ticking away?

Complete and Unabridged

LEFT The cover of the 1951 paperback book, *The Smuggled Atom Bomb,* shows the mushroom cloud hovering in the foreground above an illustration of a corpse. The story involves a graduate student who discovers a Soviet scheme to sneak briefcase-sized bombs into American cities.

RIGHT Two figures cower as a cloud rises over an unnamed city on the cover of *Doomsday Eve*. Written in 1956, this novel was set in the year 2020 in a post-apocalyptic world where people lived under the threat of a new "superbomb" that could destroy all life on earth.

ACE
DOUBLE NOVEL
BOOKS

D-215

TWO COMPLETE NOVELS 35c

WERE THESE STRANGERS IMPERVIOUS TO H-BOMBS?

DOOMSDAY EVE

ROBERT MOORE WILLIAMS

Complete & Unabridged

"IT WILL SCARE THE PANTS OFF YOU!" ....Hedda Hopper

COLUMBIA PICTURES presents

INVASION, U.S.A.

SEE New York topple!

SEE San Francisco in flame!

SEE Boulder Dam destroyed!

LEFT The poster for the 1952 film, *Invasion, U.S.A.*, which exploited fears of the Communist threat, tried to entice viewers by promoting its scenes of spectacular destruction: "See New York topple! See San Francisco in flame! See Boulder Dam destroyed!" In the low-budget black-and-white movie, the United States is attacked by an aggressor referred to only as "the enemy," but which is obviously the U.S.S.R.

OPPOSITE A monstrous ant threatens a cowering woman in a scene from the 1954 black-and-white science-fiction film, *Them!*, which starred James Whitmore, Edmund Gwenn, Joan Weldon, and James Arness. The ants, once normal-sized, were transformed into giant killers by radioactivity from atomic bomb tests. The story was set near Alamogordo, New Mexico, the city where the Manhattan Project created and tested the world's first atomic bomb.

"Mummy, what happens to us if the bomb drops?"

She looks to you for a real answer. She knows what she must do when the sirens sound at school. But what happens if they sound when she's at home? Will you be ready, like teacher is? Ready to protect her from harm? Ready to help her if she is hurt?

An atomic blast is something like a tornado, a fire and an explosion all rolled into one. Any of these may happen any day. They do happen every day, somewhere. But when they happen all at once, lots of people get hurt. Everybody needs help at the same time—and it may be hours before it comes to your home.

U. S. Civil Defense, working with doctors and atomic scientists, has developed a list of "must" disaster first-aid supplies. These few simple items may already be in your home or, if not, you can get them at any drug counter. For the sake of your children, your neighbors and yourself, these supplies should be in your home—and you should know how to use them.

BE SURE YOU HAVE THESE OFFICIAL DISASTER FIRST-AID ITEMS

- ☐ 4 Triangular Bandages
- ☐ 12 Sterile Gauze Pads (3" x 3")
- ☐ 1 Gauze Bandage (2" x 10 yds.)
- ☐ 1 Gauze Bandage (1" x 10 yds.)
- ☐ 2 Large Emergency Dressings (7 1/2" x 8")
- ☐ 100 Water-Purification Tablets (4 mg.)
- ☐ 3 oz. Antiseptic, Benzalkonium Chloride
- ☐ 1 oz. Aromatic Spirits of Ammonia
- ☐ 1 oz. Castor Oil Eye Drops
- ☐ 50 Sodium Chloride Tablets (10 gr.)
- ☐ 50 Sodium Bicarbonate Tablets (5 gr.)
- ☐ 12 Wooden Tongue Blades

Get free booklet "Emergency Action To Save Lives" from your drug counter or local Civil Defense Director.

  SPONSOR'S NAME

LEFT A worried young girl asks, "Mummy, what happens to us if the bomb drops?" in a public service newspaper advertisement produced by the Advertising Council. The question makes an eye-catching headline, but the text of the advertisement doesn't actually address the question. Instead, it tells mothers to be prepared with an array of first-aid materials should a nuclear attack occur when a child is at home. It also includes a checklist of emergency medical supplies developed by "U.S. Civil Defense, working with doctors and atomic scientists."

OPPOSITE These crayon drawings were done by schoolchildren who witnessed repeated atomic blasts because they lived near the Nevada Proving Grounds, the national bomb testing site outside of Las Vegas. The sketches were published in the June 21, 1952, issue of *Collier's*. In the center is a photograph of an actual mushroom cloud.

Rare, striking color photo of atomic explosion, by Collier's John Florea, is shown with kids' crayon versions. Clockwise from upper left, they're by Gary Buckner, 9; Dick Bower, 13; Lewis Larsen, 9; Charlotte Ray, 12, and Mary Agnes Cordova, 9

ATOMIC BLAST TO TEST FAMILY BOMB SHELTERS

Homes and Autos Set Up for Trials

BY LLOYD NORMAN

[Chicago Tribune Press Service]

Washington, March 14 — An atomic bomb exploded from a 300 foot tower will be used next Tuesday to test 12 family bomb shel-

YOU CAN SURVIVE!

In 1950, President Harry S. Truman created the Federal Civil Defense Administration (FCDA)—the predecessor to today's Department of Homeland Security—to develop strategies and programs that would serve to address American fears about atomic attacks. The public campaigns would first acknowledge that a nuclear attack was possible, and would then offer hope by telling Americans they could learn skills that would save their lives.

These two themes are evident in the 1951 Civil Defense film, *Survival Under Atomic Attack*. First, there is the recognition of the threat: "Let us face, without panic, the reality of our times: the fact that an atom bomb may someday be dropped on our cities."

Next, learn what to do if the bomb comes, and you will be safe. Specific instructions were delivered by the narrator:

OPPOSITE An article in the March 14, 1953, issue of the *Chicago Tribune* announced plans for the first government atomic bomb tests of home shelters.

If there's an impending attack, you'll hear a warning, a warbling siren blast that will last three minutes. If you are outdoors, run to the nearest building and go to the basement or cellar. If there is no building nearby, fall flat on the ground, face down, with your hands clasped tightly behind your head. Whatever you do, don't look at the bomb's bright light flash—it could blind you. If you're at home, close the front and back doors, but don't lock them. Shut the valve on the gas line. Pull the curtains. Turn off electrical appliances.

Then, in an astonishing turnabout scenario of "blame the victim," the film offered the promise of survival: "If the people of Hiroshima and Nagasaki knew what we know about civil defense, thousands of lives would have been saved."

These early campaigns to calm fears backfired. Not only did they fail to reassure Americans, they frightened people more by reinforcing the enormity of the threat. This was a paradox that the government would repeatedly attempt to resolve in its attempts to quell atomic anxiety: How could it

describe the dangers of a nuclear attack vividly enough to convince people to take action without, at the same time, convincing them that such an overwhelming force makes any action futile?

In search of a solution to this dilemma, the government turned to Associated Universities, Inc., a consortium of eight universities—Columbia, Cornell, Harvard, the University of Pennsylvania, Yale, Johns Hopkins, the Massachusetts Institute of Technology, and the University of Rochester. In 1952, the think tank delivered its findings in a 10-volume top-secret publication called *Report of Project East River*. The report recommended that the government change its message. Stop telling people what to do when the bomb drops. Instead, focus on the time *after* an attack, implicitly delivering a positive message: You will survive.

Notably, these recommendations did not address what actually needed to be done—if anything *could* be done—to protect Americans during and after a nuclear attack. Instead, they suggested ways to control

25¢ March, 1951

Russian Guns: How Good?

Save this Issue:

How to Build A "Family Foxhole"

American fears about nuclear attacks by channeling those anxieties into activity. It was a campaign of "emotion management," a campaign designed to give its citizens freedom from fear of the bomb.

The focus shifted to what you need to do now to prepare for life *after* an attack. Assemble a first-aid kit. Create "Grandma's Pantry" and stock it with emergency food supplies and water. Drill your family in emergency procedures.

It continued into the community. The newly created FCDA would work with state and local authorities to train and mobilize a civilian force of volunteers that could take over all functions necessary for the continuation of civilization after a nuclear attack. Every neighborhood would have a Civil Defense Warden to manage local mobilization. Training in first aid, firefighting, police procedures, and emergency rescue would be given in local schools and municipal buildings. Full-scale emergency drills—with and without warning—would be held. These real-life simulated attack scenarios would test the skills of the new Citizen Cold Warrior. A nuclear attack is simply another disaster, like a forest fire, flood, or earthquake. Bad? Yes. Insurmountable? No.

Millions of schoolchildren saw *Duck and Cover*, one of the earliest Civil Defense films. It expressed the two themes that are at the heart of every Civil Defense campaign: *Be Prepared. Stay Alert.* Follow these two simple rules, and there would be nothing to fear from atomic attacks. You will survive! The film opens with Bert the Turtle, a cartoon character walking upright along a path. A monkey in a tree dangles a flaming firecracker frightfully close to Bert's head.

OPPOSITE The cover story of the March 1951 issue of *Popular Science*, a do-it-yourself magazine for men, told its readers how to build a "family foxhole" in their homes to protect themselves and their loved ones in the event of an atomic attack.

Bert spots the firecracker, drops belly-down to the ground and pulls his head, arms, and legs into his shell. With a flash of light, the firecracker explodes! But Bert, enclosed in his shell, is unscathed. "Bert is a very, very careful fellow," the narrator intones. "When there's danger, this is the way he keeps from being hurt. Sometimes it even saves his life." The film cuts to a classroom full of kids and the narrator says, "That's why these children are practicing duck and cover, just as you do in your school." At the teacher's command, the kids dive under their desks, crouch down, and lock their hands behind their heads to create a "shield" against the atomic bomb.

The film, which uses a goofy cartoon turtle to calm American anxieties about the most destructive weapon ever known to man, exemplifies the bizarre disconnect that pervaded government "preparedness" campaigns. The strategy was to normalize the idea of nuclear attack by integrating it into everyday life. Yes, the narrator acknowledges, we are threatened by the atomic bomb. But we are accustomed to threats. "Fire is a danger. It can burn whole buildings if someone is careless. But we are ready for fire. We have a fine fire department to put out the fire." Lesson: If we can extinguish fires, we can handle the atomic bomb. Learn what happens when an atomic bomb hits. "There's a bright flash, brighter than the sun, brighter than anything you've ever seen. If you were not ready, if you did not know what to do, it could hurt you in different ways. It could knock you down, hard. Or throw you against a tree or a wall….But if you duck and cover, like Bert, you will be much safer."

Stay Alert. Be Prepared. The Federal Civil Defense Administration (FCDA) blanketed the country with this message using every possible medium: pamphlets, booklets, posters, newspapers, magazines, filmstrips, movies, radio and television.

At first, "preparedness" only required following a few rules. But the government was constantly ratcheting up the requirements for "preparedness," part of the strategy of "emotion management." The way to relieve anxieties was to create more activities. So knowing how and where to seek emergency shelter wasn't enough. Now you must designate and equip an area in the home to serve as a nuclear refuge, by installing shelving, cots, a first-aid kit, and a three-day supply of food and water. Soon, adapting part of your home was no longer enough. Now, to assure the safety of yourself and your family, you must build a permanent structure: a dedicated bomb shelter.

In addition to managing emotions by creating time-demanding activities on domestic, local, state, and national levels, the emphasis on preparing for post attack life served a political purpose. If Americans could be convinced to embrace the government's Civil Defense programs, they could also be convinced to support its foreign policy of "deterrence." Under this policy, America would maintain and expand its nuclear arsenal in order to "deter" the enemy from attack. This required spending billions of dollars on a never-ending arms race. The Cold War was the first war that wasn't fought with weapons. Instead, it was a conflict fought by keeping score. The "winner" would be the nation with the most, the biggest, and the best bombs.

The policy of deterrence also required convincing the U.S.S.R. that a nuclear attack would not destroy the United States. Even if tens of millions of Americans were killed, some percentage of the population would survive to rebuild the nation. So the Soviets must believe the United States had a way to shelter its people. It threw the responsibility on its citizens: Every American must prepare for nuclear attack by building a bomb shelter. A man's home would be more than his castle: It would be his bunker.

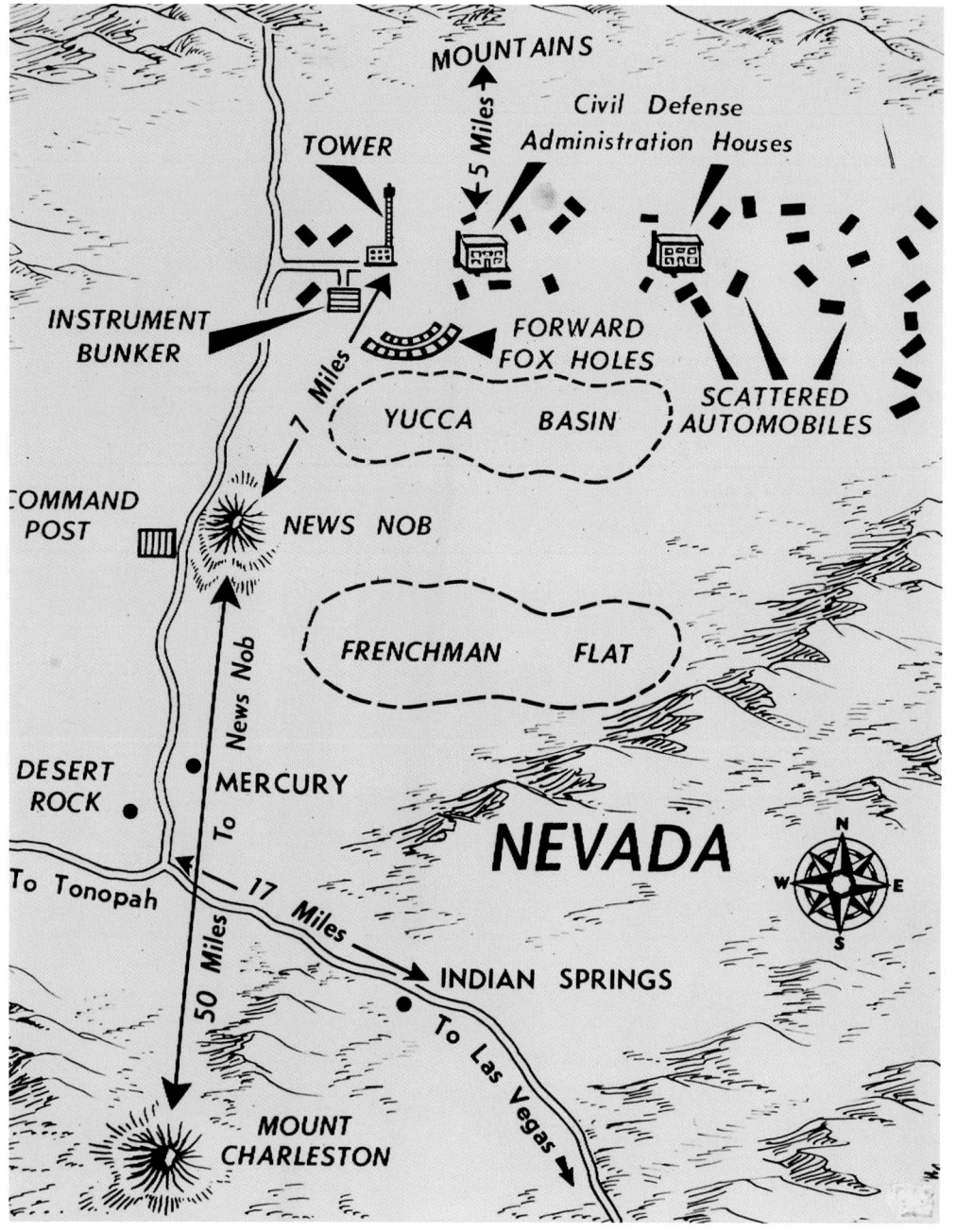

ABOVE An illustrated map shows the layout for the Operation Doorstep atomic bomb test at the Nevada Proving Grounds that took place on March 17, 1953. The shelters tested were in the basements of two wood-frame houses, identified on the map as Civil Defense Administration Houses. Reporters and photographers observed the test from an area called the News Nob, seven miles south of the blast site.

OPPOSITE The atomic bomb for Operation Cue was detonated on May 5, 1955. It was the second Civil Defense test of domestic structures at the Nevada Proving Grounds.

The FCDA orchestrated two remarkable atomic bomb tests in 1953 and 1955. The ostensible goal was to assess the performance of different types of structures in the face of an atomic blast. But the actual goal was to persuade Americans that home shelters would protect them during a nuclear attack. These tests were staged at the Nevada Proving Grounds, 680 square miles of desert about 65 miles from Las Vegas, the primary site for nuclear bomb tests in the United States. While the test site was usually closed to the public, an exception was made for these events. The press was invited and the tests were nationally televised.

The first test, on March 17, 1953, was called Operation Doorstep. Two identical houses were constructed and placed at different distances—a half-mile and a mile-and-a-half—from Ground Zero. They were designed in a reassuringly familiar Cape Cod-*cum*-farmhouse style, with a pitched roof, a red brick chimney, and double-hung windows. In the house further away from Ground Zero, a female mannequin holding a toddler was placed under the lean-to shelter in the basement. A few feet away, a nuclear mannequin family— Dad, Mom and two kids— sat in a box shelter. On the first floor of each house, other mannequins were seated around a dining table, or in the living room. Then an atomic bomb was detonated. The house near Ground Zero was destroyed.

The house farther away from the blast site was damaged, but remained standing. The mannequins in the living and dining rooms were disheveled and broken. But the mannequins, protected by their shelters, were unscathed. Civil Defense trumpeted the news: The test proved that shelters work!

In fact, the test proved nothing of the kind. The houses were not real houses. They were just wooden shells. They had no electric wiring, gas pipes, or oil burners, all of which would have immediately burst into flames from the heat of the blast. *Time* pointed out that human beings, unlike mannequins, are vulnerable to the deadly effects of radiation: "Just after the explosion, a cloud of radioactive dust settled over both houses. People huddled in the basement shelters would certainly have been killed by this silent, insidious force."

This second Civil Defense test of houses, conducted on May 5, 1955, was more elaborate than the one performed two years earlier. FCDA officials created a neighborhood called "Doom Town." Its streets were paved; one bore the name "Doomsday Drive." Six houses were built for the blast: three Cape Cods (one wood-framed; two brick), a wooden ranch; and two versions of a flat-roofed structure called "Survival House," which had been designed by architects to meet earthquake-proof specifications.

"Survival House" was less of a house than it was an aboveground bunker, with 12-inch thick concrete walls. And it lived up to its name: Though the "Survival Houses" suffered some cracked walls and blown-out windows, both were still standing after the bomb's blast.

OPPOSITE The remains of one of the six houses built for the 1955 Operation Cue bomb test still stands at the Nevada test site as a tourist attraction.

RIGHT This remarkable series of images are from a government film taken of the house closest to the detonation site during the March 1953 Operation Doorstep test. The time from the flash of the bomb's explosion, top left, to the destruction of the house, bottom right, was less than three seconds.

OPPOSITE AND ABOVE A family of mannequins, placed in this "corner room" basement shelter by Civil Defense workers, awaited the 1953 atomic bomb test blast. Two of the walls of the shelter and its ceiling were constructed of wood. The basement's corner served as the shelter's third and fourth walls. Perhaps because the detonation would have taken place before dawn, the mannequins were dressed in nightclothes. With the exception of the toddler, the mannequins are wearing bathrobes. Dad sports striped pajamas.

ABOVE The lean-to shelter was a wooden panel butted against the wall under which Civil Defense officials placed a female mannequin holding a child in her lap.

RIGHT Las Vegas businesses capitalized on the city's proximity to the Nevada Test Site by promoting the atomic blasts as tourist attractions. A postcard from Joe W. Brown's Horseshoe Club shows the sequence of a blossoming explosion.

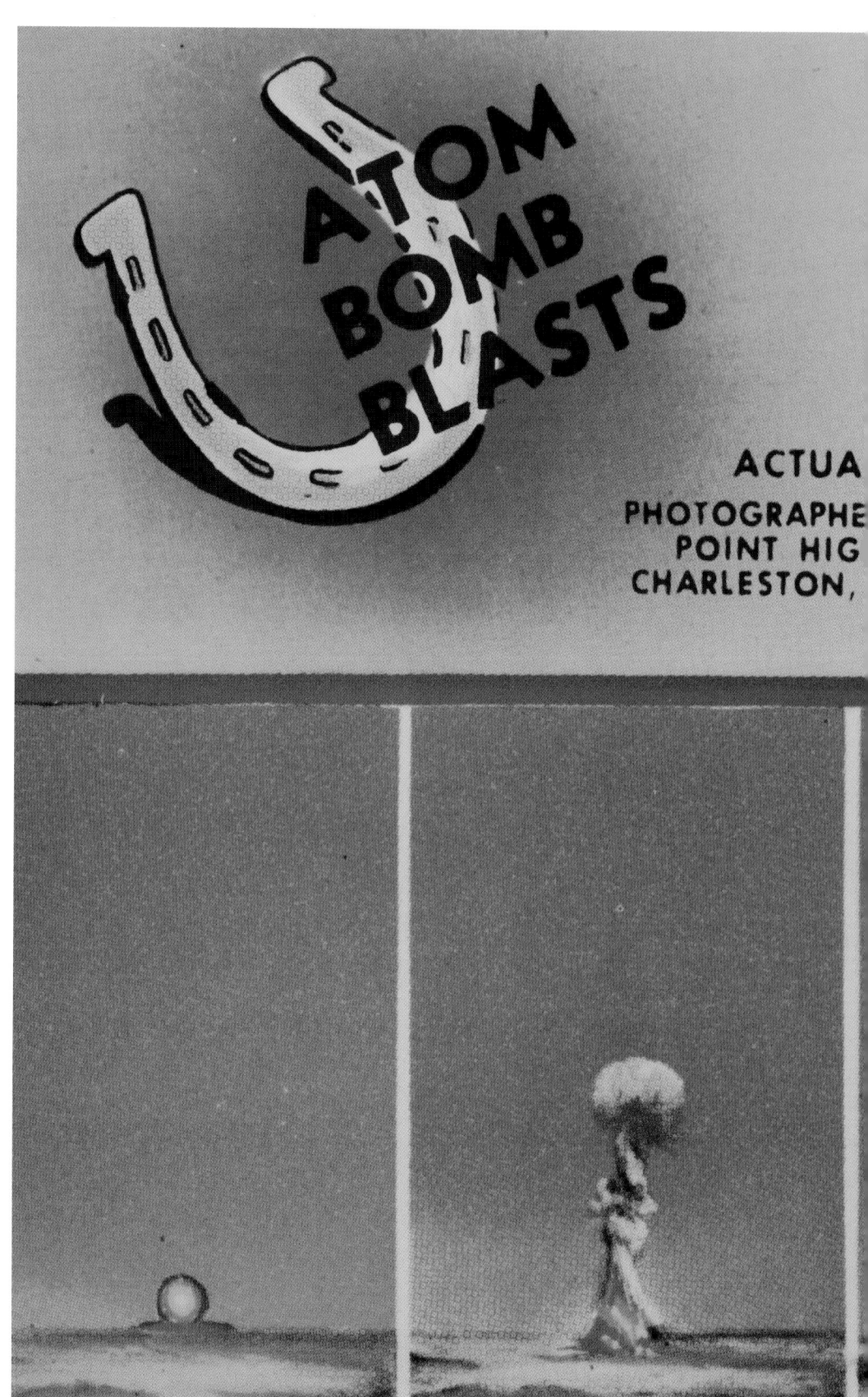

COURTESY

Joe W. Brown's

Horseshoe Club

PICTURES
FROM VANTAGE
TOP MOUNT
AR LAS VEGAS

DOWNTOWN
LAS VEGAS, NEV.

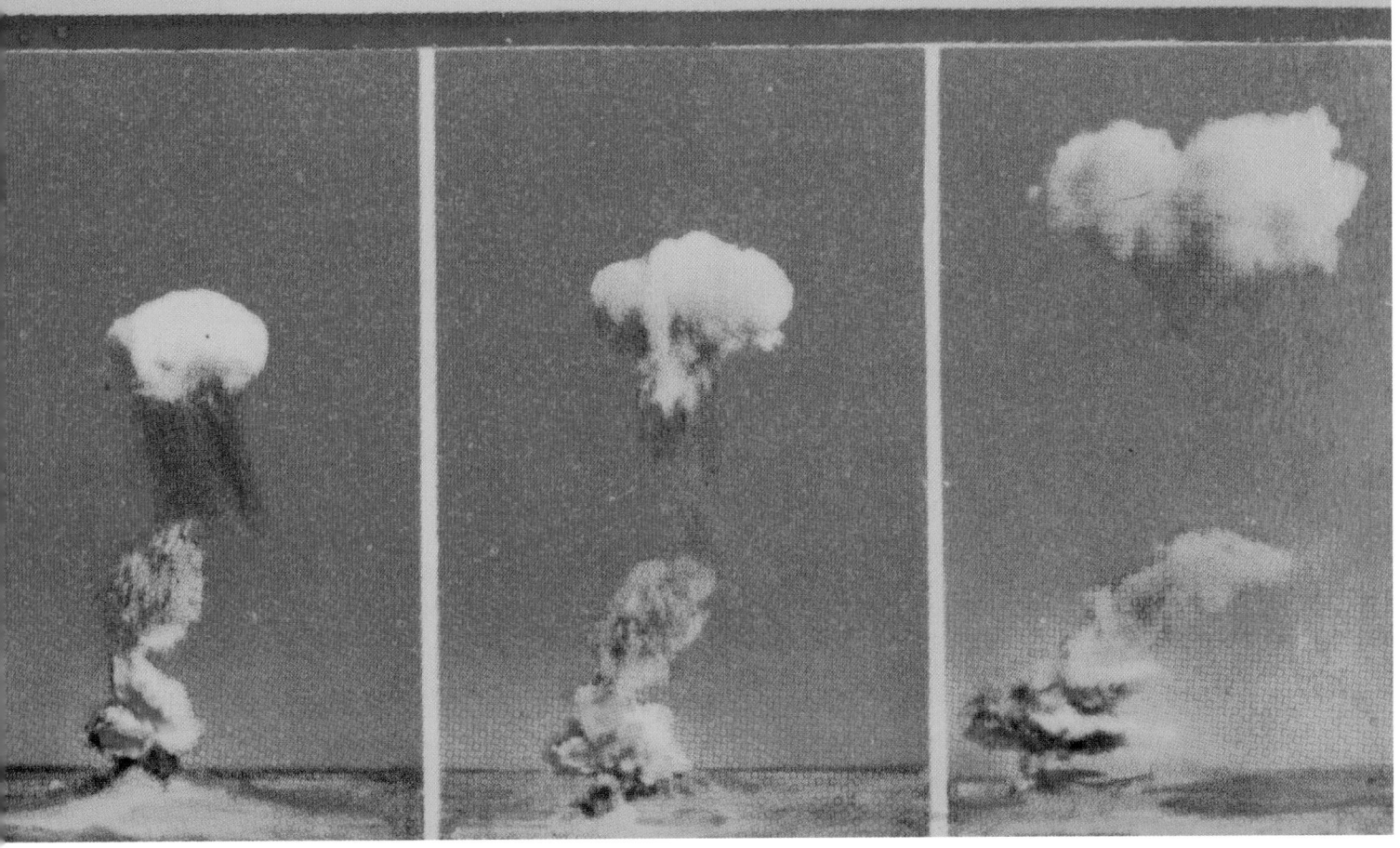

COMMUNICATIONS

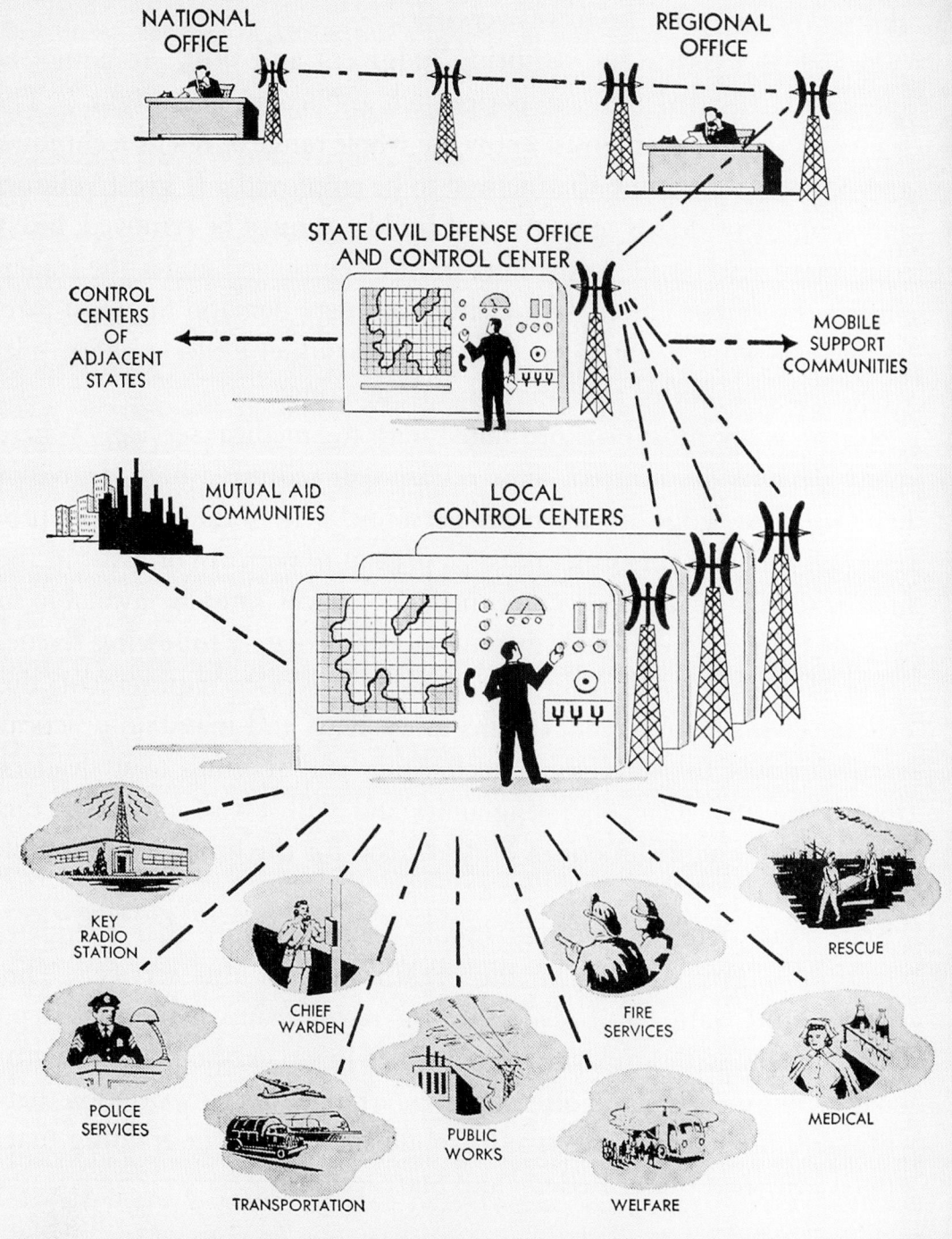

OPPOSITE An efficient communications system was essential during and after an atomic attack, as illustrated here in the 1950 publication, *United States Civil Defense*. The system was organized into three hierarchical levels: National, State, and Local. Information would originate in the National Office and be sent to the Regional Offices, which would then relay it to the Local Control Centers. These Local Control Centers would pass this intelligence on to the organizations involved in emergency response: Rescue, Fire, Medical, Welfare, Public Works and Transportation. The Center would also send information to the Chief Warden in every community, who had the responsibility for organizing his area's citizens. Radio stations would broadcast up-to-the-minute attack news to the public.

RIGHT The cover of the 1956 book *Survival: How to Protect Yourself, Your Family, Your Community in Event of Attack!* depicts a single-family home, a church, tall city buildings, and a factory dwarfed by the mushroom cloud of an atomic bomb. The text emphasizes the immediate necessity of learning survival techniques and procedures. "It has been said that after an atomic attack, there would be only two kinds of people left—those who needed help, and those who could help."

SURVIVAL

How to Protect
YOURSELF • YOUR FAMILY • YOUR COMMUNITY
IN EVENT OF ATTACK!

LEFT AND OPPOSITE This 16-page cartoon booklet was part of the "Duck and Cover" campaign, the first Civil Defense program aimed specifically at children. In 1951, three million copies were printed, to be distributed to elementary school students after they had watched the *Duck and Cover* film. Civil Defense officials said the campaign was specifically designed not to frighten children unnecessarily, as no graphic scenes of death and destruction were shown. Instead, Bert the Turtle, a friendly cartoon character, was created to tell the story of how to protect yourself against nuclear attack.

YOU HAVE LEARNED HOW TO TAKE CARE OF YOUR-SELF IN MANY WAYS-- TO CROSS STREETS SAFELY.

AND YOU KNOW WHAT TO DO IN CASE OF FIRE -- B-U-T...

THE ATOMIC BOMB IS A NEW DANGER. IT EXPLODES WITH A FLASH BRIGHTER THAN ANY YOU'VE EVER SEEN.

THINGS WILL BE KNOCKED DOWN ALL OVER TOWN, AND, AS IN A BIG WIND, THEY ARE BLOWN THROUGH THE AIR. YOU MUST BE READY TO PROTECT YOURSELF.

SO, LIKE BERT, YOU **DUCK** TO AVOID
THE THINGS FLYING THROUGH THE AIR...

...AND **COVER** TO KEEP FROM GETTING
CUT OR EVEN BADLY BURNED.

YOUR CITY AND ITS CIVIL DEFENSE WILL TRY
TO WARN YOU WITH A SPECIAL ALARM IN TIME
TO GO TO SPECIAL SHELTER...THEN...

YOU MUST GO QUICKLY AND QUIETLY TO THE
SPECIAL SHELTER AS THE BLOCK WARDEN,
YOUR TEACHER OR YOUR PARENTS TELL YOU.

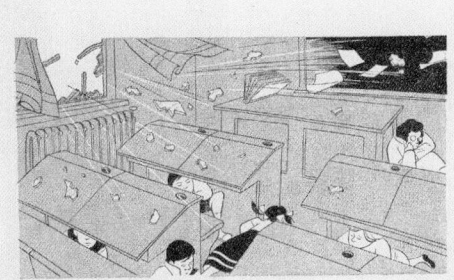

BUT SOMETIMES--**AND THIS IS VERY IMPORTANT**--
THE BOMB MIGHT EXPLODE AND THE BRIGHT FLASH
COME... *WITHOUT ANY WARNING!*

THERE IS ALWAYS **SOMETHING** TO SHELTER
YOU-INDOORS, A SCHOOL DESK, A CHAIR, A TABLE.
ALWAYS DUCK AWAY FROM WINDOWS AND GLASS DOORS.

OUTDOORS, DUCK BEHIND WALLS AND TREES. EVEN
IN A HOLLOW IN THE GROUND. IN A BUS OR AUTO,
DUCK DOWN BEHIND OR UNDER THE SEATS.

BUT REMEMBER... **DO IT INSTANTLY**...
DON'T STAND AND LOOK, DUCK AND COVER!

LEFT In this Civil Defense illustration, children are shown crouched down beneath their desks with their hands locked tightly behind their heads, correctly performing a "Duck and Cover" exercise.

BELOW LEFT A woman uses her desk as a shield against the bomb in an illustration from the 1950 book, *Atomic Bombing: How to Protect Yourself.*

OPPOSITE In this photograph published in *Collier's,* schoolchildren in Indian Springs, Nevada, twenty-five miles from the government's atomic bomb test site, practice what they have been told to do in case of an atomic attack: lie flat on the ground, shield their eyes with one arm, and protect their head with the other arm.

The safest place inside any building will be near the interior partition—

A IS FOR ATOM

Have a Plan of Action Now

A family consultation will determine each person's role

The Report to Governor Rockefeller on Fallout Protection has reached a wide and various audience.

LEFT A young boy is posed holding a booklet he is obviously too young to read: *Survival Under Atomic Attack*, a report by the New York State Committee on Fallout Protection, that was published in 1960. It was written at the direction of Governor Nelson Rockefeller, an ardent proponent of fallout shelters for everyone.

OPPOSITE In 1955, four-year-old Toni Wright of Las Vegas, Nevada, inspects her newly issued dog tag. The tags were designed to identify the missing, injured, and dead after an atomic attack. Civil Defense authorities wanted every American to wear one, although they eventually abandoned that plan.

RVICE
OFF
CIVIL
IDENTI
CD
JOHN H DOE
928 MAIN STREE
HOMETOWN OHIO
2-21-49
GET
DETAILS HERE!

LEFT A helmeted Mr. Civil Defense played the starring role in a 1956 comic book called *Mr. Civil Defense Tells About Natural Disasters*. In the 16-page publication, the cartoon character gave step-by-step instructions for creating a local Civil Defense unit to save a community in the aftermath of a calamity—whether a "flood" or an "enemy bombing."

OPPOSITE Identification cards were issued by the Civil Defense Organization of the city of Royal Oak, Michigan, to volunteers trained in the skills of first aid, firefighting, rescue, and other life-saving techniques.

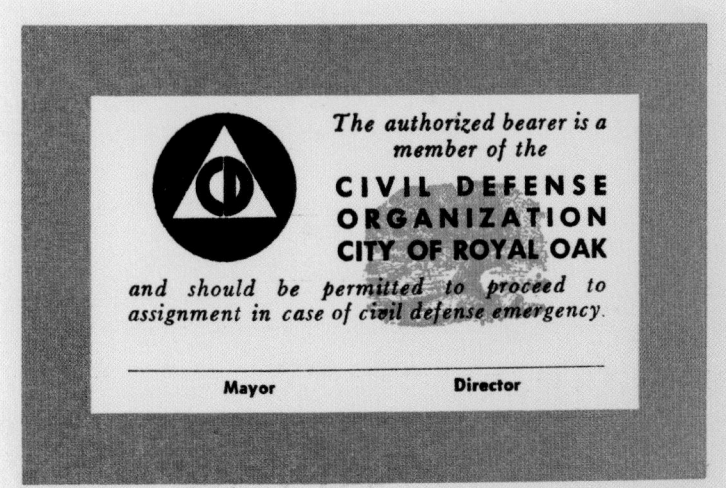

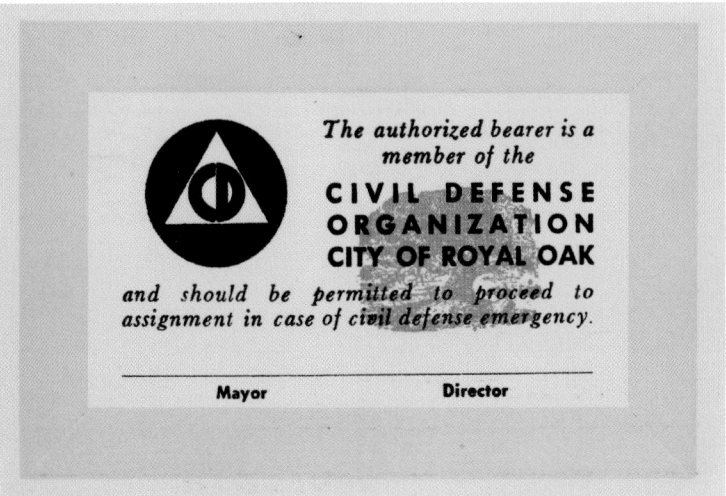

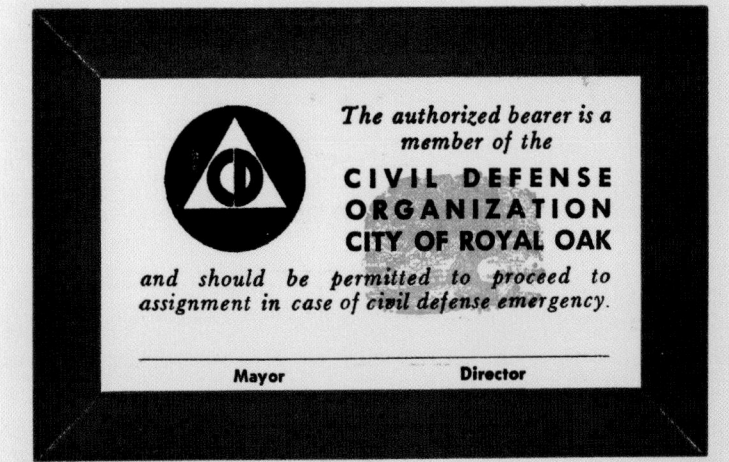

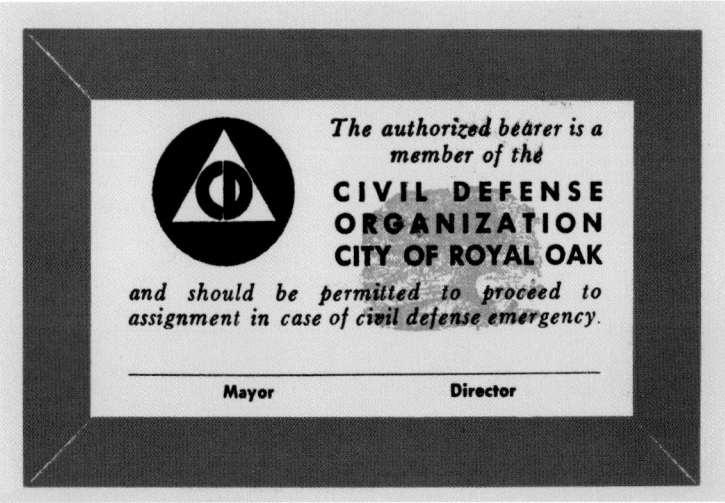

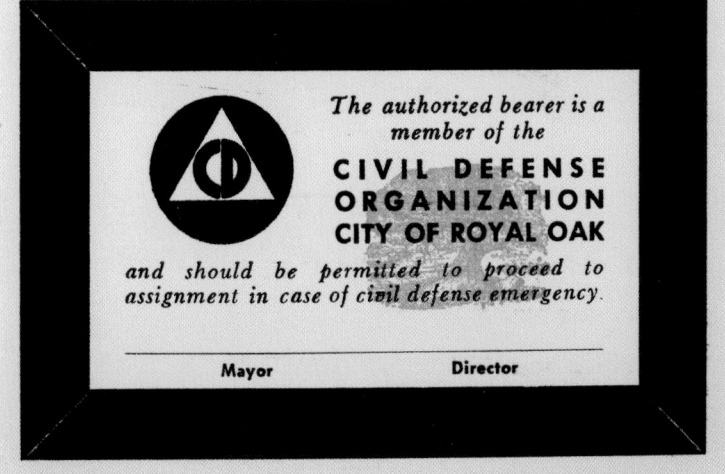

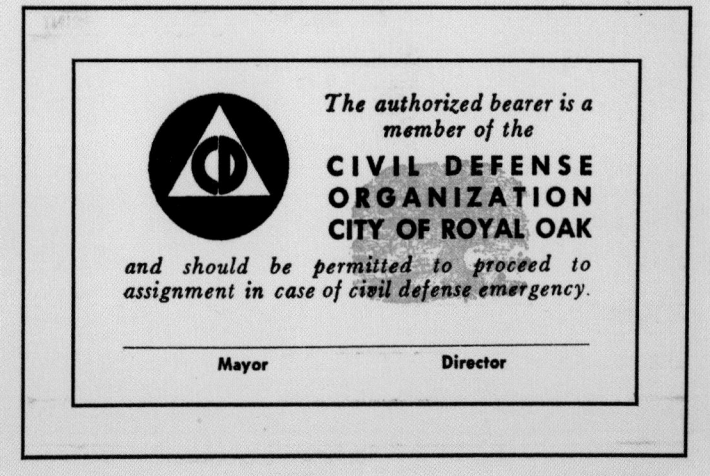

LEFT Rebecca Fowler, a rescue worker from Georgia, learns how to operate a fire extinguisher on Rescue Street at the Civil Defense Training Center in Olney, Maryland, in 1952. A city block of structures was constructed to simulate "bombed-out" living conditions after a nuclear attack. The site was used to train Civil Defense volunteers in firefighting and rescue techniques.

OPPOSITE Civil Defense Volunteer Lois E. Ruckert poses for the cover of the March 21, 1954, issue of the *Baltimore Sun*'s Sunday magazine. She is standing in front of a map of Baltimore inside the city's underground Civil Defense center, the place that would serve as the city's emergency command center in case of a nuclear attack. The article called the center "the Safest Place in Baltimore" and explained its function: "This is the nerve center from which the authorities would direct the removal of building debris from the streets, the rescue of trapped victims, the location of lost children, the housing and feeding of the homeless, and all the other things which would attend an attack on the city." It was equipped for around-the-clock operation and had an independent electricity generator to supply power.

MAGAZINE

THE SUNDAY SUN

BALTIMORE, MD.   METROGRAVURE   MARCH 21, 1954

Young
Defender

OPPOSITE A Civil Defense poster used an illustration of a mushroom cloud floating above a city set aflame by a nuclear bomb blast to motivate citizens to attend classes and to learn how to protect themselves against radioactive fallout.

RIGHT In this brochure, Civil Defense authorities in the coastal city of Annapolis, Maryland advocated the use of boats as fallout shelters. Keeping the boat moving was advised. That way, any radioactive material that might fall on the boat would be blown away by the wind.

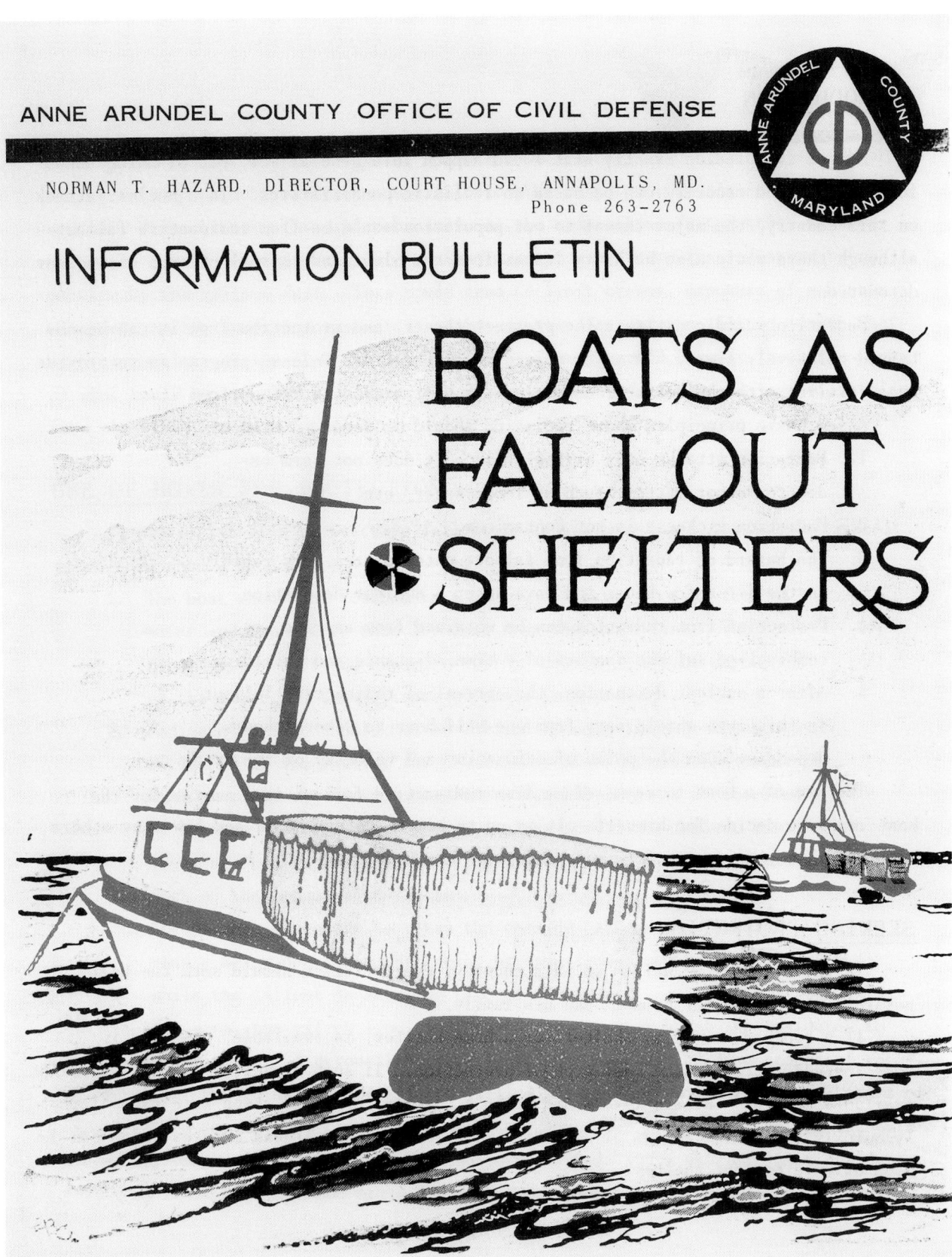

ANNE ARUNDEL COUNTY OFFICE OF CIVIL DEFENSE

NORMAN T. HAZARD, DIRECTOR, COURT HOUSE, ANNAPOLIS, MD.
Phone 263-2763

INFORMATION BULLETIN

BOATS AS FALLOUT SHELTERS

Have good maps of your city and the surrounding areas. In an evacuation, maps will be important, since it may be necessary for the official traffic broadcasts to route you over roads you do not know.

Your car can be your shopping center

In an emergency you may not be able to buy food for several days. Have an adequate supply on hand to make your family self-sufficient. The food you'll need can be based on the 7-day supply suggested by the Federal Civil Defense Administration in its "Grandma's Pantry" program. Keep these emergency rations in a carton, ready to be put into the car trunk.

Know what would be needed in the way of water containers, first aid kit, clothing, and blankets. See that it is available in your home and make it the responsibility of one member of the family to see that no item is forgotten if an emergency arises.

A few cautions about Civil Defense driving

In an evacuation, only courtesy, cooperation, and careful driving can prevent disastrous traffic jams. Learn and observe these rules:

- Obey police, civil defense auxiliaries, and other authorities.
- If you have room, pick up walking evacuees.
- Don't crowd or try to beat the other fellow.
- If your car becomes disabled, try to get off the road.
- If traffic gets stalled, don't lean on the horn. Your impatience may become someone else's panic. That cost lives!

For sale by the Superintendent of Documents, U. S. Government Printing Office, Washington 25, D. C. - Price $2.25 per 100 copies

U. S. GOVERNMENT PRINTING OFFICE: 1955—O-362833

YOUR CAR AND CIVIL DEFENSE

4 wheels to survival

FEDERAL CIVIL DEFENSE ADMINISTRATION

Your car can be "four wheels to survival" for you and your family in a civil defense emergency. How well your car serves this purpose depends on a few commonsense advance preparations—things which may spell the difference between life and death for you and your family.

Your car helps you move away from danger

Many civil defense actions, especially pre-attack evacuation, depend on your ability to move away from a probable area of danger. Properly used, your car can move you and as many others as can be comfortably seated many times as far as the strongest of you could go on foot. To do this:

Keep your car in the best possible mechanical condition.

 *Keep your tires properly inflated.*

Be sure the battery is always in tip-top shape.

 *Keep your gas tank more than half-full at all times.*

Most cars today can move some 250 miles on a full tank of gasoline. You may not need to move that far at any one time under emergency conditions, but it may be difficult to obtain additional gasoline for quite a while after an attack.

Ways to conserve gasoline:

- Keep your engine in proper mechanical adjustment.
- Learn the most efficient operating speed of your engine. Usually between 30 and 40 miles per hour.
- Remember—you can push or pull another car with little increase in your own gasoline consumption.

Your car helps shelter you

Tests under an actual atomic explosion in Nevada proved that modern cars, especially those with turret top construction, give a degree of protection against blast, heat, and radiation.

Before an attack, roll the windows down to equalize pressures and to prevent glass breakage. Crouch or lie down, below the level of the windows. After an attack, windows should be raised to keep out as much dust as possible; it may be contaminated by radio-active fallout.

Shelter in on unexpected blast is a bonus you get from your car. More importantly, the car provides a small movable house. You can get away in it—then live, eat, and sleep in it in almost any climatic conditions, if necessary, until a civil defense emergency is ended.

Your car is your information center

Under the CONELRAD system of emergency radio broadcasting, your car radio will be your source of official information. Be sure it is working and marked with the civil defense frequencies of 640 and 1240.

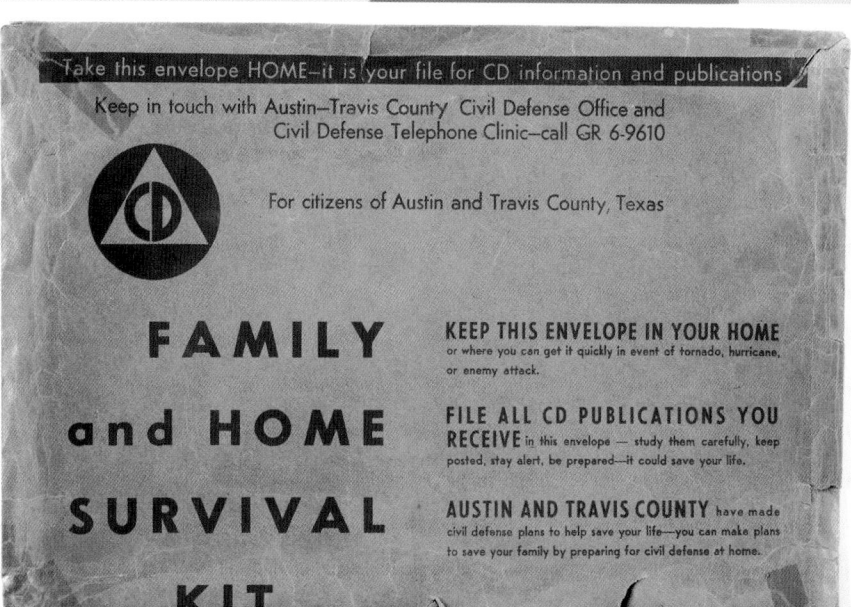

Take this envelope HOME—it is your file for CD information and publications

Keep in touch with Austin–Travis County Civil Defense Office and Civil Defense Telephone Clinic—call GR 6-9610

For citizens of Austin and Travis County, Texas

FAMILY and HOME SURVIVAL KIT

KEEP THIS ENVELOPE IN YOUR HOME or where you can get it quickly in event of tornado, hurricane, or enemy attack.

FILE ALL CD PUBLICATIONS YOU RECEIVE in this envelope — study them carefully, keep posted, stay alert, be prepared—it could save your life.

AUSTIN AND TRAVIS COUNTY have made civil defense plans to help save your life—you can make plans to save your family by preparing for civil defense at home.

Take this envelope HOME—it is your file for CD information and publications

CIVIL DEFENSE INSTRUCTIONS STUDENTS SHOULD KNOW

 **ATTACK WARNING SIGNAL**

WAILING TONE OR SERIES OF SHORT BLASTS. NATION IS UNDER ATTACK. TAKE PROTECTIVE ACTION.

 **ALERT SIGNAL**

STEADY TONE—3 TO 5 MINUTES. LISTEN FOR ESSENTIAL INFORMATION VIA RADIO OR PUBLIC ADDRESS SYSTEM.

THIS SIGN MARKS ALL FALLOUT SHELTERS. IF YOU DO NOT HAVE A SHELTER AT HOME, YOU AND YOUR FAMILY SHOULD KNOW THE LOCATIONS OF PUBLIC FALLOUT SHELTERS IN YOUR NEIGHBORHOOD.

AT SCHOOL, FOLLOW INSTRUCTIONS. GO TO YOUR ASSIGNED SHELTER AREA UNTIL YOU ARE TOLD IT IS SAFE TO GO HOME.

OPPOSITE ABOVE The Civil Defense pamphlet, *4 Wheels to Survival,* pointed out the utility of the family car: "Shelter in an unexpected blast is a bonus you get from your car. More importantly, the car provides a small movable house."

OPPOSITE BELOW FAR LEFT The Austin-Travis County Civil Defense Office provided an oversized envelope to store the information required to maintain a "Family and Home Survival Kit."

OPPOSITE BELOW LEFT Schoolchildren in New York State could protect their textbooks with an informative book cover provided by the New York State Civil Defense Commission.

RIGHT *Women in Civil Defense*, a 1952 booklet, described the special role that females must play. "Whether you are a housewife, secretary, business executive, or nurse, Civil Defense looks to you, as a woman, to take an active role in protecting your home. No one else can do that job for you."

ABOVE FAR RIGHT The booklet, *Survival in a Nuclear Attack,* delivered grim news to the residents of Austin, Texas: "Death and destruction from a 20-megaton surface explosion can be absolute within a five-mile radius of ground zero."

RIGHT The early 1950s booklet, *What About You and Civil Defense?*, posed the question: "Can we Survive a Grand-Slam Attack on Our Country?" The answer: "Certainly—if we are prepared on the home front."

LEFT *The Seattle Civil Defense Manual* sponsored by the city's KVI radio station and local businesses, and published in 1951, portrays the city in flames beneath a giant mushroom cloud. It called for residents to volunteer for the Seattle Civil Defense Corps with the promise that, "in a city properly alerted and organized for Civilian Defense, the death toll can be cut as much as 50 percent."

OPPOSITE A 1955 Civil Defense pamphlet entitled *Facts About Fallout* attempted to alleviate American fears about the new threat unleashed by the hydrogen bomb—lethal radioactive fallout that can drift for thousands of miles and fall to ground for months, even years, after the explosion. It promised that the government would alert Americans when fallout was coming, giving them enough time to either leave the area, or seek shelter.

YOU CAN'T HEAR IT

YOU CAN'T TASTE IT

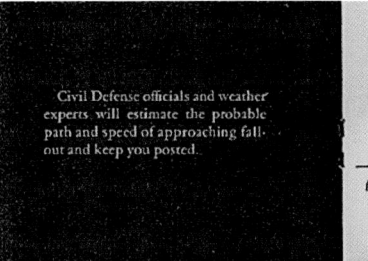

Civil Defense officials and weather experts will estimate the probable path and speed of approaching fallout and keep you posted.

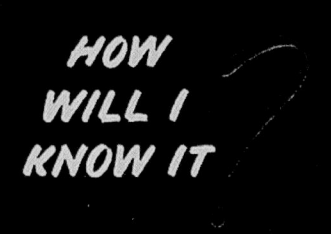

HOW WILL I KNOW IT?

YOU CAN'T TOUCH IT

Tune your AM radio to 640 or 1240 kilocycles, your Conelrad stations, for official Civil Defense news and instructions.

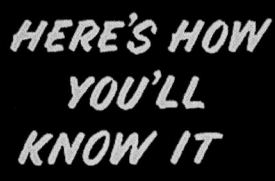

HERE'S HOW YOU'LL KNOW IT

YOU CAN'T SMELL IT

OFTEN YOU CAN'T EVEN SEE IT

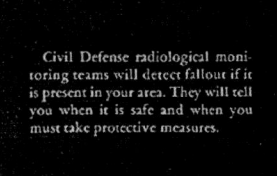

Civil Defense radiological monitoring teams will detect fallout if it is present in your area. They will tell you when it is safe and when you must take protective measures.

An old-fashioned root cellar is ideal. Stock it with such staples as Grandmother used and water supplies, first-aid kits, blankets, a lantern, fuel . . . .

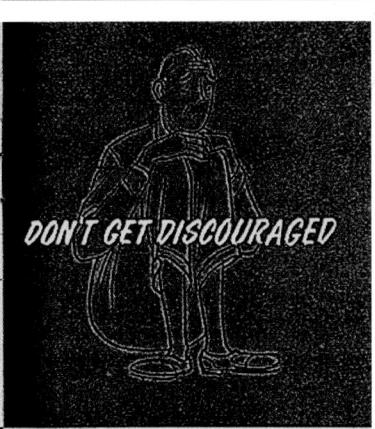

DON'T GET DISCOURAGED

IF IT COMES MY WAY, WHAT DO I DO THEN?

If there is enough warning time, your local Civil Defense director may order a general evacuation of the area to get away from the bomb or its effects, before it comes.

IF YOU DON'T HAVE TIME TO EVACUATE, SEEK THE BEST AVAILABLE SHELTER

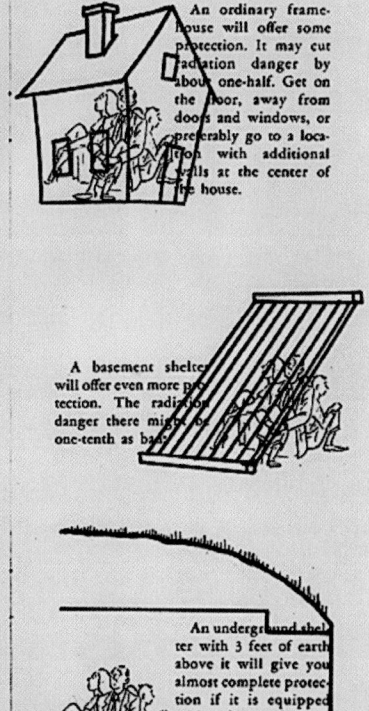

An ordinary frame house will offer some protection. It may cut radiation danger by about one-half. Get on the floor, away from doors and windows, or preferably go to a location with additional walls at the center of the house.

A basement shelter will offer even more protection. The radiation danger there might be one-tenth as bad.

An underground shelter with 3 feet of earth above it will give you almost complete protection if it is equipped with a door and an air filter.

EVERYTHING YOU NEED TO LIVE IN IT FOR A FEW DAYS

DON'T GET PANICKY

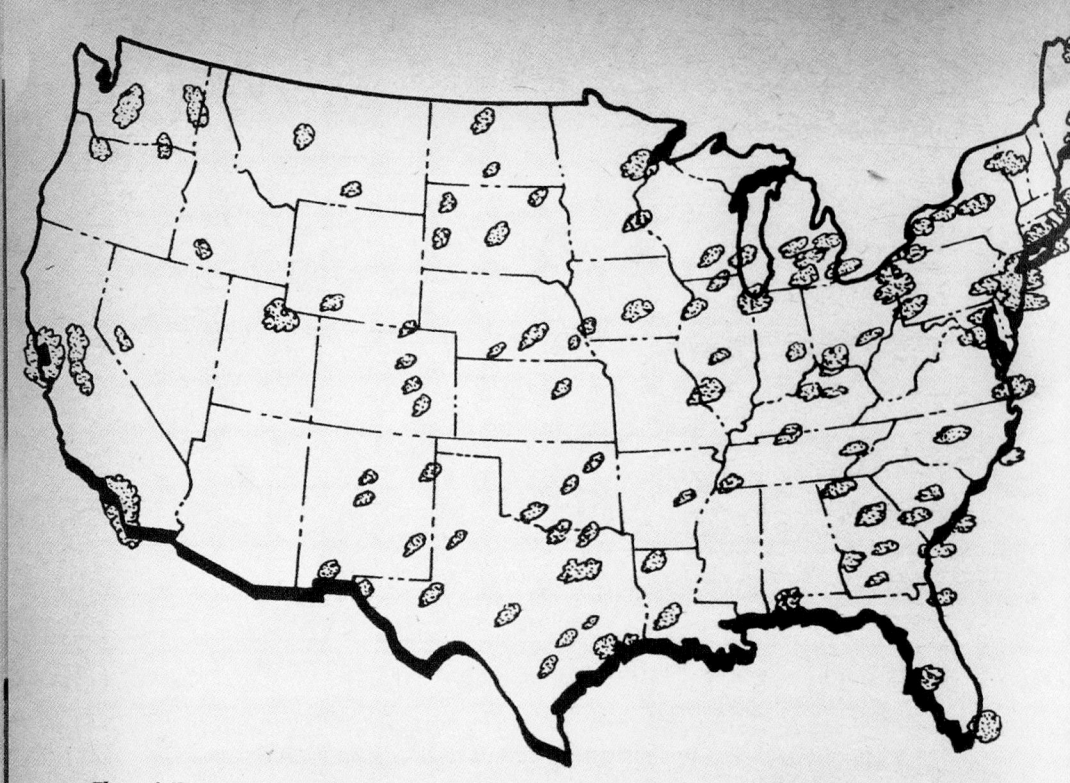

These fallout zones would exist one hour after the first detonations of nuclear weapons over the U. S.

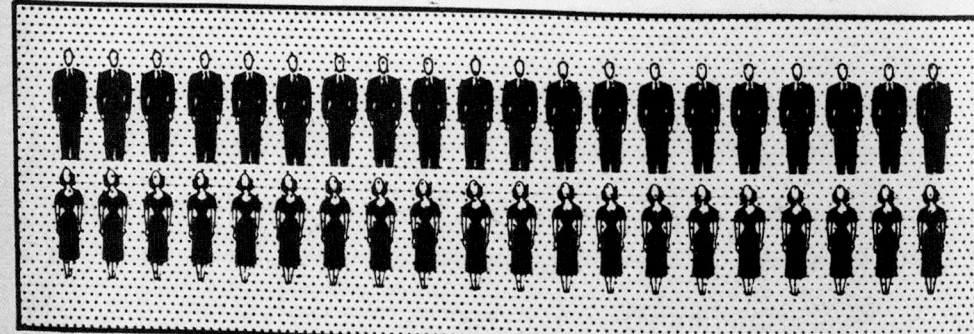

0-100 ROENTGENS - NO OBVIOUS EFFECTS

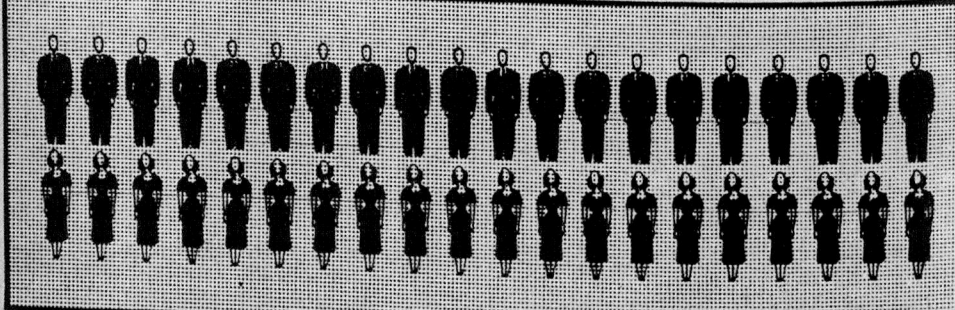

100-200 ROENTGENS - SOME SICKNESS

48

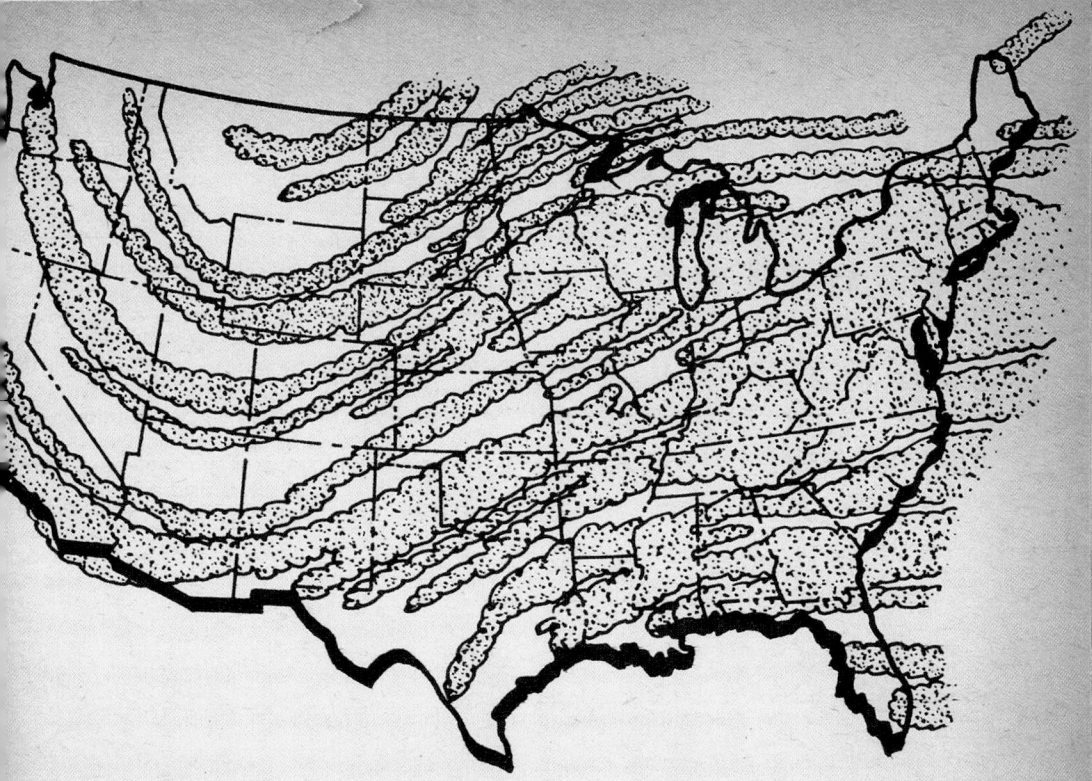

The same clouds, twenty-four hours later, could be spread over the shaded areas shown in this drawing.

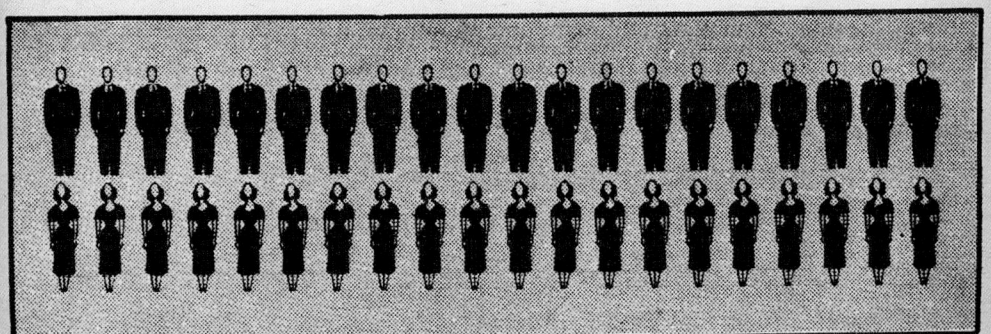

200-300 ROENTGENS - SICKNESS AND SOME DEATHS

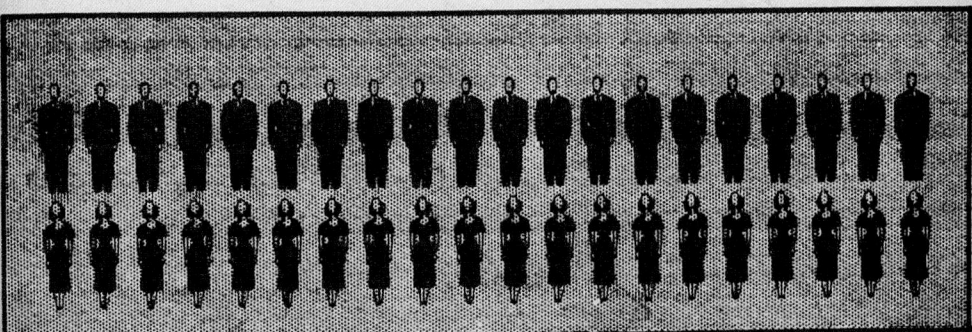

300-600 ROENTGENS - SEVERE SICKNESS AND MANY DEATHS

49

LEFT The effects of radioactive fallout, illustrated in the 1962 *Family Fallout Shelter Handbook* by Chuck West, were based on information provided by Civil Defense authorities. Included were two maps that represented the United States after a nuclear attack. The dotted areas indicate the dispersal of radioactive fallout one hour after an attack, left, and, twenty-four hours after an attack, right. The figures below the maps describe the disease and deaths to be expected after a twenty-four-hour exposure to various levels of radiation expressed here in roentgens, a unit of measurement named after Wilhelm Roentgen, the man who discovered x-rays in 1896. Exposure to 100 roentgens would produce "no obvious effects," 100 to 200 roentgens would produce "some sickness," 200-300 roentgens would produce "sickness and some deaths," and 300-600 roentgens would result in "severe sickness and many deaths."

ABOVE In 1946, a cake of angel food puffs in the shape of a mushroom cloud sparked a firestorm of controversy at a party commemorating the dissolution of the Army-Navy task force that conducted the Operation Crossroads atomic bomb tests in the Bikini Islands. Vice Admiral W.H.P. Blandy and his wife cut the cake while Rear Admiral F.J. Lowry stood by. "If I had the authority of a priest of the Middle Ages, I would call down the wrath of God upon such an obscenity," said the Reverend A. Powell Davids after he saw this photograph in the *Washington Post*.

OPPOSITE On May 24, 1957, Lee Merwin, a showgirl at the Copa Room of the Sands Hotel in Las Vegas, posed for this photograph and was dubbed "Miss Atomic Bomb" by the Las Vegas News Bureau, the city's publicity agency. She was the last in a series of atomic pin-up girls that began in 1952 with Miss Atomic Blast.

FALL-OUT SHELTER- -Mr. and Mrs. Paul Miller, left, with children Bobbie, on dad's shoulder, Betsy and Paul Jr., show building progress of their front-yard fall-out shelter to Joseph J. Micciche, director of the L.A. office of Civil Defense, and Ray Toland, who is the president of the Nuclear Survival Corp.

BUILDING FALLOUT SHELTER

Family Hopes to 'Waste' $2,500

BY SPENCER CRUMP

RANCHO PARK —A family here is investing more than $2,500 in a project which it hopes never will be used.

But from the knowledge they gained while serving the FBI as underground agents in the Communist party, Paul Miller and his wife, Marion, fear that the trend of world events will bring their radiation fallout shelter into use.

In Front Yard

The shelter, being built by a contractor under the front yard of their home at 10716 Esther Ave., is expected to be completed late this month.

~~ining 100 sq. f~~

"Frankly, we hope the shelter will end up as a storeroom." he says. "But having been members of the Communist Party and seen its operation, we're frightened of what's being planned for America.

The Millers revealed five years ago they had been members of the Communist Party as a service to the FBI. Their adventures will be told in Mrs. Miller's recently-completed book, "I Was a Spy," to be published in the fall.

Their fallout shelter is being built of reinforced cement. Three of the walls will be 8 in. thick while the fourth, containing the entrance from the

stairs, will be 16 in. in thickness. The roof and floor each will contain four layers of steel in cement.

Cost 'Worth It'

"We're not wealthy people," he says, "but we think the cost of the shelter is worth the expenditure for our own protection as well as to point out the dangers of nuclear attack to other people."

Miller reports that while some of his neighbors have "shrugged their shoulders and remained complacent," others have taken an interest in the project and are considering their own shelters.

BETTER HOMES & BUNKERS

In George Orwell's *1984*, citizens of the totalitarian state of Oceania were required to accomplish the impossible task of holding two contradictory ideas in their minds and accepting both of them: *War is peace. Freedom is slavery. Ignorance is strength.* Orwell called this "Doublethink." Similarly, Citizen Cold Warriors in the United States were expected to be able to reconcile these two diametrically opposed thoughts: *A nuclear war can destroy all life on earth. You will survive if you build a family fallout shelter.*

But the family fallout shelter's ostensible purpose—to ensure survival during and after a nuclear attack—was impossible to achieve. That wasn't why it was created. It was part of the propaganda campaign to convince the American people that they could survive a nuclear war.

OPPOSITE On July 24, 1960, the *Los Angeles Times* ran an article explaining why Paul and Marion Miller decided to install a 100-square-foot shelter in the front yard of their house in Rancho Park, California.

No one knows exactly how many shelters were built. But tens of thousands of Americans—maybe even hundreds of thousands—actually did build shelters. Millions considered doing so. Why? How could so many people believe that hiding in an underground concrete cube would save their lives during a nuclear attack? And then, if they somehow did survive, why did they believe they could function when they emerged into a post-apocalyptic world with fires raging, cities destroyed, and a landscape littered with the dead and injured? Because by the time the Federal Civil Defense Authority launched its Family Fallout Shelter campaign in 1958, Americans had spent nearly a decade steeped in Civil Defense campaigns, posters, films, classes, and emergency drills. The idea of being a Citizen Cold Warrior had become embedded in the American psyche. People built shelters because doing so seemed to be their best hope; it was a desperate grab for empowerment in the face of the unthinkable. Doing something felt better than doing nothing.

The roots of the family fallout shelter can be traced back to 1952, when the U.S. created a new bomb—the hydrogen bomb—that was 1,000 times as powerful as the bomb dropped on Hiroshima. This bomb would destroy an atomic bomb shelter as easily as the wolf blew down the house of straw in the fairy tale, *The Three Little Pigs*.

The world witnessed the astounding power of this new weapon on March 1, 1954, when it was exploded above the Marshall Islands in the Pacific. The blast vaporized the island below it and carved out a crater a half-mile wide and several hundred feet deep.

The bomb also threw several million tons of radioactive fallout into the atmosphere. After a nuclear bomb is detonated, it sucks dirt, water, and other matter into the explosion and transforms it into radioactive particles that can be as large as snowflakes or so small as to be invisible. Fallout can drift in unpredictable directions for thousands of miles over a period of years.

No longer was a nuclear bomb's killing power limited to the place where it was detonated. Now everyone, everywhere was

a potential victim of radioactive fallout.

The following year, the U.S.S.R. exploded *its* first hydrogen bomb. Fear of fallout gripped the nation. The government acknowledged that a bomb shelter would be useless against a direct hit by the H-bomb. However, it said, you can protect yourself against fallout. During a nuclear attack, go into your fallout shelter and stay there for two weeks, until the radiation in the atmosphere has dropped to a safe level.

In 1958, President Dwight D. Eisenhower declared: "The National fallout shelter policy is based *firmly* on the philosophy of the obligation of each property-owner to provide protection on his own premises."

The family fallout shelter was a direct descendent of the atomic bomb shelters that Americans built after the U.S.S.R. exploded its first atomic bomb in 1949. These shelters took many forms. Some were prefabricated, like the one modeled on the Andersen Shelter, a small steel shed distributed by the British government to more than two million households during World War II to protect against the Luftwaffe bombings during the Blitz of 1940-1941. These floorless structures were dug into the yard and covered with earth. Others were contractor-built, like the poured-concrete cube installed underground, which was essentially a swimming pool with a concrete lid. Others were re-purposed objects, like the converted septic tank shelter.

In 1959, the government published and distributed millions of copies of a 32-page booklet called *The Family Fallout Shelter*. It included step-by-step instructions for building the Concrete Block Shelter, a cube constructed of concrete block and mortar. *The Family Fallout Shelter* was more than a how-to manual. It was a call to arms for the

Cold Warrior: "We do not want a war. We do not know whether there will be a war. But we know that forces hostile to us possess weapons that could destroy us if we were unready. These weapons create a new threat—radioactive fallout that can spread death anywhere. That is why we must prepare. No matter where you live, a fallout shelter is necessary insurance. It will not be needed except in emergency. But in emergency it will be priceless—as priceless as your life."

The Concrete Block Shelter could be installed in the basement. But for optimum protection against radiation, it should be buried in the backyard and covered with three feet of earth. Entry was to be through a ground-level hatch door. Drawings, photographs, and both miniature and full-size models of this shelter were disseminated in brochures, posters, television shows, Civil Defense films, public exhibitions, lectures, architectural journals, print advertisements, and large-circulation magazines. It became the iconic family fallout shelter.

Americans saw it on television in a show called *Walt Builds a Family Fallout Shelter*, produced by The National Concrete Masonry Association, the trade group representing the concrete block industry. The host was Walt Durbhan, the folksy, handyman star of the how-to television show, *Walt's Workshop*. The show depicts him constructing the iconic shelter in his basement, one concrete brick at a time. Building a structure designed to save your life during a nuclear attack is presented as though it were just another do-it-yourself project, like a backyard shed.

Millions of Americans saw photographs in *Life* of Governor Nelson Rockefeller, a messianic proponent of fallout shelters, sitting in a mockup of the Concrete Block Shelter in a New York City bank in 1960. Rockefeller installed shelters in his homes in Pocantico, New York, Washington, DC, and in the Governor's mansion in Albany,

New York. He even tried, unsuccessfully, to pass a law that would have required every New York State resident to have a family fallout shelter.

Sensing opportunity in the shelter market, materials makers leapt onto the bandwagon. The National Lumber Manufacturers Association published a booklet called *Family Fallout Shelters of Wood*, which included plans for a buried cubic room that required 2300 linear feet of lumber. Anticipating arguments that wood's vulnerability to water makes it unsuitable for a structure to be buried underground, the brochure recommends "mopping the exterior with hot asphalt" before installing it. In *Steel Shelters for Fallout Protection*, the American Iron and Steel Institute promoted the portability advantages of a steel shelter. Because it is constructed of panels that are bolted or screwed together, "a shelter of steel does not saddle you with a permanent, hard-to-move 'monument' in your basement or yard when the current emergency is over." For people who didn't want to go the do-it-yourself route, there was a dizzying array of prefabricated shelters from which to choose. They came in the form of cubes, domes, lozenges, cylinders, and pods, and were made of steel, pour-in-place concrete, concrete block, wood, and fiberglass. But whether built or prefabricated, shelters didn't come cheap. The Concrete Block Shelter, for example, could cost more than $10,000 in today's currency. But cost be damned! Building a shelter isn't throwing money away; it is a prudent and patriotic step that every American must take to ensure his and his family's survival. As the Civil Defense publication *Individual and Family Preparedness* emphasized, "Protection of our people is not new in the United States. When a free America was being built by our forebears, every log cabin and every dwelling had a dual purpose—namely, a home and a fortress."

RIGHT Built in 1951 by the American Safety Bomb Shelter Company in Los Angeles, this igloo-shaped structure was an early and unusual example of a bomb shelter. It served as both a sales model and an office for the firm. It is notable in several ways: It had decorative stepped-back walls flanking the entrance; it was an early example of the use of concrete block in a residential bomb shelter, a building material that would come to play a major role in the construction of the family fallout shelter; and it had a full-size entrance door.

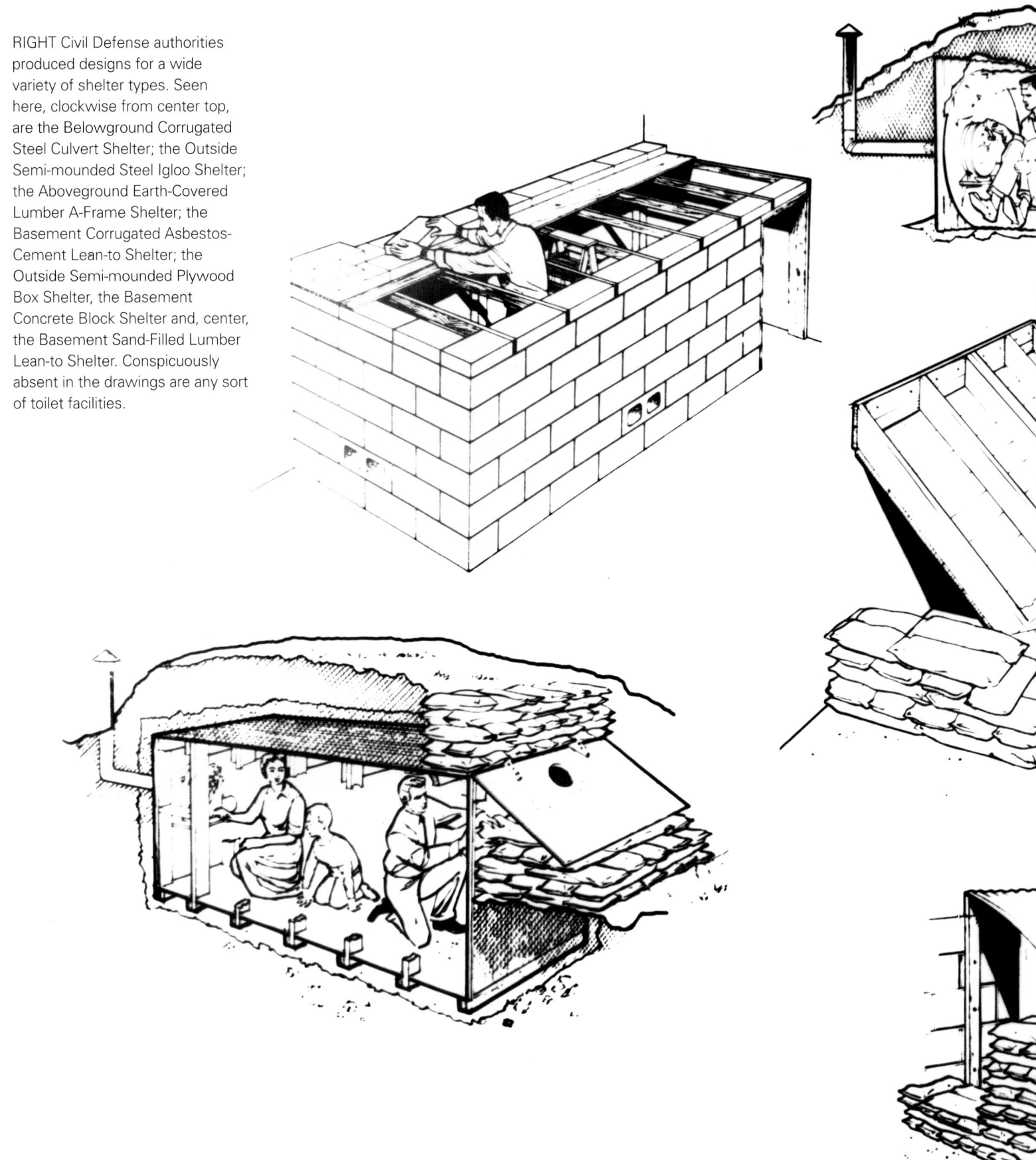

RIGHT Civil Defense authorities produced designs for a wide variety of shelter types. Seen here, clockwise from center top, are the Belowground Corrugated Steel Culvert Shelter; the Outside Semi-mounded Steel Igloo Shelter; the Aboveground Earth-Covered Lumber A-Frame Shelter; the Basement Corrugated Asbestos-Cement Lean-to Shelter; the Outside Semi-mounded Plywood Box Shelter, the Basement Concrete Block Shelter and, center, the Basement Sand-Filled Lumber Lean-to Shelter. Conspicuously absent in the drawings are any sort of toilet facilities.

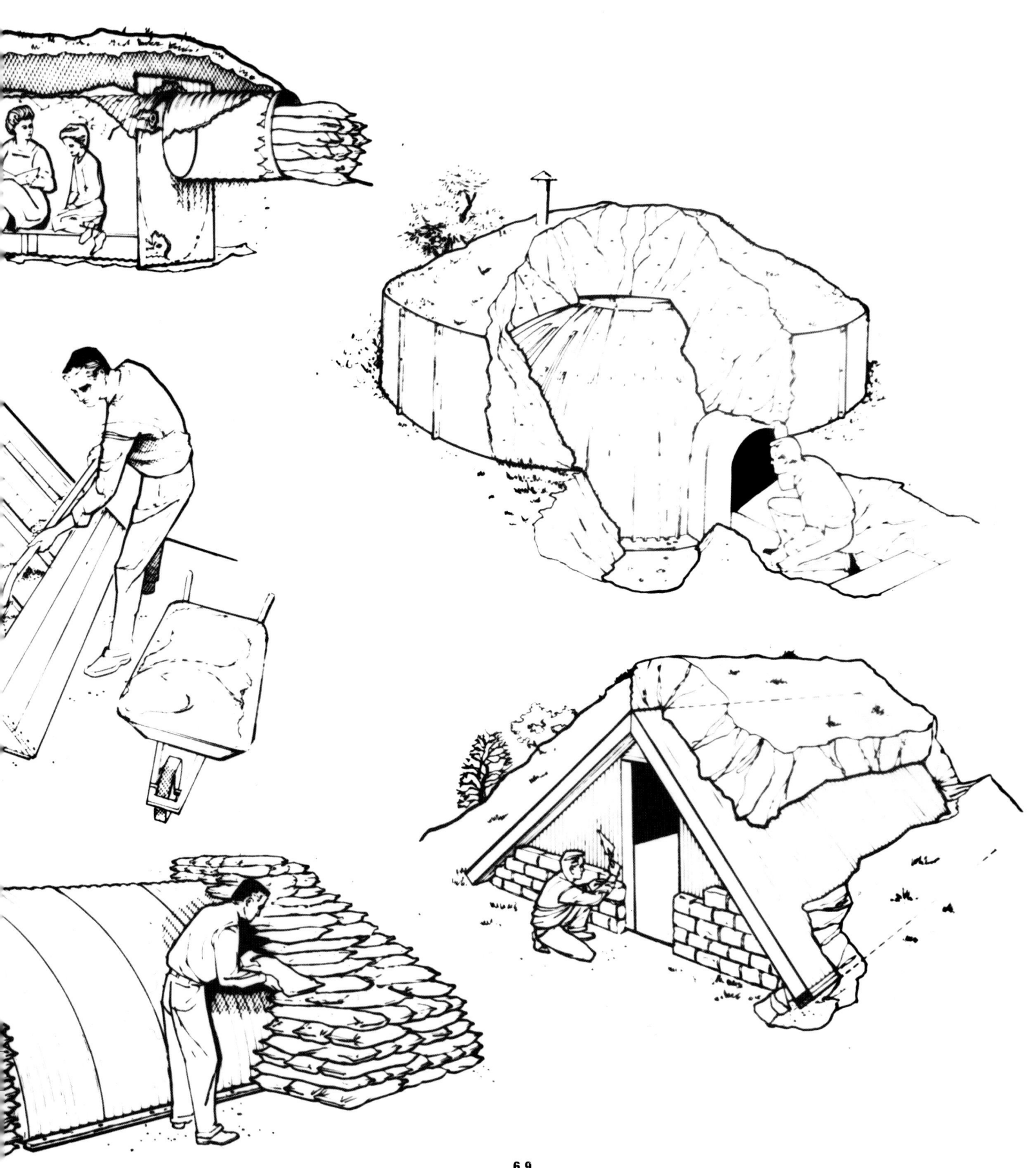

YOU
CAN
PROTECT
YOUR
FAMILY

AGAINST

FALLOUT!

KELSEY-HAYES CO. • FALLOUT SHELTERS
NOW AVAILABLE FROM HENRICH LUMBER, INC. · 465 CORNWALL AVE. · BUFFALO, N. Y.

OPPOSITE A sales brochure for the Kelsey-Hayes Company's basement shelter promised: "You Can Protect Your Family Against Fallout." On the cover, a family is seen silhouetted in a shelter barely tall enough to stand up in. Dad, sitting in a Danish modern armchair, smokes a pipe while Mom relaxes in her Eames Eiffel base rocking chair.

RIGHT Children sit in a basement shelter in this image from the 1951 Civil Defense film, *Atomic Alert*, which was shown to schoolchildren in an attempt to alleviate their fears about the Bomb. The wavy lines represent radioactivity. In the film, the narrator says reassuringly, "These children are protected. Concrete walls help stop radioactivity."

BELOW RIGHT An image from the early 1960s pushes the needs of protection a step further: Earth must be piled high enough to cover a house's foundation in order to provide proper shielding from fallout.

OVERLEAF A 1959 Civil Defense poster promoted *The Family Fallout Shelter*, a thirty-two-page booklet that detailed step-by-step instructions for building a Concrete Block Shelter.

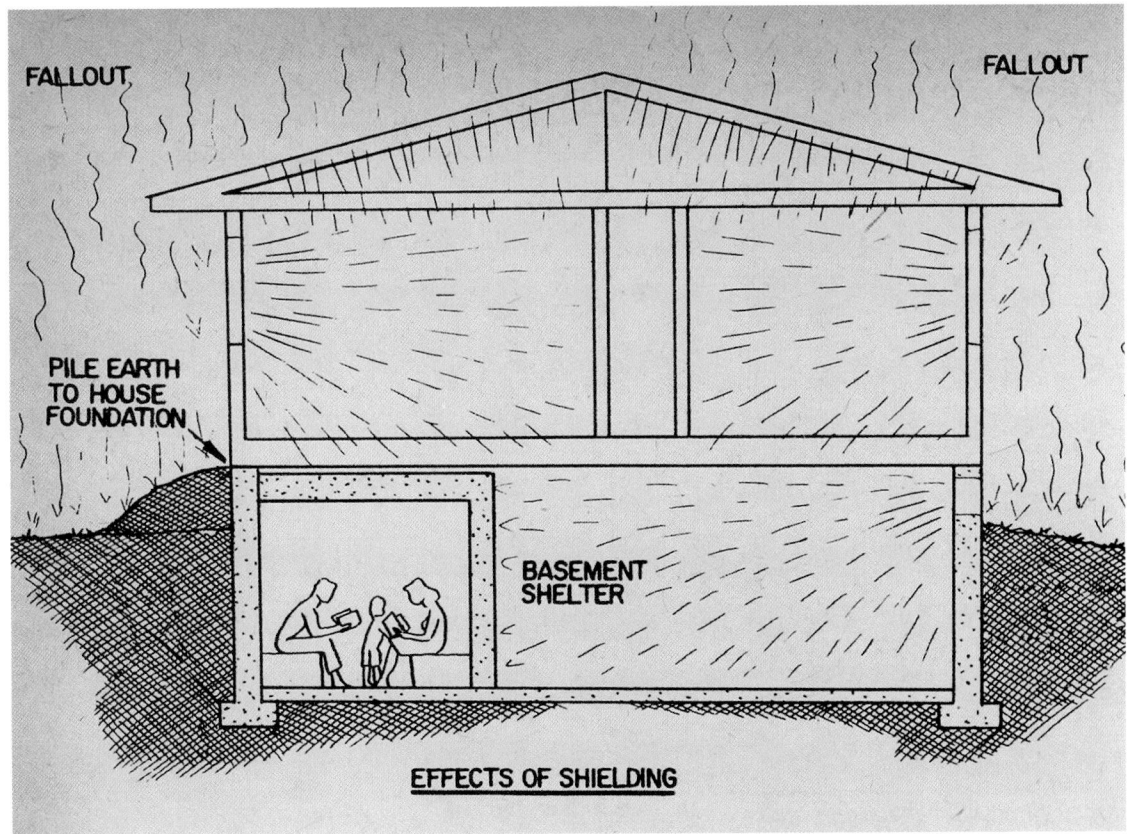

FALLOUT   FALLOUT

PILE EARTH
TO HOUSE
FOUNDATION

BASEMENT
SHELTER

EFFECTS OF SHIELDING

OCDM—P-2

your one defense against

FALLOUT

GET FREE BOOKLET
FROM LOCAL CIVIL DEFENSE

☆ U.S. GOVERNMENT PRINTING OFFICE : 1959 O—519760

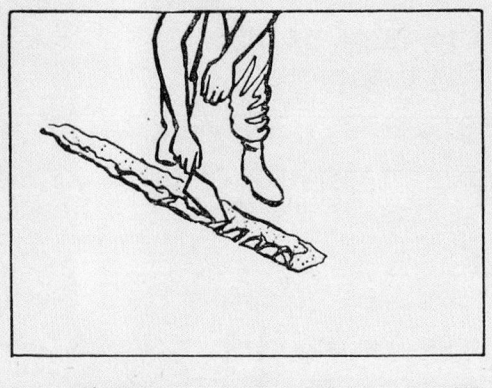
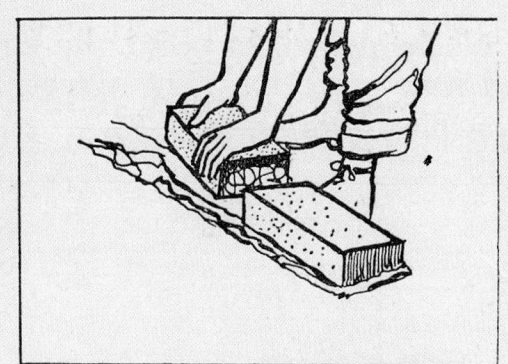
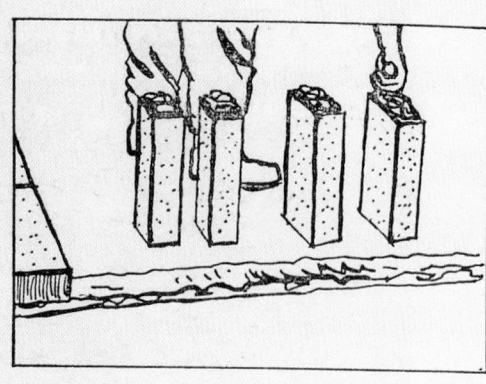
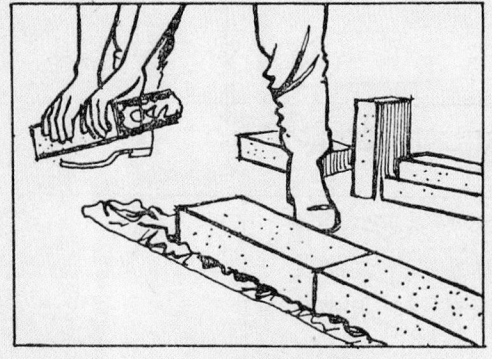

ABOVE Building the Concrete Block Shelter was depicted in these step-by-step illustrations in *The Family Fallout Shelter* as a simple do-it-yourself project. However, it was no easy task. It required assembling a daunting amount of materials. The shopping list for a six-person shelter included: 475 solid concrete blocks, each measuring 4 x 8 x 16 inches; sixty concrete blocks, each measuring 4 x 8 x 8 inches; eight cubic-foot bags of ready-to-mix cement; 95 feet of one-inch thick wood; fourteen lengths of lumber in a variety of dimensions for building beams, posts and joists; ten bolts; and six pounds of nails.

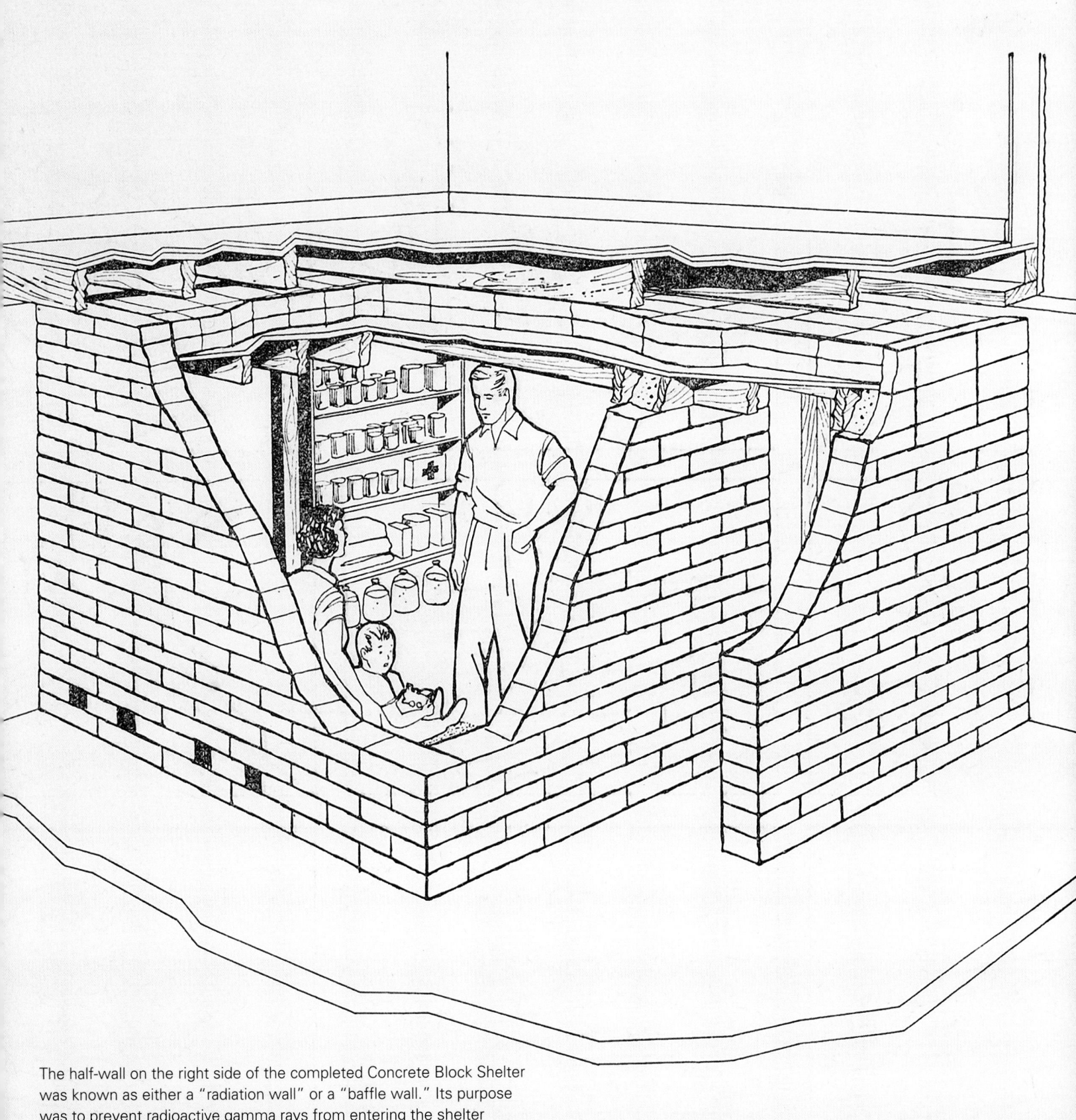

The half-wall on the right side of the completed Concrete Block Shelter was known as either a "radiation wall" or a "baffle wall." Its purpose was to prevent radioactive gamma rays from entering the shelter through the doorway, which is partially visible in this drawing to the left of the radiation wall.

TEMPORARY BASEMENT FALLOUT SHELTER

OPPOSITE A look of panic fills the faces of a family waiting for the worst in their Temporary Basement Fallout Shelter, built from Civil Defense plans. The structure was based on the same plan as the Concrete Block Shelter, but was constructed with less permanent materials. The walls were made of stacked wood and sandbags to provide shielding against radiation.

RIGHT The Kelsey-Hayes Shelter was designed for easy assembly. The copy promised: "No excavating! No stones to lay. Simply bolt the prefabricated panels together in your basement and fill with sand and gravel or earth." Components of the shelter are shown in the schematic drawing, left. The photograph, above right, shows the completed shelter.

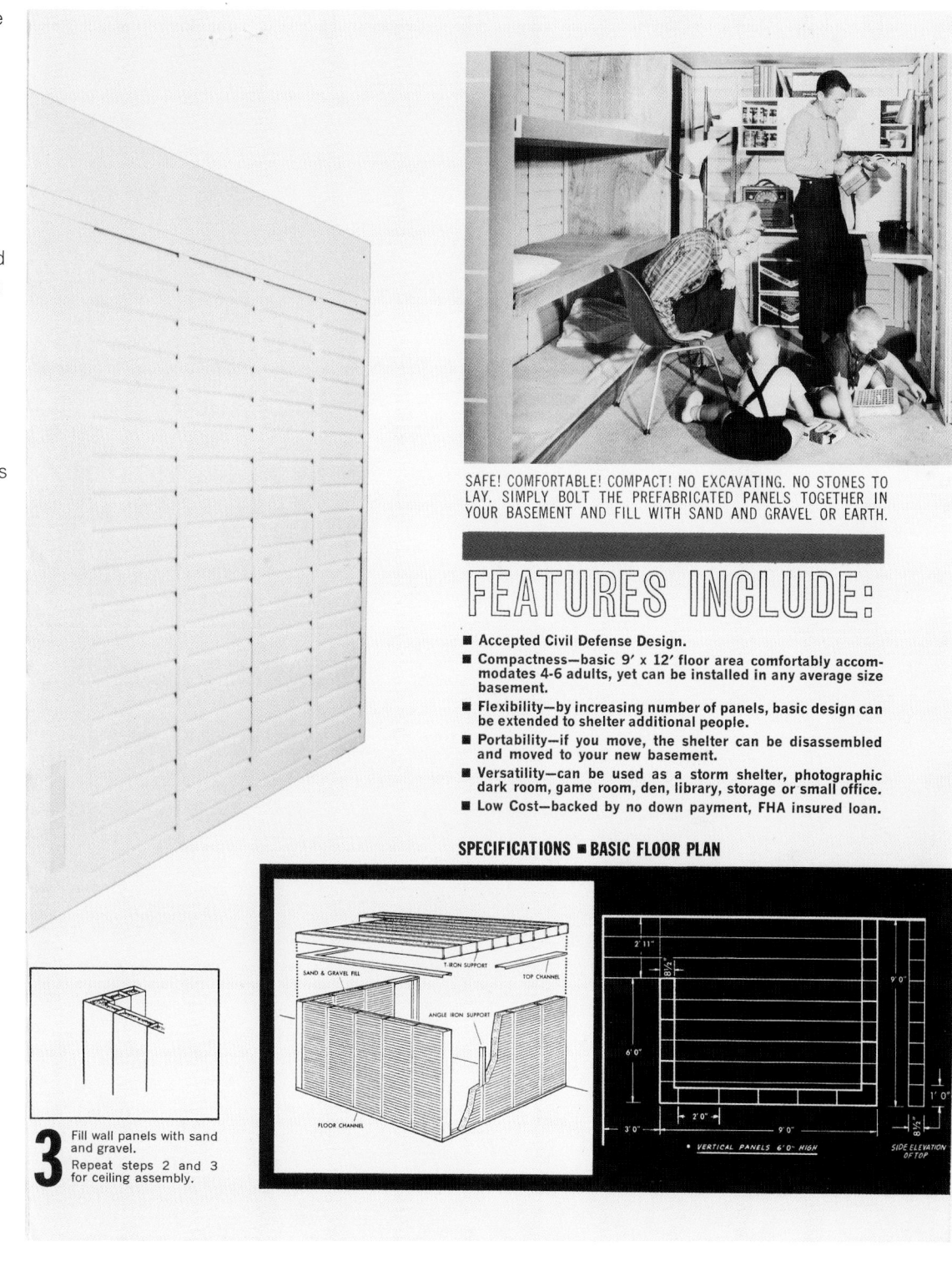

SAFE! COMFORTABLE! COMPACT! NO EXCAVATING. NO STONES TO LAY. SIMPLY BOLT THE PREFABRICATED PANELS TOGETHER IN YOUR BASEMENT AND FILL WITH SAND AND GRAVEL OR EARTH.

FEATURES INCLUDE:

- Accepted Civil Defense Design.
- Compactness—basic 9' x 12' floor area comfortably accommodates 4-6 adults, yet can be installed in any average size basement.
- Flexibility—by increasing number of panels, basic design can be extended to shelter additional people.
- Portability—if you move, the shelter can be disassembled and moved to your new basement.
- Versatility—can be used as a storm shelter, photographic dark room, game room, den, library, storage or small office.
- Low Cost—backed by no down payment, FHA insured loan.

SPECIFICATIONS ■ BASIC FLOOR PLAN

3 Fill wall panels with sand and gravel.
Repeat steps 2 and 3 for ceiling assembly.

SAND & GRAVEL FILL
T-IRON SUPPORT
TOP CHANNEL
ANGLE IRON SUPPORT
FLOOR CHANNEL

2' 11"
8½
9' 0"
6' 0"
3' 0"
2' 0"
9' 0"
1' 0"
8½
• VERTICAL PANELS 6' 0" HIGH
SIDE ELEVATION OF TOP

RIGHT A drawing illustrates a family creating a "covered foxhole." This instant and inexpensive shelter was developed by Civil Defense authorities in response to public complaints about the high cost of fallout shelters recommended by the government. When an attack warning was issued, family members would work as a team to quickly dig, equip, and cover an underground burrow. Dad is shown handling the digging while Son arranges dirt (to provide extra shielding) on a newly-laid wooden plank. Mom and Daughter carry a second plank from the house to complete the hole's roof. Once the hole is dug, the family would step in, sit down, pull the final plank over their heads, and wait underground until the lethal fallout had passed. As shown at the left of the foxhole, homeowners were instructed to have on hand: a battery-operated radio, a can of water, and a basketful of canned goods to take into their grim hideaway, which would have neither lighting nor a toilet.

After staking out the excavation area, a man uses a shovel to dig a 5 x 9 foot, two-foot-deep hole for the main body of the shelter.

Two men lay a 20 x 30 foot piece of plastic sheeting which would line the hole. It would be wrapped around the structure after installation.

Photographs from federal Civil Defense archives demonstrate how a homeowner could install a corrugated steel shelter in his backyard. Although the structure weighed five hundred pounds, captions on the photographs assured it can "easily be carried to the excavation by the homeowner and three friends and neighbors using rope slings. Also, one or two persons can slide or roll the shelter to the site."

OPPOSITE The shelter is now finished. One of the builders demonstrates how its occupants would close the shelter opening, which has no door. Once inside, the occupants will drag the thirty 12 x 20-inch sandbags that had been stored inside the structure to its "doorway," using them to seal the opening shut.

Three men standing on a flatbed truck prepare to roll the shelter down the inclined boards, and then onto the ground.

After attaching two horizontal posts to the steel tube, four men carry it to the site and drop it into place.

Once the plastic sheeting was pulled up to cover the top of the shelter, a man begins shoveling earth onto it to provide shielding against radiation

Sandbags placed around the shelter entrance were supposed to keep the two-foot-thick layer of earth that would cover the shelter in place. The shelter's ventilation tube is visible at far right.

OPPOSITE The Lancer Survival Corporation claimed its prefabricated fiberglass shelter would protect against both blast and fallout. Installation required several steps. First, a bulldozer dug a large hole. Then, a nine-inch-thick layer of concrete was poured to create a base twelve feet in diameter. Next, the dome was dropped onto the base, and then more concrete was poured to encapsulate the shelter within a nine-inch-thick shell. After the entire structure was wrapped in a cocoon of plastic sheeting for waterproofing, the excavated earth was used to completely bury the structure. Ventilation was provided by two steel tubes that extended above ground. The entrance to the shelter was through the large tube at left, which would either be connected directly to the basement, or to another tube that would emerge at ground level with a hatch door.

ABOVE In 1962, two steel igloo shelters were connected to create an unusual twin-domed shelter that was installed in MacLean, Virginia, behind the home of Adam Yarmolinsky, a special assistant to Secretary of Defense Robert S. McNamara. Yarmolinsky played a prominent role in promoting family fallout shelters during President John F. Kennedy's administration. The shelter was constructed of curved steel panels that were bolted together to form a dome. It could be installed outdoors, as shown here, or in a basement, where it would be covered with an eighteen-inch-thick layer of sand, either loose or in bags.

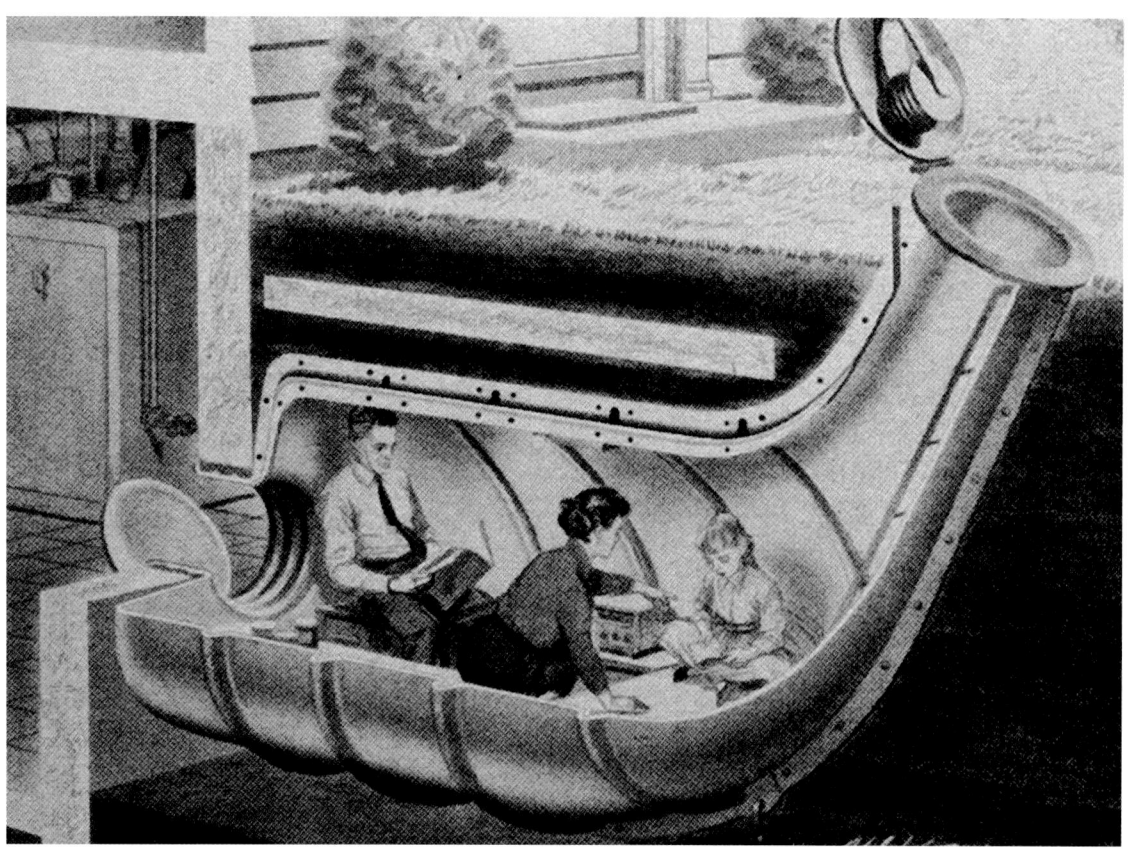

LEFT Engineer Willard Bascom wanted to make an inexpensive fallout shelter available to Americans, so he designed the Bascom shelter seen in this drawing. He intended it to be mass-produced and made of plastic but it was never manufactured.

BELOW LEFT A Civil Defense illustration depicts a family calmly ensconced in its Steel Tube Shelter. Mother is shown wearing a suit, heels, and pearls. Atypically, the shelter is shown buried in the front yard.

OPPOSITE A cylindrical shelter of corrugated steel could either be buried below ground or built above ground and covered completely with earth.

BELOW GROUND

RIGHT Rather than reprint simple line drawings of fallout shelters from Civil Defense publications, *Life* commissioned cartoon artist and advertising illustrator Elmer Wexler to create illustrations that would be more appealing to readers. One was this drawing of the Pre-Shaped Metal Shelter, which was published in the September 15, 1961, issue. To render the spartan shelter more appealing, Wexler depicted it in a pastoral landscape, with a fieldstone path leading through a verdant lawn to its entrance. Homey details included daylilies in bloom, a split-rail fence, and a farmhouse adjacent to a barn and silo. But *Life*'s title, "Big Pipe in the Backyard Under Three Feet of Earth," quickly undercut the bucolic fantasy.

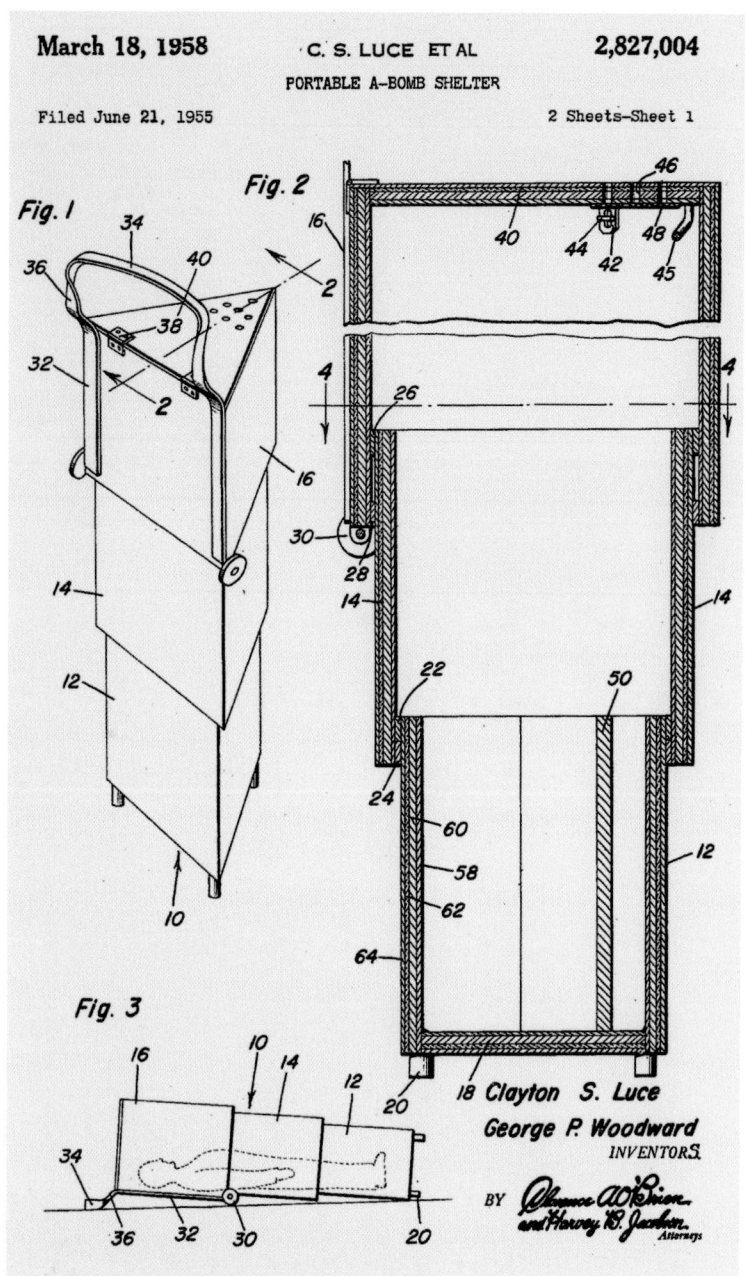

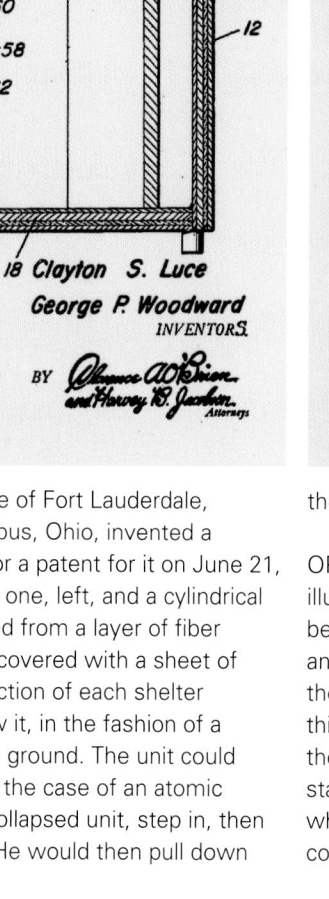

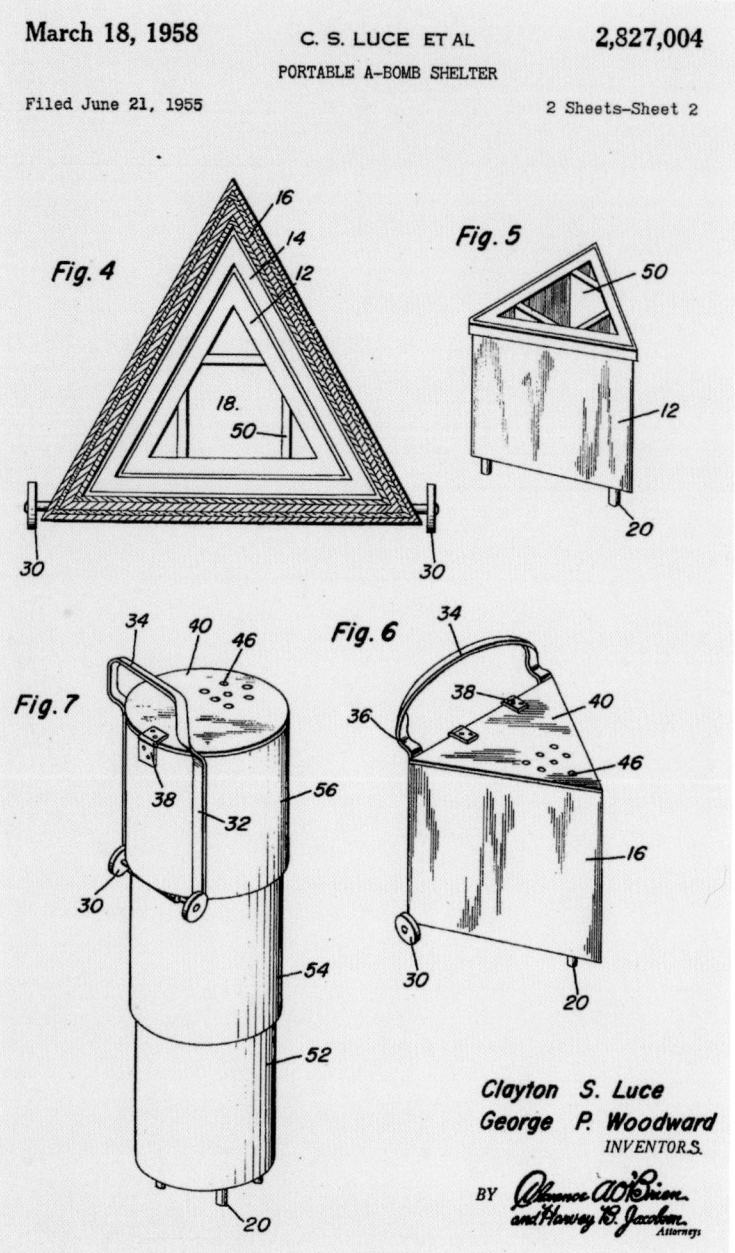

March 18, 1958   C. S. LUCE ET AL   2,827,004
PORTABLE A-BOMB SHELTER
Filed June 21, 1955   2 Sheets-Sheet 1

Fig. 1 Fig. 2 Fig. 3

Clayton S. Luce
George P. Woodward
INVENTORS
BY
Attorneys

March 18, 1958   C. S. LUCE ET AL   2,827,004
PORTABLE A-BOMB SHELTER
Filed June 21, 1955   2 Sheets-Sheet 2

Fig. 4 Fig. 5 Fig. 6 Fig. 7

Clayton S. Luce
George P. Woodward
INVENTORS
BY
Attorneys

ABOVE AND ABOVE RIGHT Clayton S. Luce of Fort Lauderdale, Florida, and George P. Woodward of Columbus, Ohio, invented a portable atomic bomb shelter and applied for a patent for it on June 21, 1955. There were two versions: a triangular one, left, and a cylindrical one, right. The shelter was to be constructed from a layer of fiber attached to plywood, which would then be covered with a sheet of asbestos and an aluminum skin. The top section of each shelter collapsed down to enclose the pieces below it, in the fashion of a telescope, allowing the wheels to touch the ground. The unit could then be tilted and pulled with the handle. In the case of an atomic attack, a person would open the lid of the collapsed unit, step in, then pull the telescoping pieces up around him. He would then pull down

the lid, which was equipped with ventilation holes, over his head.

OPPOSITE A plan for a one-man barrel shelter made of wood was illustrated in a 1954 book called The Bomb, Survival and You. It was to be constructed of vertical two-by-fours held together with metal straps and covered with a one-inch-thick plywood top. "In the emergency, lift the lid, hop in, and drop the lid. A whole house can fall down on top of this husky barrel with its two-by-four walls and no harm will come to the occupant," the book says. "Shelter of this type may be left standing in institutions, or even in children's play areas in the home, where it could serve as a table." The smaller drawing shows the components of the shelter tucked into a corner for storage.

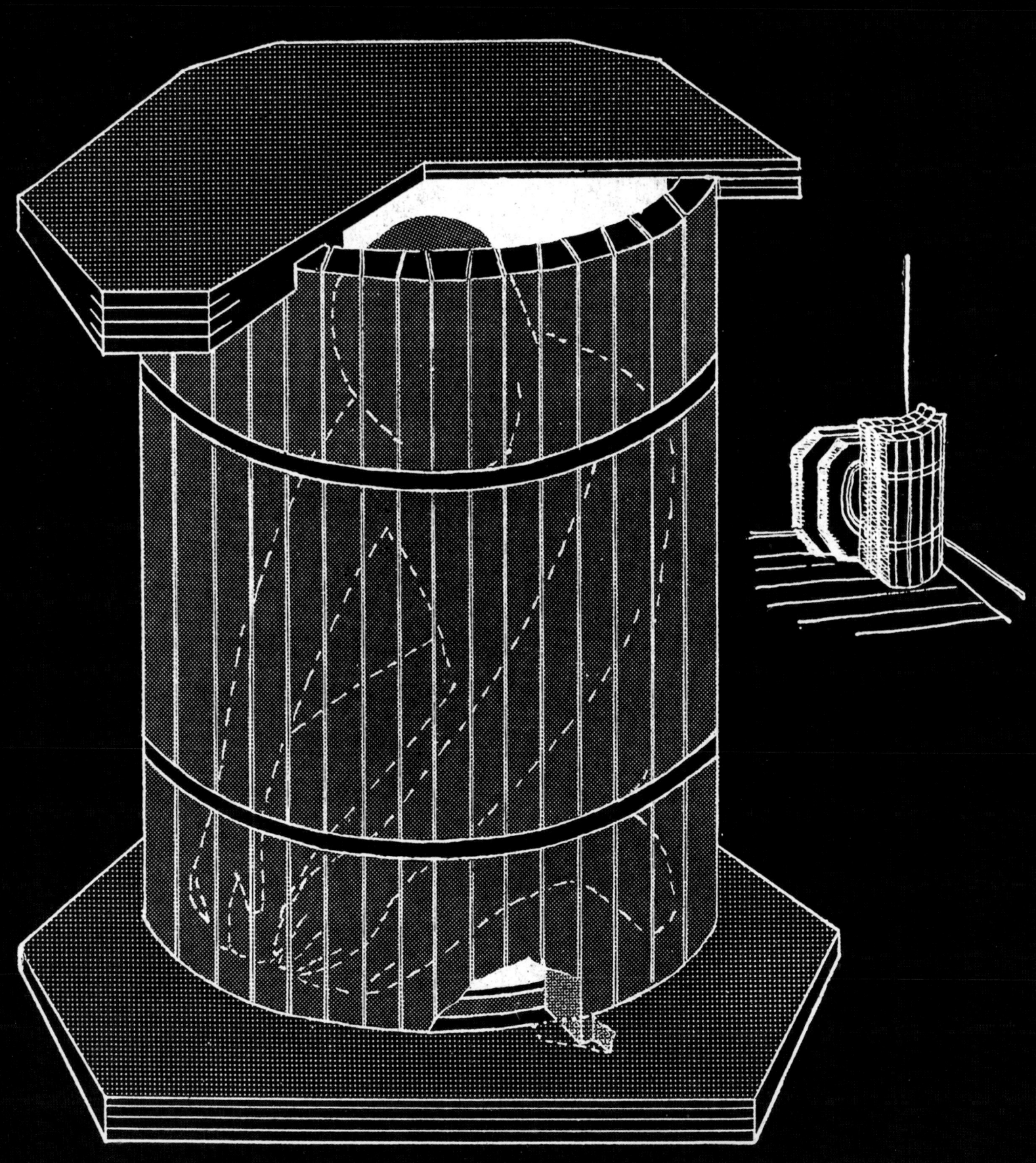

CD Chief Urges Early Plans To Preserve Home In Attack

By FRANCIS V. SCANLAN

Does the thought that members of your family might die because of your ignorance bother you?

If not, then don't read any further.

If, however, you are one of those people who think that a few hours of work is not too much to exchange for the lives of yourself and your children, then it would be worthwhile to see what the experts say on how to save your life in case of a nuclear attack.

If you think that someone is going to help you get organized when the bomb hits, you must be naive indeed.

Fill Tank

This may sound callous, but imagine, if you can, that a nuclear bomb is about to hit this area. Do you think that the "gas" ~~tion~~ attendant is going to hang ~~fill your~~

the family together is the best plan if time permits. Schools will close and children will be sent home.

Signal To Take Cover

A wobbly blast means duck and cover. There won't be enough time to go home. The only thing to do is take the "best available" cover. For this reason it is necessary that employers have a plan for an orderly movement to a pre-designated shelter area.

2. Use your radio. All stations except the CONELRAD stations at 640 and 1240 will go off the air. The civil defense authorities will give an exact evaluation of the situation and any local instructions which may be pertinent.

3. Have a family plan. Try to imagine all the possible situations in which you might be caught and ~~~~ which best solves

NUCLEAR HOUSEKEEPING

In the era of the atomic bomb, the term "nuclear family" took on a new meaning: It was to be the basic unit of defense in America's Cold War civilian army. Judging from the illustrations in Civil Defense publications, the Nuclear Family was never African-American, Hispanic, Native American, Asian, gay, or disabled. It was always Wonder Bread, Leave-it-to-Beaver white. The Nuclear Family shown in these leaflets reflected the stereotypical gender roles of the time: Dad was the provider, Mom was the homemaker.

Instead of referring to the shelter as a home fallout shelter or a domestic fallout shelter, the government chose to call it a *family* fallout shelter. No matter what time of day or night an attack would come, the family would be together, nestled safely in

OPPOSITE In an article in the June 14, 1959 issue of the *Hartford Courant,* Civil Defense official Thomas Shortell argues: "Families are always planning things together—vacations, picnics, trips and so forth. Why shouldn't they take the same amount of care to plan for defense in case of emergency?"

their shelter. Mom, as the Atomic Housekeeper, had the biggest role to play. "A house that is neglected is a house that may be doomed in the atomic age," warned the Civil Defense film, *The House in the Middle*. To keep her family out of harm's way, Mom had to be a combination nurse, cook, morale booster, and supply administrator. She had to know, for example, that an ironing board could serve as a stretcher for the injured or wounded. The shelter had to be furnished and equipped. But that was no easy task. Mom had to buy and install beds, chairs, tables and shelving; she had to stock the shelter with a two-week supply of foodstuffs that did not require refrigeration, like canned goods, cereals, cookies, crackers, peanut butter, and coffee. These conventional pantry items could be supplemented with foods created specifically for the shelter, like "Survival Biscuits," life-sustaining crackers with an endless shelf-life. Not only did Mom have to assemble a first-aid kit containing more than twenty essential items, she had to be

well-versed in fire prevention. The house must be kept tidy, because a messy house is more likely to catch fire during an atomic attack. Clear out rubbish! Clean out the attic! Don't let newspapers pile up! The pamphlet *Fire Fighting for Households* advised getting rid of things that burn easily, like "curtains, draperies, tablecloths, bedclothes, lamp shades, coats, suits, dresses, wicker and wooden furniture, rags, and linoleum." The pamphlet *Atomic Blast Creates Fire: Are You Prepared?* preached, "Good, clean housekeeping is Civil Defense Housekeeping." Mom must also fireproof the fabrics in her home: "Dissolve nine ounces of Borax and four ounces of boric acid in a gallon of water. Dip your curtains, drapes and slipcovers in it."

Post-attack, the Nuclear Family had to be prepared to take on all the functions normally handled by society, from medical care to traffic control to firefighting. One family member should be appointed Family Fire Marshall and learn firefighting tools and methods. Another must take on

MEAT
PRODUCTS

WATER
14 QTS

CEREAL

MEAT
2 CANS

CRACKERS

VEGETABLE
OIL

SHORTENING
1 CAN

COOKIES
2 BOXES

the role of medic and be trained in first-aid treatment for likely injuries, including broken bones, burns, external and internal bleeding, poisoning, and shock. And since the family had to be prepared for living without electricity, a battery-powered radio for receiving up-to-the-minute reports from CONELRAD (acronym for CONtrol of ELectronic RADiation), the government's emergency broadcast system, was necessary, as were battery-operated lamps.

Another essential item was a manually operated "air blower," a fan equipped with a "fallout filter" that, when you turned its hand crank, would pull "clean" air into the shelter. To determine when it would be safe to leave the shelter, the family needed a dosimeter, a pen-sized scope that measured radiation levels in the air, and its battery-operated charger. The shopping list went on and on: sheets, blankets, coats, gloves, paper plates, light bulbs, toilet paper, sanitary napkins, washcloths, towels, soap, matches, and more. It seemed to never end. And don't forget the can opener! A crowbar, a pick-ax, and a shovel were essential tools for digging through post-attack debris that could block the door when it was time to emerge from the shelter. The motto for the Atomic Housekeeper might as well have been "Shop 'til you drop."

Publications promoting shelters portrayed time spent in a fallout shelter as something between a campout and a vacation. On the cover of *The Fallout Shelter Handbook*, the Nuclear Family is

OPPOSITE A photograph published in the *Chicago Sun-Times* on October 27, 1962, shows Mary Mitchen, a checkout clerk at the Jewel Food Store, holding the cash register receipt for the groceries spread out in front of her. This is the amount of food that Illinois Civil Defense officials said must be stocked for each family member in preparation for a two-week stay in a shelter.

shown enjoying domestic harmony in their buried backyard shelter. Dad smokes a pipe. Mom, wearing a dress, apron and heels, puts dishes away. Daughter sets the table. It's as though the family room—with its mid-20th century modern furnishings—had been magically lifted out of the house and buried in the backyard.

However, the reality of life in a fallout shelter was something else altogether. To promote shelters, sellers staged publicity stunts, offering prizes to people who would stay in one and then rave about it to the press. In 1959, Florida newlyweds Melvin and Maria Mininson spent two weeks in a shelter for a stunt sponsored by a store in Miami. When they emerged, they became famous as the atomic Honeymoon Couple, before departing on their prize trip to Mexico. Years later, in an interview, they confessed how uncomfortable the shelter actually was, with its temperature reaching over 90 degrees.

Some people who stayed in shelters as part of Civil Defense-sponsored demonstrations gave similarly grim descriptions of their time underground. Harold Peters, an editor for the *Boston Globe*, spent a week in a nine-by-twelve foot underground shelter with his wife and three daughters. Humidity and the lack of ventilation were their biggest complaints. "The Peters' belongings were damp and covered with mildew," wrote the newspaper. "The soles of their shoes were coming apart from the rot induced by the dampness." Anne Peters, 17, gratefully emerged from the weeklong stay saying, "This is the best thing in the whole world, fresh air." A Houston family who spent 72 hours in a shelter complained about the lack of light and sanitation. "We had small-wattage bulbs in there. My eyes, after a few days, started stinging through eye strain," Stanley Christmas recalled decades later. "But the biggest problem was one that no one really thinks about.

They gave us two chemical toilets, and we filled those in two days. On the third day we had to use cans and bottles and any other containers we could find."

Thomas A. Powner, his wife Madelin, and their three small children spent two weeks in a simulated shelter at Princeton University in Princeton, New Jersey, as part of a Civil Defense-sponsored study in 1959. They reported awakening with headaches because of the lack of oxygen. At the end of the two weeks, the couple said they were able to cope with the pressures of the stay only by drinking whiskey and giving tranquilizers to their children.

Comedian Woody Allen cleverly captured the spirit of these exercises in a routine performed on the satirical comedy television show *That Was the Week That Was*, when he described a two-week-shelter stay with his wife:

> We entered the air raid shelter on
> Monday morning at 11:30.
> We went in, my wife and me, we shut
> the door, we sat down, we faced each
> other, and we chatted, and we read,
> and we ate three very nice meals; and
> by then, already, it was noon.
> She was beginning to get on my nerves.
> Tuesday we spent most of our time
> just standing in the center of the
> room shrieking.
> Wednesday we played gin rummy,
> and she came at me with an ax.
> Thursday my wife's spirits began to
> lift perceptibly; she woke up Thursday
> morning; she was smiling, she was
> laughing.
> She laughed straight through until the
> following Wednesday.
> She woke up on the next Thursday
> and she said to me, 'Does the
> King suspect?'
> I left the shelter. She's still there. It's
> been four years.
> You can write to her if you want to.

A FAMILY ACTION PROGRAM

HOME PROTECTION
exercises

MP-2-1
(Misc. Publication)

EXECUTIVE OFFICE OF THE PRESIDENT
Office of Civil and Defense Mobilization

(Revised September 1958)
(Reprinted May 1959)

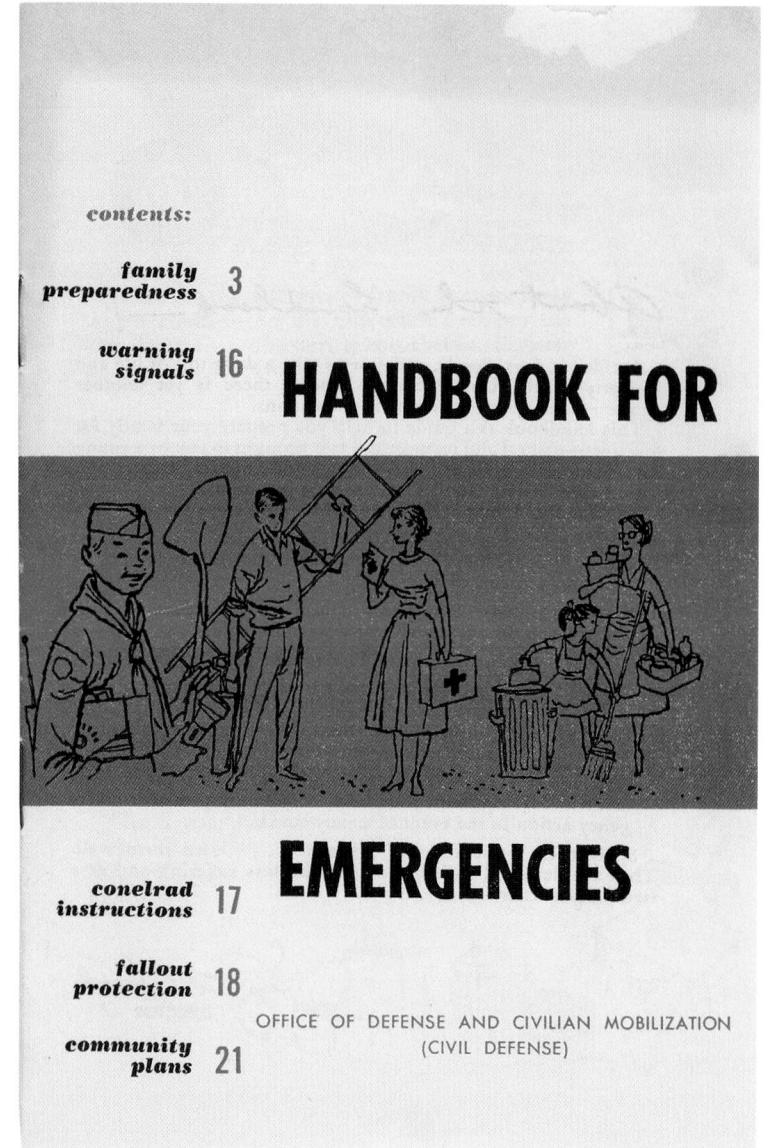

HANDBOOK FOR EMERGENCIES

OFFICE OF DEFENSE AND CIVILIAN MOBILIZATION
(CIVIL DEFENSE)

ABOVE A domestic battle plan was outlined in the 1958 Civil Defense publication *Home Protection Exercises: A Family Action Program.* Every family member was assigned specific tasks, such as unplugging appliances, closing windows, drawing blinds and curtains, and assembling an emergency evacuation kit. Mom was responsible for holding regular drills so the family would know what to do during an attack. "Talk over the rehearsals afterward and decide how each performance can be improved," the publication instructed. "Drill any lagging members of the family again."

ABOVE The Civil Defense *Handbook for Emergencies* was distributed to families by the Boy Scouts of America, an organization whose motto has always been "Be prepared." A uniformed scout, left, is equipped with a shovel, flashlight, and a radio for tuning in to CONELRAD broadcasts.

OPPOSITE As depicted in *Home Protection Exercises: A Family Action Program*, a house was a firetrap just waiting to happen. First step: Go through the rooms and remove all fire hazards—throw out old paint rags, check electrical fixtures, and remove rubbish and trash. Once that's done, assemble firefighting tools: a fire extinguisher, hose adapters for all indoor faucets, containers of sand, water buckets, a shovel, and a ladder.

REMOVE HOME FIRE HAZARDS

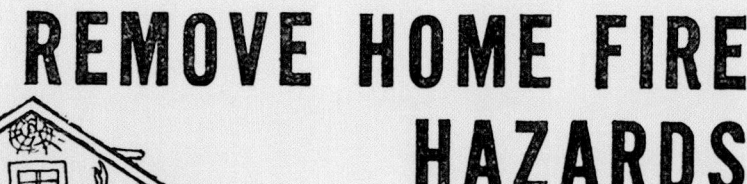

Chimney and roof in good condition?

Attic a junk pile?

Stairs or halls cluttered?

Trash and rubbish near your house?

Is your basement a fire hazard?   Paint rags?

Shavings near work bench?

Fuel within 3 ft. of furnace?

Open paint or oil cans?

Piled-up paper and rubbish?

Electrical circuits and fixtures OK?

THEN

When your house is cleared of fire hazards assemble your fire fighting tools

A fire extinguisher

Hose adapter for inside faucets

Sand, covered water buckets, and shovel

A good hose near at hand

A ladder in good condition

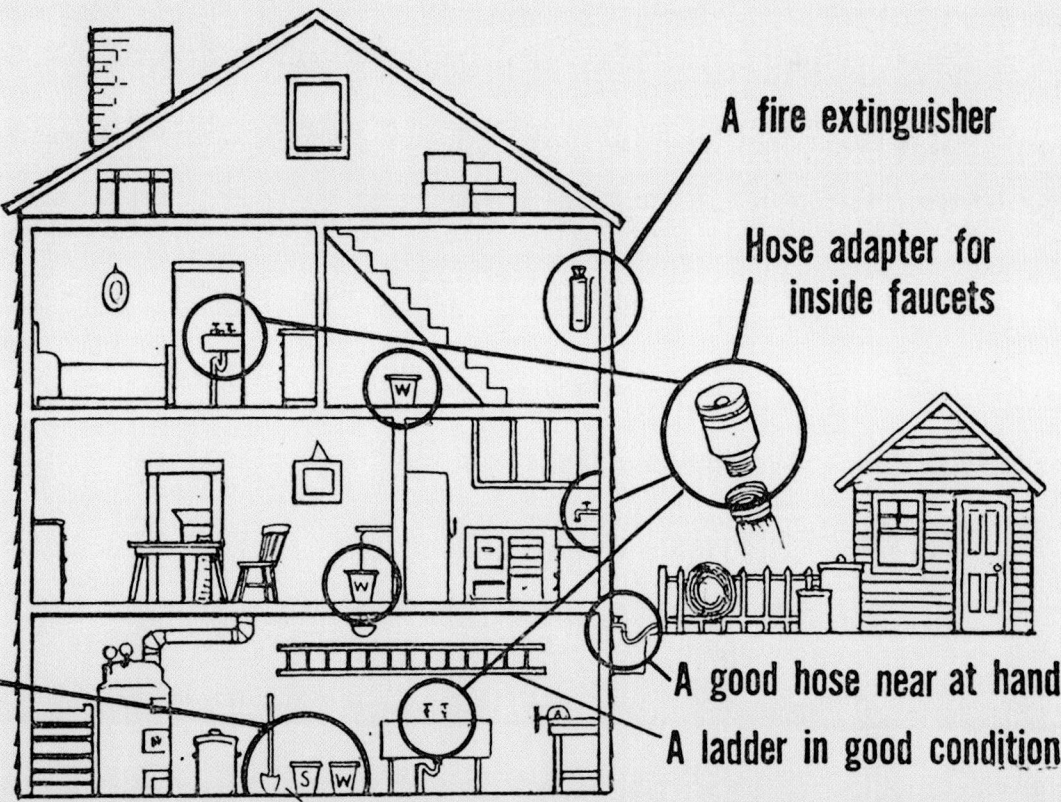

BEFORE DISASTER STRIKES

YOU SHOULD KNOW....

Where to find safe water	How to dispose of garbage
How to turn off water service valve	How to dispose of human wastes
How to purify water	How to make soil bags
What foods to store and how to prepare them	What to do with frozen foods
What foods are unsafe	

YOU SHOULD HAVE....

Stored water or other liquid (7 gals. per person)	A covered pail for bathroom purposes
A 2-week supply of proper foods, paper plates and napkins	Toilet tissue, paper towels, sanitary napkins, disposable diapers, soap
Cooking and eating utensils, measuring cup, can and bottle openers, pocket knife and matches	Rubber sheeting and special equipment for the sick
Special foods for babies and the sick	Grocery bags, week's supply of newspapers for sanitary uses, waterproof gloves
Large garbage can to keep garbage	2 pts. of house-hold chlorine, 1 qt. of 5 per-cent DDT
Smaller can for human wastes	Wrench, screwdriver, shovel, and other tools

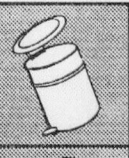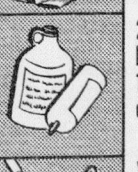

TEAR OUT THIS PAGE FOR YOUR CHECKLIST

ABOVE An illustrated checklist called "Before Disaster Strikes" was included in the Civil Defense publication, *Emergency Sanitation at Home: A Family Handbook*, as a pullout centerfold in 1958. Readers were urged to remove it from the booklet and use it as a guide to ready their shelters. Preparedness activities were split into two categories. The first one was called "You Should Know." It required learning how to purify water, how to determine when foods are unsafe, and how to properly dispose of garbage and human wastes. The second one, entitled "You Should Have," required gathering a daunting amount of supplies and equipment, starting with containers of water (seven gallons for every shelter occupant); continuing through the necessities for cooking and eating—plates, cutlery, a measuring cup, can and bottle openers, a pocket knife, and matches. The list ended with a set of tools—a wrench, screwdriver, and shovel.

RIGHT This illustration of shelter necessities was published in 1963 in a 131-page Civil Defense manual called *Personal and Family Survival*. Supplies and equipment deemed "essential" are shown against a gray background. These included: sanitation and medical supplies; food, water, and a can opener; a radiation meter and a battery-operated radio; baby bottles; a flashlight; batteries and Civil Defense manuals. The lower-priority items, shown against a light background, included bedding, clothing, diapers, eating utensils, a calendar, a clock, and an array of tools, such as an ax, a crowbar, a screwdriver, a saw, a wrench, and a shovel.

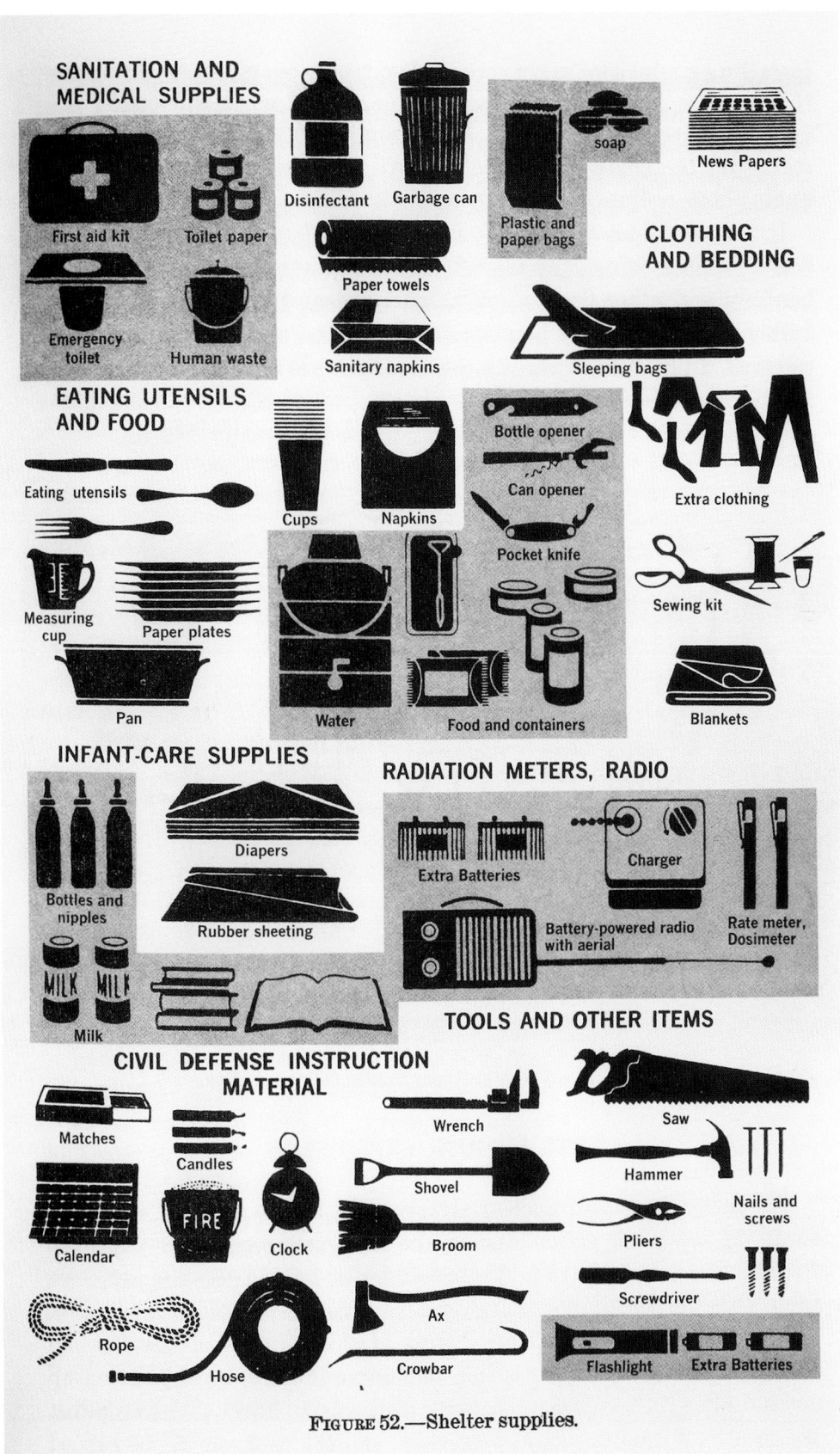

FIGURE 52.—Shelter supplies.

LEFT The September 15, 1961, issue of *Life* published this photograph of Art Carlson, a New York plumbing contractor, with his wife and three children in a fully stocked Kelsey-Hayes basement fallout shelter. The photograph was designed to demonstrate how a family could share responsibilities in order to keep the family shelter in a state of readiness. Dad Carlson is in charge of making sure tools are in tip-top shape, as well as monitoring the supply of bottled gas to be used for cooking. His wife—identified only as Mrs. Carlson—maintains the larder of canned food and water on the shelves behind her. Each of the children has also been assigned tasks. Charlene, left, handles the bedding for the folding cots and bunks. Claude keeps an eye on the battery-operated lamps and the radio. Judy, as the "shelter librarian," is responsible for providing books and games to keep the family entertained during their post-attack stay. The person who staged the pose may have had the Grant Wood painting *American Gothic* in mind. In it, the archetypal farmer holds a pitchfork; here, the patriarch of the nuclear family wields a shovel, to dig his way out after the blast.

YOUR FAMILY SURVIVAL PLAN

PA—578

Federal Extension Service, U S. Department of Agriculture in cooperation with the Office of Civil Defense, Department of Defense.

LEFT On the cover of *Your Family Survival Plan*, a Civil Defense pamphlet, Mother, aided by Daughter, is depicted stocking canned food on shelves, while Dad sits passively on the side. Civil Defense publications always represented Mother as the active member of the Nuclear Family unless a construction project was involved, in which case the focus would be on Dad. The leaflet unfolds to reveal a 15 x 21½-inch wall chart that is meant to serve as the family's preparedness battle plan. It had a detailed checklist of necessary shelter items called, "Check What Your Family Has Now…Note What You'd Need for Emergency Survival."

OPPOSITE On June 24, 1960, the *Chicago Daily Tribune* published a detailed menu plan recommended for the atomic homemaker in an article headlined, "Meals for Two Days in Fallout Shelter." The menu was created by Jeanne Bryant, a home economist from Armour & Company, a manufacturer of canned meat products. Predictably, the meals included a lot of meat. She is shown preparing a meal in a prototype shelter. The recommendations were specific: Stock canned food in sizes sufficient to feed the family for only one meal in order to eliminate leftovers that would require refrigeration, and choose foods that don't require water for cooking, because water supplies would be limited.

Meals for Two Days in Fallout Shelter

Luncheon for four, two adults and two children under 10, includes cream of vegetable soup, deviled ham spread on crisp crackers, and for dessert canned bing cherries. Beverages could be coffee, tea, or hot chocolate. Paper plates and cups also are suggested.
[TRIBUNE Photos by John Austad and Earl Gustie]

Foods and Menus for a Family of Four

MENUS

Four Servings for 6 Meals and Snacks

BREAKFAST
Pineapple-Grapefruit Juice
Corned Beef Hash
(Corn Flakes with Milk for Children)
Coffee or Tea   Hot Chocolate

BREAKFAST
Orange and Grapefruit Sections
Creamed Dried Beef on Melba Toast
Coffee or Tea   Hot Chocolate

LUNCH
Fried Sliced Luncheon Meat
Stewed Tomatoes
Brown Bread
Coffee or Tea   Hot Chocolate

LUNCH
Cream of Vegetable Soup
Deviled Ham on Crackers
Bing Cherries
Coffee or Tea   Hot Chocolate

DINNER
Beef Stew
French Fried Onion Rings
Peach Melba
Coffee or Tea   Hot Chocolate

DINNER
Chopped Ham Slices
Sweet Potatoes   Peas
Pear Halves
Coffee or Tea   Hot Chocolate

FOODS

CANNED MEATS AND VEGETABLES
1 can (12 ounces) chopped ham
1 can (15½ ounces) corned beef hash
1 can (12 ounces) luncheon meat
1 can (24 ounces) beef stew
1 jar (2½ ounces) sliced dried beef
1 can (12 ounces) corned beef
2 cans (3 ounces each) deviled ham
1 can (16 ounces) sweet potatoes
1 can (16-17 ounces) peas
1 can (6 ounces) french fried onions
1 can (16-17 ounces) stewed tomatoes

CANNED FRUITS
1 can (16-17 ounces) pear halves
1 can (1 pint) pineapple-grapefruit juice
1 can (16-17 ounces) cling peach halves
1 can (16 ounces) orange, grapefruit sections
1 can (16 ounces) bing cherries, pitted

MISCELLANEOUS
6 cans (14½ ounces) evaporated milk
1 jar (2 ounces) instant coffee
1 jar (¾ ounce) instant tea

1 can (8 ounces) chocolate sirup
1 can (3½ ounces) coconut
1 jar vanilla pudding for infants
1 can (11 ounces) brown bread
1 box (7½ ounces) soda crackers
1 box (8 ounces) rye wafers
1 box (6 ounces) melba toast
2 cans cream of vegetable soup
1 can candy
1 can peanuts
1 pint salad oil
1 box (8 ounces) corn flakes
Flour, salt, pepper and sugar

You Can Serve Variety of Nourishing Dishes

BY MADELINE HOLLAND

SHELTERS offering protection against nuclear bomb fallout have been like the weather up to now. Many people talked about them, but few did anything.

Robert O. LeRoy, president of a construction company in Lyons and a prisoner in a nazi concentration camp during World War II, is among those who have done something about shelters. He has constructed, at a cost of $5,000, a prototype underground shelter fully equipped with every necessity for complete protection.

Known as a "foldup fallout shelter," it is equipped with chairs, beds, tables, and other furnishings that fold up to provide more space as needed.

Because food is an important factor, LeRoy contacted home economists of Armour & Co. who worked out menus in accordance with recommendations of the office of civil defense mobilization.

To dramatize the shelter, the Walter Williams family of Harvey spent two days and two nights in the shelter, living, eating, and sleeping under actual confinement conditions.

As a result of their experience, Armour home economists adjusted the menus to provide ample nourishment for a family of four — two adults and two children under 10 years of age — in the shelter.

In planning the menus, Jeanne Bryant of Armour & Co. selected foods that store easily, keep without refrigeration, are easily prepared, and require little cooking. She was concerned with providing variety in the meals, as well as a low fat and low starch diet for a family with only a minimum of exercise.

Menus also had to be planned around the equipment in the shelter and minimum water requirements. As suggested by the civil defense office, the basic equipment is: one or two cooking pans; disposable tableware, paper plates, cups, and napkins; measuring cup; bottle and can opener; pocket knife, matches, a small cooking unit which produces a small flame and uses little oxygen.

According to the civil defense experts, the minimum requirement of water for drinking and food preparation is ½ gallon a person a day. Therefore, foods requiring the minimum addition of water for preparation were selected.

Another major concern of the menu makers was refuse. Cans and jars of foods in sizes to meet family needs for only one meal were selected for meat, poultry, fish, vegetables, fruit, evaporated milk, and other foods which deteriorate rapidly unless refrigerated after the container is opened. This also helped to eliminate the problems of leftovers.

The basic survival needs of a fallout shelter are a 2 weeks' supply of food and water, cooking and eating utensils and equipment, fuel, clothing, bedding, first aid supplies, special medicines [if required by chronic illness], sanitation supplies and equipment, and a battery powered radio.

The major requirement of a home shelter for protection from radioactive fallout is that the top and sides be covered with enough dense material [concrete, earth] to shield the occupants from penetrating gamma radiation. Other requirements include proper entrance design [not more than two feet wide], ventilation, adequate space, and sanitation facilities.

Jeanne Bryant, home economist, Armour & Co., cooks canned luncheon meat on the bottled gas cook stove in the compact but complete cooking area of the "fold up fallout shelter." The cooking area also includes small sink, water, battery powered spotlights, and cooking utensils. Within reaching distance are first aid kit, geiger counter, hand pump for filtering contaminated air, folding card table and chairs, survival kit, and fold up cots.

For this dinner, sliced canned chopped ham, drained sweet potatoes, and canned peas are cooked together in a skillet until heated thru. Canned pear halves are served as dessert with beverage.

A typical fallout shelter breakfast doesn't differ too much from the ordinary: orange and grapefruit segments from a container, creamed dried beef on packaged melba toast, and choice of beverages.

OPPOSITE An unidentified woman prepares to take a bite of a "Survival Biscuit," a cracker created by Civil Defense authorities to serve as a food substitute after a nuclear attack. The article accompanying this photograph, which was published in the *Chicago Daily News* on March 14, 1962, said seventy tons of the biscuits would be stored in empty warehouses until they could be moved to public shelters.

RIGHT Emergency life-sustaining rations—"survival crackers" and "carbohydrate food supplements"—were manufactured in the early 1960s to be stocked in public shelters. The crackers in this sample package, purchased on eBay nearly fifty years later, are a bit crumbled, but have held up remarkably well.

City of Detroit
Office of Civil Defense
PUBLIC FALLOUT SHELTER SUPPLIES

Designated public fallout shelters in Detroit can give radiation protection to over 600,000 persons in a civil defense emergency. Hundreds of shelters are stocked with food, water drums, medical and sanitation supplies and radiation detection equipment.

The two food items enclosed in this package are samples of food stored in the shelters.

1. **Survival Cracker**—a flour base cracker containing approximately 30 calories. When this is the only food item in the shelter, each shelteree receives 36 crackers daily.

2. **Carbohydrate Food Supplement**—a sugar base candy-like item. When it is part of the shelter food supply, each shelteree receives 12 pieces of this supplement and 24 survival crackers.

For 196-CA (12-64)

Take a Lesson from Grandma's Pantry··

make an emergency Preparedness Plan

FOR FURTHER INFORMATION CONTACT YOUR

LEFT This Civil Defense poster from the 1950s advises housewives to "Take a Lesson from Grandma's Pantry." It was part of a preparedness campaign created to persuade the homemaker to have a seven-day supply of food on hand to sustain herself and her family after an atomic attack.

BELOW LEFT Mrs. W.C. Bruner is shown in her basement fallout shelter holding a container of saltine crackers in a photograph published on November 16, 1962, in *The Knoxville News-Sentinel*, with the caption "Prepared for the Worst." She has stocked the shelves with canned fruits and vegetables (commercial and homemade), canned meats (Spam), soft drinks (Coca-Cola and Pepsi), and jars of water. Her eight-year-old daughter, Rhonda, is lying on the wooden bunk that will serve as a bed.

OPPOSITE A woman posed in a model shelter is running through a checklist of necessary supplies, including a variety of canned foods stored on shelves, a first aid kit, a battery-operated lantern, and a foot-pedal garbage can. Visible at top left is a hand-crank blower which was designed to pull fresh air into the shelter via an attached tube that extended aboveground.

ABOVE Having enough water in a shelter was an absolute must. The labels on the privately produced U.S. Aqua, left, and the government issued Emergency Drinking Water, right, both claimed that the water would stay potable for years and the U.S. Aqua label claims the can is "impervious to nuclear fallout."

OPPOSITE A man serves "Emergency Drinking Water" to a few people. Emergency public shelters were to be stocked with large cans of water like the ones shown here.

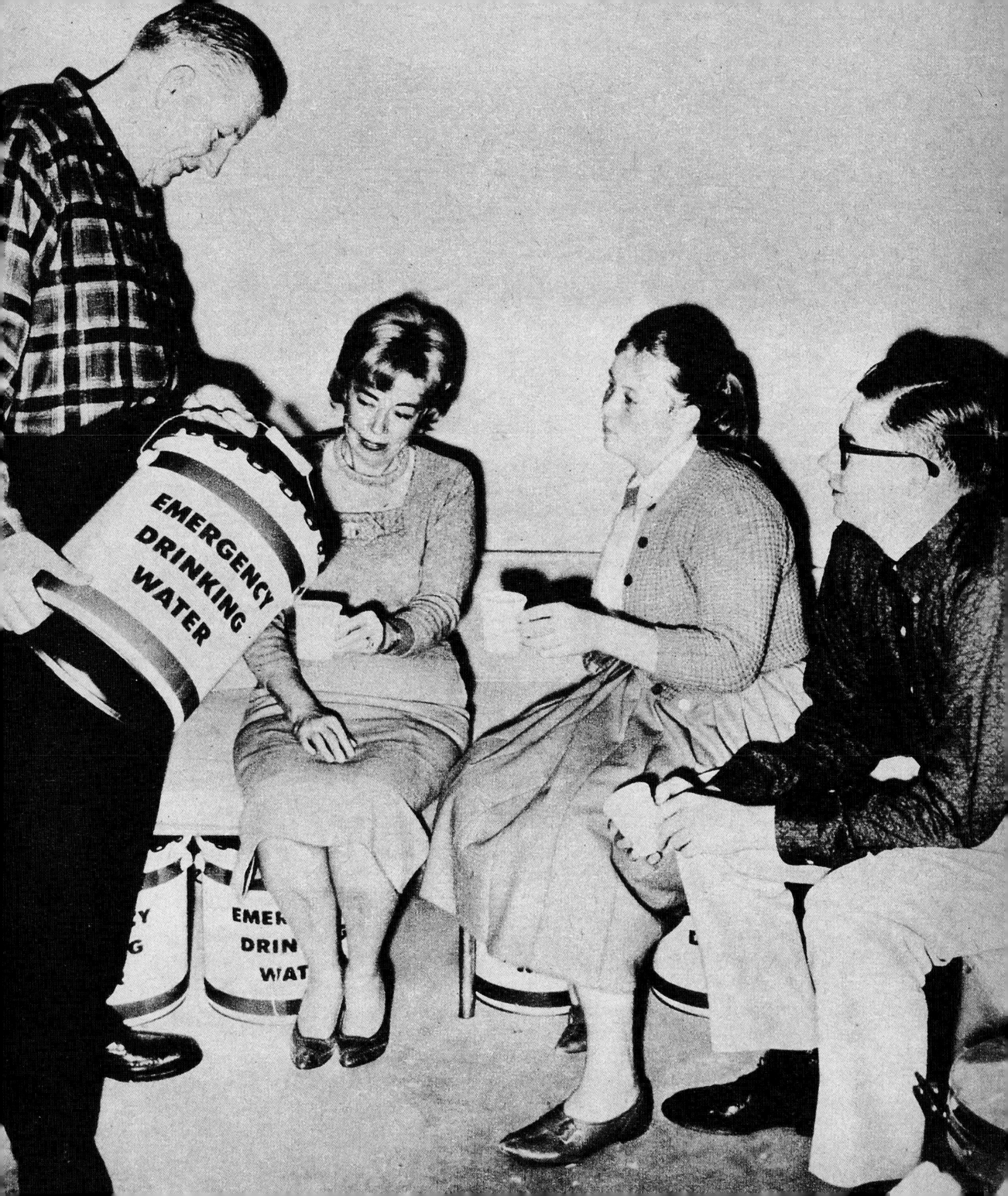

OPPOSITE The U-238 Atomic Energy Lab was an educational toy manufactured for the budding nuclear scientist in the early 1950s by the A.C. Gilbert Company. Among its contents were four types of uranium ore, a Geiger counter, an instruction manual, and a comic book called *Dagwood Splits the Atom*.

RIGHT A Colonial dollhouse with a fallout shelter, manufactured by Marx Toys, was included in the 1962 Sears Christmas catalog (bottom right). The accompanying copy described it as "one of the most up-to-date toys you can give little girls." The furniture for the shelter, including folding cots, was sold separately.

405 Bluebird Lane

Eight-room luxury house built of steel. Two-story colonial style boasts these features .. ringing doorbell, living room light, vinyl-framed walk lined by plastic shrubs and a plastic picket fence around the swimming pool.

Colorful steel house has 22 plastic doll inhabitants. Scaled-to-size, they're made to be moved to any of the 8 rooms: bath, nursery, bedroom, family room, kitchen, laundry room, living-dining area. Attractive appointments include cloth draperies that frame 5 windows; 3 window awnings; plastic shutters and porch. Plus sports car. 52 plastic pieces furnish 8 rooms, include record cabinet, bed, buffet, tableware, washer, lawn pieces, etc. Unassembled. 44x14x18 inches high.
79 N 1424L—Wt. 17 lbs......$15.88
79 N 4660—"D" Batteries. Order 2 for house lights. Wt. 4 oz.. Each 16c

$15⁸⁸
without batteries

7-room Northern Colonial Metal House with sun porch
$9⁹⁹

Steel house is painted to look like red clapboard and white brick, with "landscaped" exterior. Portico has simulated wrought iron door. Rooms include family room, living-dining area, kitchen, utility room, bedroom, bath, nursery. Has 51 scaled-to-size plastic pieces. Awnings shade second floor. 4 plastic figures. Unassembled. 44x15x18 inches.
79 N 1412L—Shpg. wt. 10 lbs......$9.99

Colonial Metal House has fall-out shelter
$6⁴⁴

Conversation-piece design has its own fall-out shelter! This 15x8x38-inch house makes one of the most up-to-date toys you can give little girls. They like the other special features, too, like the plastic Dutch door that opens as one piece or swings open only at the top or bottom, and the breezeway. There are eight more attractive rooms, including the patio, den, living and dining room, bedroom, nursery, kitchen and bath. Rooms are tastefully furnished with 35 plastic pieces including chairs, sofas, tables, beds, etc., all colorfully designed and each one scaled to size. Assembles easily.
79 N 1419C—Shipping weight 9 pounds...................$6.44

384 SEARS SOL.

RIGHT Ventilation for a shelter was to be provided by a "blower," a fan contained in a housing that would pull air into the shelter via a pipe extending aboveground. A sales brochure entitled *The Fallout Protection Kit* from the Champion Blower & Forge Company in Lancaster, Pennsylvania, offered six different options, ranging from a simple twelve-pound blower to a larger blower with ten feet of flexible three-inch hose, a hundred-foot roll of masking tape, and an "absolute filter" that the company claimed would prevent fallout from entering the shelter.

ABOVE In an advertisement for the Buffalo Forge Company, a boy turns the hand crank on a shelter blower to power a fan within the unit. The blower's function was to pull air into the shelter via a tube that opens at ground level. The advertisement features two blowers – a small one for the home shelter and a larger one for a group shelter.

OPPOSITE Inside a shelter, a woman demonstrated how to pedal a stationary bicycle that generated power to operate the blower.

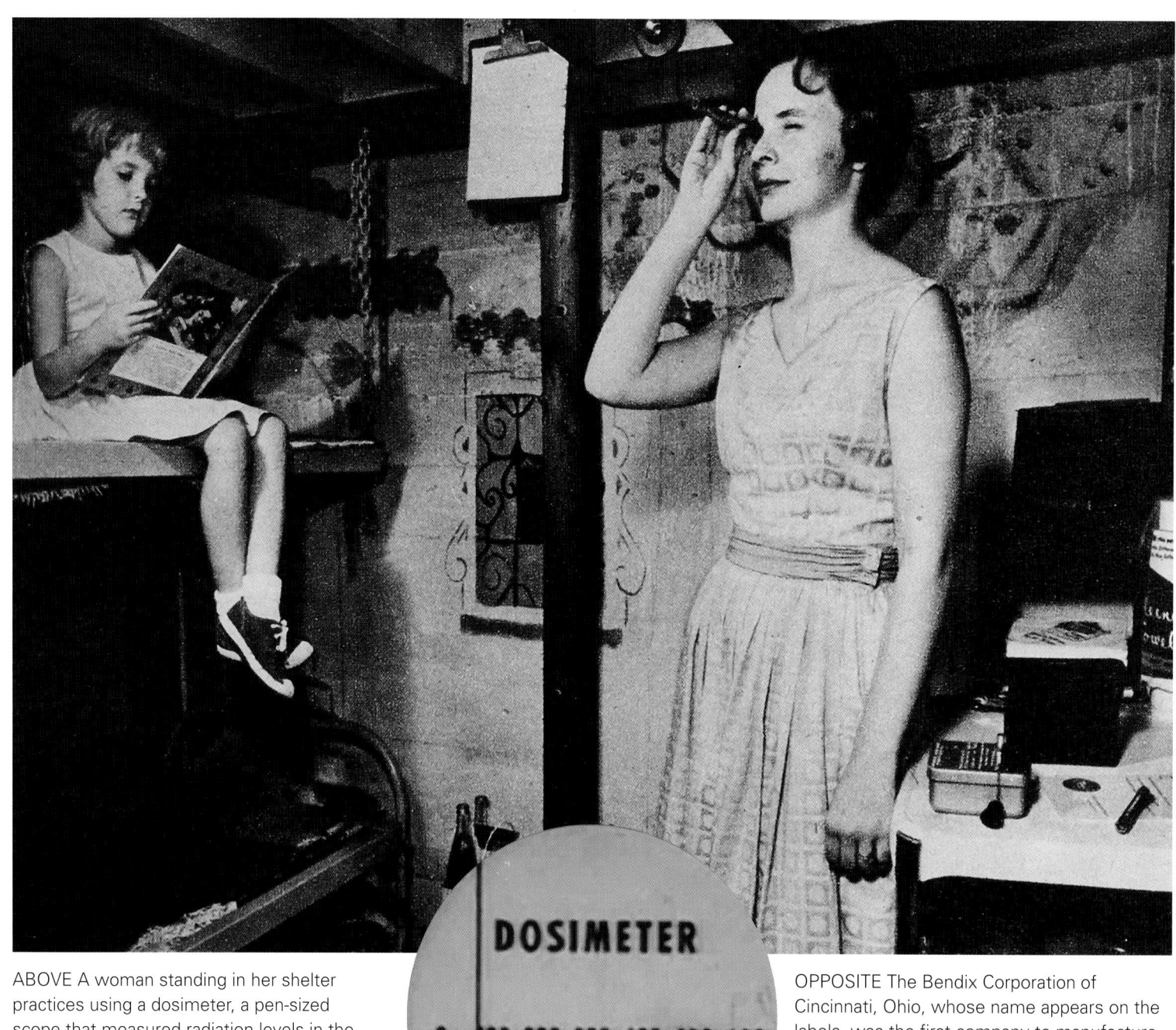

ABOVE A woman standing in her shelter practices using a dosimeter, a pen-sized scope that measured radiation levels in the atmosphere. After an attack, she (or a family member) would go outdoors and use it to determine whether it was safe to leave the shelter.

DOSIMETER

0 100 200 300 400 500 600

ROENTGENS

ABOVE This image represents what she would see in the dosimeter. The instrument indicates the level of radiation in the air as measured in roentgens.

OPPOSITE The Bendix Corporation of Cincinnati, Ohio, whose name appears on the labels, was the first company to manufacture dosimeters specifically designed for family fallout shelters.

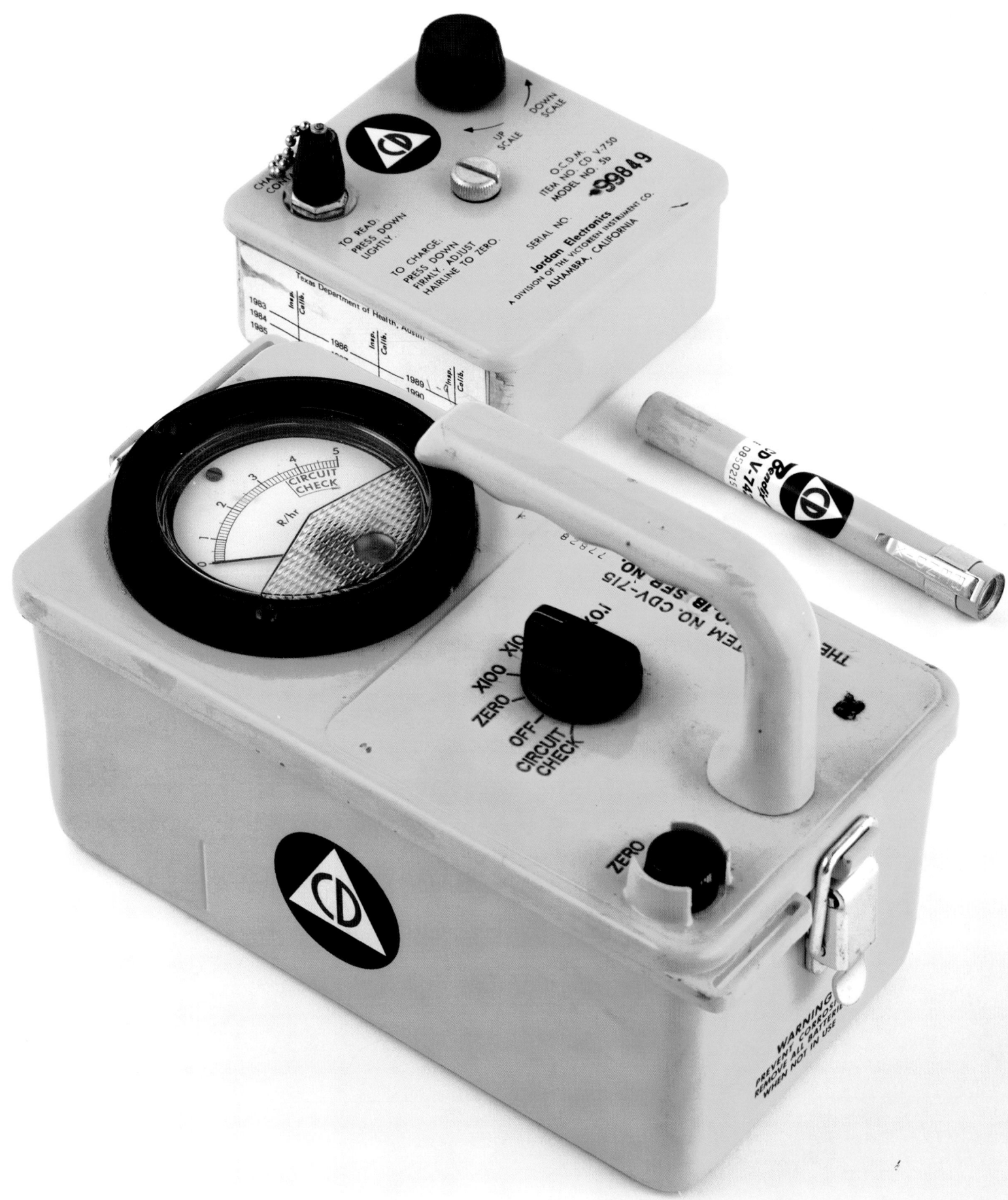

OPPOSITE The object with the handle is a radiation meter, a device that Civil Defense workers would use after an attack to detect levels of lethal radiation in the atmosphere. The findings would be visible in the round screen. It was manufactured by the Victoreen Instrument Company. It was a far more sophisticated device than the pen-sized dosimeter, right, that was designed for home use. The dosimeter required regular charging in order to function. The box-like charger, left, operated on flashlight batteries. The user would unscrew the cap at top left, remove it, and insert the end of the dosimeter into a small chamber. This one was made by Jordan Electronics, a division of the Victoreen Instrument Company.

TOP RIGHT A grim illustration in *Protection from Radioactive Fallout*, a booklet published by the New York State Civil Defense Commission, graphically depicts the effect of exposure to various levels of radiation during twenty-four hours. The "R" stands for roentgens, the unit of measurement for radioactivity.

RIGHT A chart from the *Family Fallout Shelter Handbook* utilizes groups of human figures to deliver similar information.

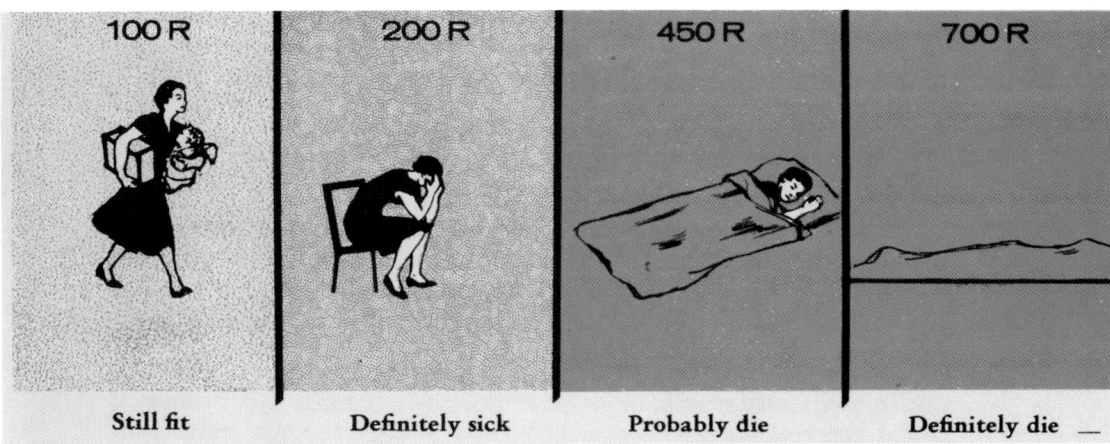

100 R	200 R	450 R	700 R
Still fit	Definitely sick	Probably die	Definitely die

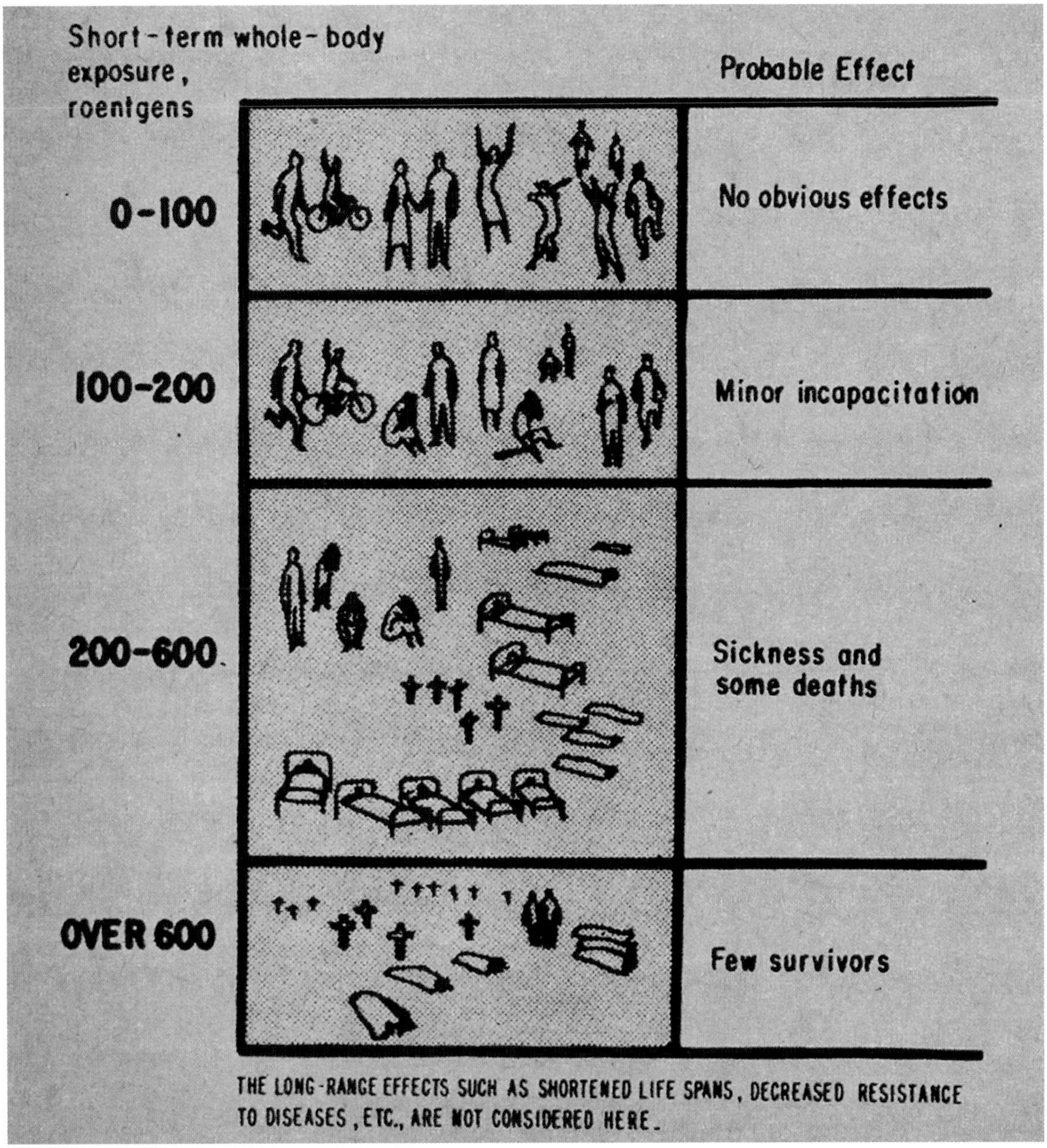

Short-term whole-body exposure, roentgens / **Probable Effect**

0-100	No obvious effects
100-200	Minor incapacitation
200-600	Sickness and some deaths
OVER 600	Few survivors

THE LONG-RANGE EFFECTS SUCH AS SHORTENED LIFE SPANS, DECREASED RESISTANCE TO DISEASES, ETC., ARE NOT CONSIDERED HERE.

CASTRO CONVERTIBLES

SPLIT SECOND *Jet Beds*

They're absolutely unique in design! You can place them in ANY area that has a 6-foot head-room — and they are a-b-c simple to attach to ANY surface (steel, concrete, brick, wood) with only 4 bolts! Once attached, it takes less than 2 seconds to ready them for comfortable sleeping! NOT ordinary folding cots for in-a-pinch use; they're 3-inch thick Poly-foam** mattresses on buoyant springs! When closed, Jet* Beds extend a mere 5 inches from the wall, giving you the most compact, out-of-the-way storage possible!

THE UNIQUE BEDS OF 101 USES

STYLE 4000 CLOSED WITH CURTAINS

LOWER UNIT USED AS COUCH

STYLE J-4000

Additional Styles Available

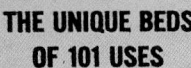

Each bed operates as an **independent unit** (pull down one or both, as the occasion demands). AND, the lower unit can be used as a restful couch! Each Poly-foam** mattress is a full 3-inches thick and is 27 by 74 inches. Helical springs of heavy-gauge steel and link-spring construction. Convenient, folding guard rail. Extends only 5 inches from wall when closed!

TABLE OPEN

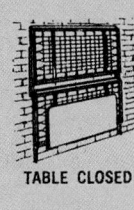

TABLE CLOSED

HANDY JET* TABLE ATTACHMENT

You can attach it quickly to the Jet* Bed unit! Gives you dining and work area in space-saving way! Snaps open in seconds, seats up to 5! 24 x 60 inches; ¾-in. Plywood top (or heat- and stain-resistant Extronic† in choice finishes). Folds for neat, out-of-way storage.

FOR ADDITIONAL INFORMATION AND ILLUSTRATED BROCHURE WRITE:

THE INCOMPARABLE   AMERICA'S TOP NAME IN CONVERTIBLE FURNITURE

Castro Convertibles

1990 JERICHO TURNPIKE, NEW HYDE PARK, N. Y.

Copyright 1961 by Castro Convertible Corp., New Hyde Park, N. Y.   *Trade-Mark Reg. U. S. Pat. Off.   †Trade-Mark   **Polyurethane foam

9

LEFT In a magazine advertisement, Castro Convertibles promoted its Split Second Jet Bed, a two-bunk unit that provided spaces for sleeping at night, and, in the morning, could flip up to rest flat against the wall. Its user could then pull down an attached table to eat breakfast.

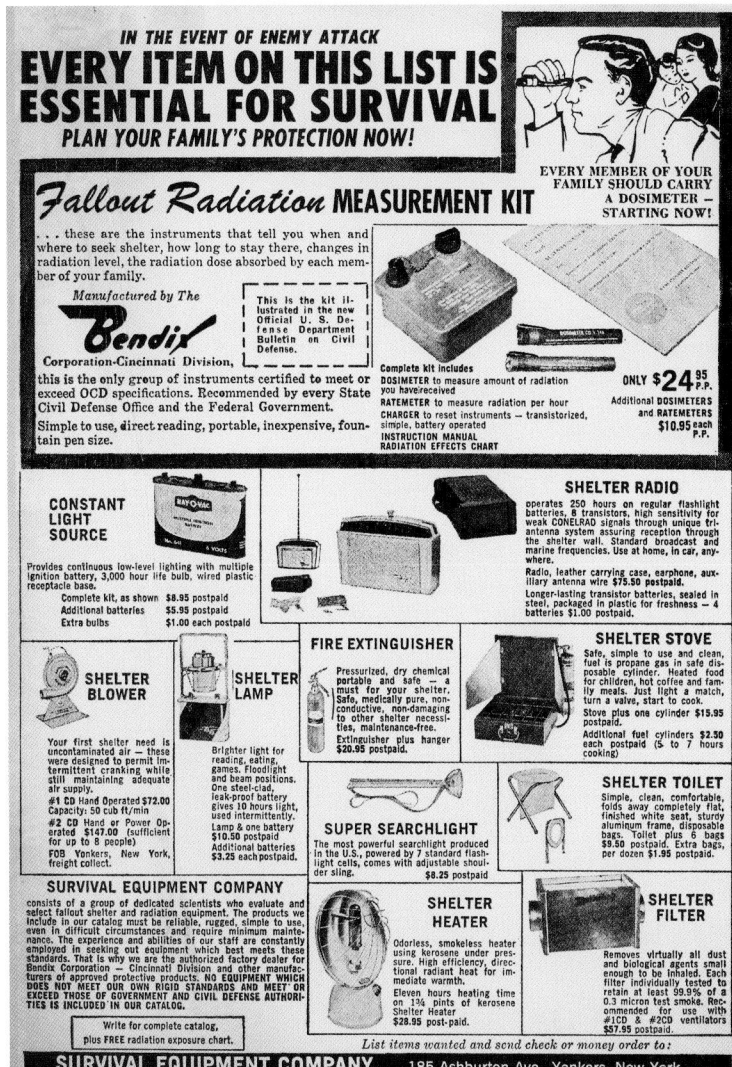

ABOVE A Tilley Heaters newspaper advertisement touted its suitability for a fallout shelter, despite the fact that it produced lethal carbon monoxide that would have killed the occupants. Civil Defense publications maintained that supplementary heaters were unnecessary because accumulated body heat would warm the shelter.

ABOVE An advertisement for the Survival Equipment Company provided one-stop shopping: A homeowner could buy all his shelter basics by mail order, and would receive a free bonus—a radiation exposure chart.

ABOVE An advertisement from the Garelick Manufacturing Company promoted the Port-O-Biff portable toilet, a folding stand equipped with a toilet seat and plastic bags. Originally created for camping, its manufacturer saw a new sales opportunity in the fallout shelter market.

ABOVE RIGHT The Age Corporation's advertisement explicitly addressed the subject Civil Defense publications typically glossed over—the elimination of human body wastes. Proclaiming "every fallout shelter must have toilet facilities!" the advertisement promised that the "Age" Chemical Toilet could efficiently process waste for two weeks.

OPPOSITE This patent application for a flush toilet designed specifically for a fallout shelter was filed with the U.S. Patent office in 1961 by two Californians, Robert F. O'Brien of Monterey Park, and Kenneth A. Milette of La Puente. To flush the toilet, the user would pull the handle depicted above the toilet three or four times. This would draw water into the toilet bowl from a holding tank hidden beneath the platform. The unit also included a urinal, washbasin, and shower. Because the water supply would be limited after a nuclear attack, the patent application noted the shower should be used sparingly, "only in the event that one of the occupants is exposed to fallout."

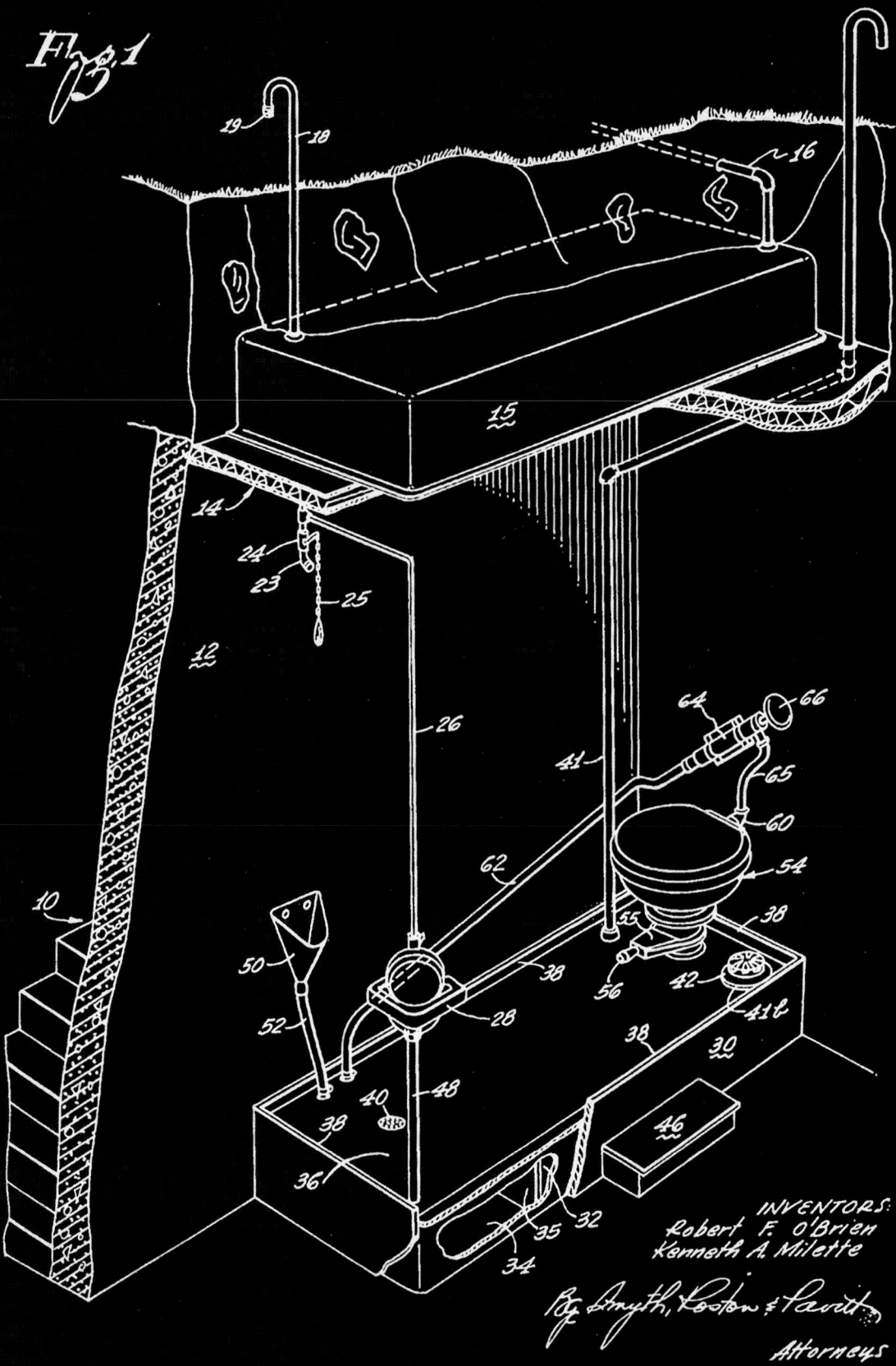

Fig.1

INVENTORS:
Robert F. O'Brien
Kenneth A. Milette

By Smyth, Roston & Pavitt

Attorneys

Fallout Shelter Fills Dual Role as a Recreation Room

BY JOSEPH ZULLO

[Chicago Tribune Press Service]

New York, Dec. 26—A compact fallout shelter that doubles as a recreation room has been designed by the American Institute of Decorators in coöperation with the Office of Civil and Defense Mobilization.

It will be exhibited for the first time in the lobby of the Merchandise Mart, Chicago, for three weeks beginning Jan. 2.

Marc T. Nielson of Chicago, former president of the A.I.D., designed the shelter to government specifications and called it "the family room of tomorrow."

Meets Specifications

The basement family shelter and water, sanitary facilities, and basic shelter equipment.

At the same time the room provides attractive and serviceable quarters for year around use, with equipment including a sofa, bunk bed with storage drawers, trundle bed, transistor television set, Conelrad radio, work table, and hopscotch board inlaid in the vinyl flooring.

A Shelter for All

Leo A. Hoegh, director of the government agency, said it is the belief of administration officials that every home should have shelter from radioactive fallout.

This kind of shelter can

DROP-DEAD GORGEOUS

The government's campaigns to convince people to install fallout shelters wasn't working. Americans couldn't be persuaded to welcome something into their homes that they saw as a daily reminder of nuclear apocalypse. So Civil Defense officials opted for no more gloom and doom. It's time to give the shelter a makeover. Goodbye bunker, hello, glamorous guest room! To create this fallout shelter facelift, the government sought professional help from the American Institute of Decorators, commissioning it to design schemes for transforming the Iconic Concrete Block Shelter into an irresistible and cozy enclave. The resulting designs—a hobby room, a sewing room, a library—were uninspired and predictable, with a single exception: the one from the Chicago-based designer Marc T. Nielsen, the organization's one-time

OPPOSITE On December 26, 1959, the *Chicago Daily Tribune* ran an article that described "The Family Room of Tomorrow, a decorated model shelter commissioned by the Office of Civil and Defense Mobilization.

president. The scheme offered everything Civil Defense officials could have hoped for. It was playful, utilitarian, attractive and, most of all, optimistic. Nielsen called it "the Family Room of Tomorrow," which, of course, carried the happy news that there would indeed *be* a tomorrow.

The room was as efficient as a ship's cabin—appropriate, perhaps, for a structure that is the land-based equivalent of a lifeboat. Nielsen squeezed function out of every square inch, employing built-ins, the designer's favorite space-saving trick. So, a built-in banquette sofa doubled as a bed; a built-in bookshelf held a battery-operated television set and radio; two built-in closets were fitted with shelving to store canned food and supplies.

Nielsen also employed another designer technique: multi-functionality. A drop-leaf table served as desk, a dining table, and a kitchen counter; a long, cushioned seating unit doubled as a bed; and, mindful of the need to keep the kids entertained, Nielsen inlaid a shuffleboard court in the linoleum floor.

The designer must have had a wry sense of humor. The fabric on the banquette, with its pattern evoking the prehistoric paintings discovered in 1940 inside the caves of Lascaux in France, was an allusion to man's earliest shelter, the cave. In addition, the maps of the earth on the closet doors were comforting reminders of the world outside, to which the shelter's occupants would (hopefully) soon return, using the pick-ax and shovel (decoratively arranged on the wall) to dig their way out, post-blast. Millions saw photographs of this shelter in *Life,* which proclaimed, "A family could live comfortably enough in this room for two weeks until radiation decreased outside." It said the shelter, complete with built-in cabinets, would cost $2,500, the equivalent of $19,000 in today's dollars.

The bunker-like characteristics of the shelter were spun into positives. No windows? No problem! It's a perfect darkroom! Still, a fallout shelter remained a tough sell.

But not to a Texas builder named Jay Swayze. In 1962, the town of Plainview hired

Swayze to build a model fallout shelter using Civil Defense plans. After he'd finished the rudimentary shelter, he was appalled by its claustrophobic austerity: "I decided that if modern man, with his high standard of living, had come to the point of driving himself into a six-by-eight foot hole in the ground just to *survive*, there *had* to be a better way! I was determined to find it."

So Swayze created a subterranean house for the nuclear age. Combining the words "atomic" and "habitat," he dubbed it the "Atomitat." Its design was inspired by, he explained, a "ship in a bottle." In this particular case, the "ship" was a full-size 2,800-square-foot ranch house, and the "bottle" was a 3,400-square-foot steel-reinforced poured-concrete shell buried three feet underground.

The entrance was through an above-ground garage that would be followed by a walk down a flight of steps that led to the shelter's front door. When that door was opened, one would find oneself in the foyer of a traditional four-bedroom home. It seemed like any other suburban house—except for the fact that the views outside the window were not of a backyard and sky, but of a *trompe l'oeil* landscape painted on the interior of the concrete shell. Swayze came to believe passionately that subterranean life was far superior to its aboveground alternative. With his wife and two daughters, Swayze lived in the house for four years. Beyond offering protection against nuclear attacks, tornados, and other disasters, his ship-in-a-bottle home gave him the Godlike power to completely control his environment. He could design the landscape and the views, and micromanage the lighting, temperature, weather conditions, and air quality. Because there

was no rain, snow, sleet or hail, the house never needed "exterior" maintenance. And the air was cleaned so efficiently that the house was virtually dust-free: a boon for his daughter's asthma.

A reclusive Texan named Girard B. Henderson, at the time one of America's richest men, visited Swayze's home and also became a convert to underground living. He commissioned Swayze to build subterranean homes for him in Las Vegas and in Boulder, Colorado. But Swayze wasn't satisfied. One convert was not enough. He wanted to convince everyone of the benefits of the buried lifestyle —no tornadoes! no fires! no *fallout!*—and he needed a forum for spreading the gospel. He decided that the upcoming 1964-1965 New York World's Fair, to be held in Flushing, New York, would be the perfect venue. So, with Henderson's financial backing, he created the Underground World Home Exhibit.

The exhibit he designed was a smaller version of his own house in Plainview. To reach it, visitors would enter a small, undistinguished aboveground pavilion and descend down a wide spiral staircase to discover a three-bedroom ranch house surrounded by a landscaped "yard" complete with a patio with a bubbling fountain. All of this was contained within an oblong steel-reinforced concrete shell that measured about 30 yards wide and 43 yards long. During the run of the fair, uniformed guides gave tours in fifteen languages. Not everyone shared Swayze's enthusiasm. The press coverage was largely derisive, as exemplified by this piece in the *New Yorker:*

"This structure, or excavation, is the ultimate article in fallout shelters, being a richly appointed ten-room burrow with a steel double door….On the whole it is an anomalous piece of domestic architecture, combining the small, familiar pleasures of the hearth with the headier excitements of Doomsday. It will not suit every temperament. It does not suit ours." The

exhibit was one of the least-visited at the fair, not surprising, since the main attraction—the house itself—was invisible to passersby, and also because it was dwarfed by its neighbors. To its west was the soaring Hall of Science, with its dramatic undulating concrete wall façade studded with thousands of shards of cobalt-blue glass. And to its east loomed the Chrysler exhibit, one of the largest installations at the fair. It sprawled across five islands linked by bridges set in a six-acre artificial lake. The single-story Underground Home pavilion paled in comparison.

In an effort to boost attendance at the fair during its second year, exhibits stayed open longer hours, well into the night. A clever promoter took advantage of the Underground Home's, well, undergroundness, and transformed it into a Hell-themed discothèque that was open from 10 pm until 2 am. Visitors were greeted at the door by a man wearing a black satin cape and rubber devil horns who led them down to the underground terrace. There, they were seated and served cocktails by waitresses clad in black mesh tights, high heels, and red velvet Playboy Bunny-style costumes with a curled Devil's tail affixed to their derrières.

The fair closed on October 17, 1965. The exhibits would be torn down and the fairground was to be transformed into a park. Exhibitors were given ninety days to clear their sites, which meant removing everything down to four feet below the surface. Because of the high costs of demolition, exhibitors typically met the minimum requirements and no more. As per the rules, the Underground Home's aboveground pavilion was demolished. However, it seems unlikely the exhibitor would have gone to the expense of digging out and removing a 130-foot-long concrete shell that weighed several tons. So a tantalizing mystery remains: Is the Underground House still there?

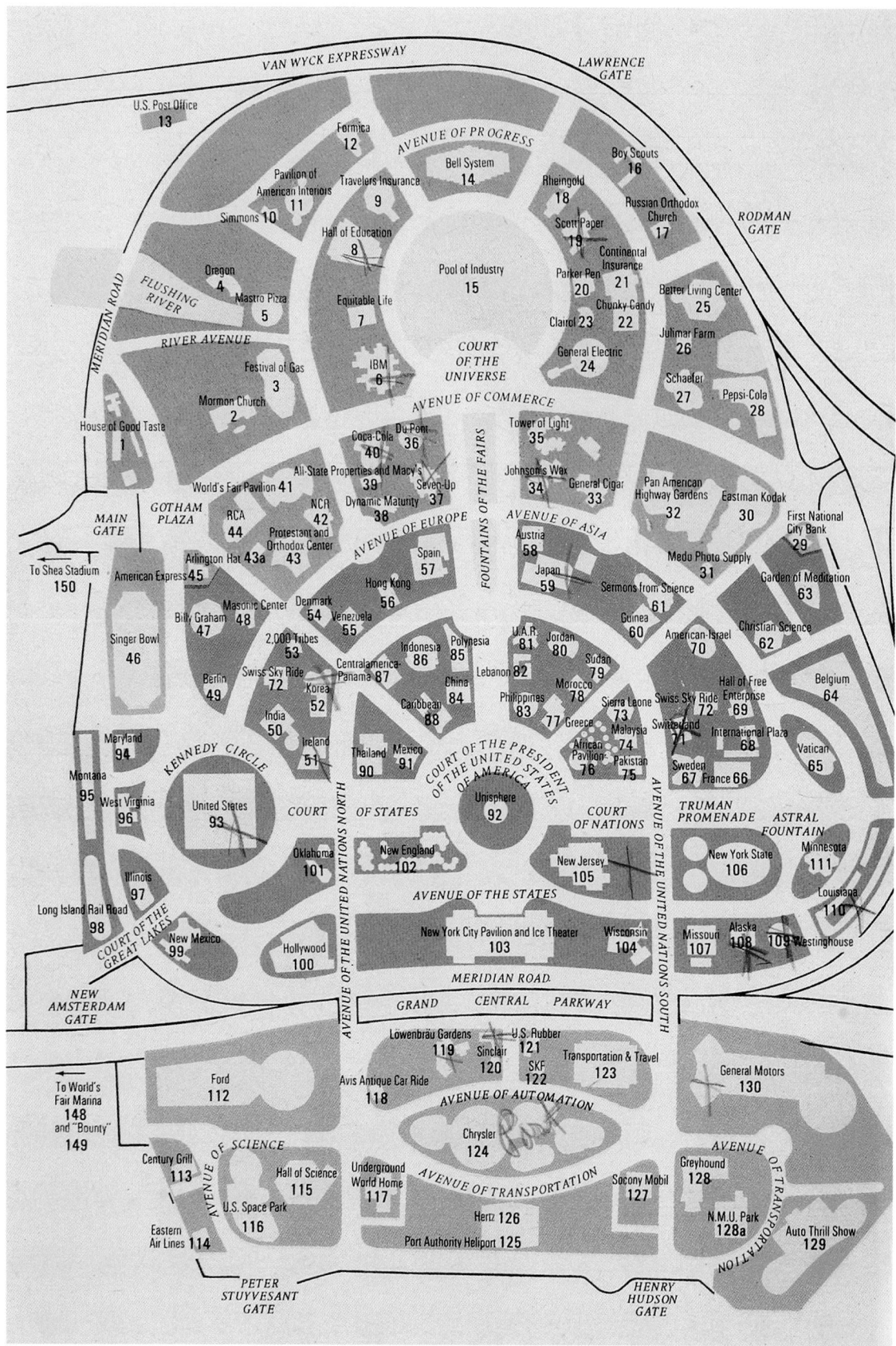

VAN WYCK EXPRESSWAY

LAWRENCE GATE

RODMAN GATE

U.S. Post Office 13

Formica 12

AVENUE OF PROGRESS

Boy Scouts 16

Pavilion of American Interiors 11

Travelers Insurance 9

Bell System 14

Rheingold 18

Russian Orthodox Church 17

Simmons 10

Hall of Education 8

Scott Paper 19

Continental Insurance 21

Oregon 4

Pool of Industry 15

Parker Pen 20

Better Living Center 25

FLUSHING RIVER

Mastro Pizza 5

Equitable Life 7

Chunky Candy 22

Julimar Farm 26

RIVER AVENUE

Clairol 23

General Electric 24

Festival of Gas 3

IBM 6

COURT OF THE UNIVERSE

Schaefer 27

Pepsi-Cola 28

MERIDIAN ROAD

Mormon Church 2

AVENUE OF COMMERCE

House of Good Taste 1

Coca-Cola 40

Du Pont 36

Tower of Light 35

FOUNTAINS OF THE FAIRS

World's Fair Pavilion 41

All-State Properties and Macy's 39

Seven-Up 37

Johnson's Wax 34

General Cigar 33

Pan American Highway Gardens 32

Eastman Kodak 30

GOTHAM PLAZA

RCA 44

NCR 42

Dynamic Maturity 38

AVENUE OF EUROPE

AVENUE OF ASIA

Austria 58

Medo Photo Supply 31

First National City Bank 29

MAIN GATE

Protestant and Orthodox Center 43

Arlington Hat 43a

Spain 57

Japan 59

Sermons from Science 61

Garden of Meditation 63

To Shea Stadium 150

American Express 45

Hong Kong 56

Guinea 60

American-Israel 70

Christian Science 62

Masonic Center 48

Denmark 54

Venezuela 55

U.A.R. 81

Jordan 80

Billy Graham 47

2,000 Tribes 53

Indonesia 86

Polynesia 85

Sudan 79

Hall of Free Enterprise 69

Belgium 64

Singer Bowl 46

Berlin 49

Swiss Sky Ride 72

Centralamerica-Panama 87

Korea 52

Lebanon 82

China 84

Morocco 78

Swiss Sky Ride 72

Philippines 83

Sierra Leone 73

Switzerland 71

International Plaza 68

Vatican 65

India 50

Caribbean 88

Greece 77

Malaysia 74

Sweden 67

France 66

Maryland 94

Ireland 51

Thailand 90

Mexico 91

COURT OF THE PRESIDENT OF THE UNITED STATES OF AMERICA

African Pavilion 76

Pakistan 75

Montana 95

KENNEDY CIRCLE

West Virginia 96

United States 93

COURT OF STATES

Unisphere 92

COURT OF NATIONS

TRUMAN PROMENADE

ASTRAL FOUNTAIN

Minnesota 111

Illinois 97

Oklahoma 101

New England 102

New Jersey 105

New York State 106

Louisiana 110

Long Island Rail Road 98

COURT OF THE GREAT LAKES

New Mexico 99

Hollywood 100

AVENUE OF THE STATES

New York City Pavilion and Ice Theater 103

Wisconsin 104

Missouri 107

Alaska 108

Westinghouse 109

NEW AMSTERDAM GATE

MERIDIAN ROAD

GRAND CENTRAL PARKWAY

Lowenbräu Gardens 119

U.S. Rubber 121

To World's Fair Marina 148 and "Bounty" 149

Ford 112

Avis Antique Car Ride 118

Sinclair 120

SKF 122

Transportation & Travel 123

General Motors 130

AVENUE OF AUTOMATION

Century Grill 113

AVENUE OF SCIENCE

Hall of Science 115

Underground World Home 117

Chrysler 124

AVENUE OF TRANSPORTATION

Socony Mobil 127

Greyhound 128

AVENUE OF TRANSPORTATION

U.S. Space Park 116

Hertz 126

N.M.U. Park 128a

Auto Thrill Show 129

Eastern Air Lines 114

Port Authority Heliport 125

PETER STUYVESANT GATE

HENRY HUDSON GATE

AVENUE OF THE UNITED NATIONS NORTH

AVENUE OF THE UNITED NATIONS SOUTH

LEFT A map of the 1964–65 New York World's Fair in Flushing, New York, shows the location of the Underground World Home exhibit created by the most enthusiastic proponent of underground living, Jay Swayze. It is number 117 in the Transportation section at bottom left, between the Hall of Science and the Chrysler exhibitions.

RIGHT The aboveground pavilion of the Underground World Home exhibition is shown in an architectural rendering on the cover of a promotional leaflet. But what is not seen is its main attraction, which is buried beneath the pavilion: a full-size three-bedroom ranch house contained in a steel-reinforced concrete shell.

BELOW RIGHT AND BOTTOM Because the main event—the house itself—was buried underground, it was easy for a fairgoer to walk right by the aboveground building without being tempted to go inside. Later in the fair's run, an outdoor café called the Soup 'n Salad Bar drew more attention to the exhibit, as did two large signs, seen on the roof.

LEFT A walkway winds through the "yard" of the Underground Home to a patio and fountain "outside" of the Underground Home itself. To the right of the path is one of the home's "exterior" walls.

OPPOSITE Swayze's designs for the World's Fair exhibit were featured in this article in the March 29, 1964, edition of the *New York Times*, entitled "Experiment in Atomic-Age Housing Will Be Exhibited at the World's Fair." The drawings at far right show the house in plan, above, and in section, below.

Experiment in Atomic-Age Housing Will Be Exhibited at the World's Fair

Foyer of underground house in Dallas built by John Swayze of Plainview, Tex. Structure provides an atmosphere that is conducive to plants, right.

Living room includes view of covered terrace, which is set up to simulate daylight and darkness.

FALLOUT SHELTER BECOMES A HOME

Texas Builder's Family Has Lived for 9 Months in One

By DUDLEY DALTON

During the tense moments of the Cuban crisis in 1962, many persons in the country seriously considered building underground shelters to protect their families and themselves from the dangers of nuclear warfare.

The officials of Plainview, Tex., went so far as to ask John Swayze, a home builder and lumberyard owner, to build a municipal bomb shelter. What they had in mind was a rather Spartan, tank-like shelter designed strictly to keep out atomic fallout.

Mr. Swayze felt that a plain underground shelter was not enough, however, and began planning a shelter that offered all of the comforts of home.

One idea led to another, and after nine months Mr. Swayze had built an underground home for himself, his wife and their two teen-age daughters. Since that time, he has built two other underground homes—one in Dallas and the other in Colorado.

Mr. Swayze is now building an underground home at the World's Fair, which will open on April 22.

Advantages Noted

The underground home has many features not found in houses above ground. For example, homeowners would be able to create their own private world, shutting out noise, intruders, storms, pollen and air pollution. Housewives would have to dust only once a month.

There is also the conservation of land. Virtually all of the land above the house is free for lawns, gardens, tennis courts or even another house. As a result, the homeowner would get double use of his land.

Like a ship in a bottle, the

Continued on Page 2, Column 1

Members of Swayze family, above, in underground kitchen that might be in a conventional house. World's Fair version (floor plan, right) will measure 130 by 90 feet and will be built in a concrete shell (cross section, below) sunk three feet below earth's surface.

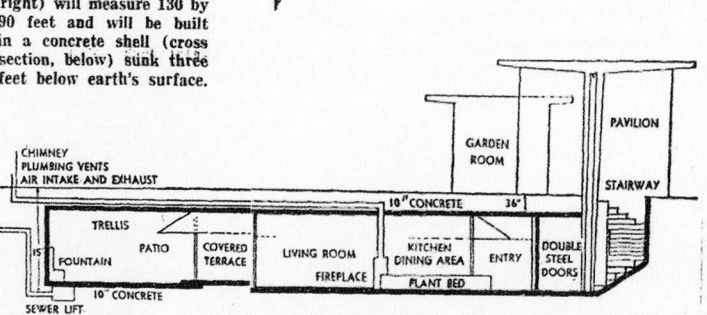

RIGHT Two women enjoy a subterranean cup of tea on the "outdoor" patio of the Underground Home. Between them stands a working fountain.

OPPOSITE TOP A visitor would enter the Underground Home through this door.

OPPOSITE CENTER One of the bedrooms featured this ornate circular seating unit and its coordinating canopy.

OPPOSITE BOTTOM Twin beds flank a window in one of the house's three bedrooms. Curtains are pulled back to reveal the view "outdoors."

FALLOUT SHELTER HANDBOOK

By CHUCK WEST

509 A FAWCETT BOOK

75¢

Diets and Food Kits
Surviving an Atomic Attack
Underground Shelters You Can Build or Buy
Basement and Garage Shelters
Medical Hints and First Aid
Evacuation Techniques
Sources of Water Supply
Above-Ground Shelters
Fallout Detection Devices

LEFT An illustration on the cover of the *Fallout Shelter Handbook* by Chuck West depicted the Concrete Block Shelter interior as a study in mid-century modernism. Two clean-lined sofas that would have looked at home in an *Arts & Architecture* Case Study house abutted a corner table on top of which sat a gooseneck lamp. Were it not for the hand-crank air blower on the wall next to the sofa at left, the scene could have been out of a family room in a suburban home. Shelters were always illustrated in cutaway, creating a visual impression of lightness and openness that belied the grim reality: An underground shelter—airless, dark, and damp—bears an inescapable resemblance to a tomb.

OPPOSITE An illustration from Swayze's book *Underground Gardens and Homes* emphasized the refuge-like qualities of subterranean living. Aboveground, the mushroom cloud of a nuclear bomb, along with a tornado, wreak havoc. Belowground, a swimmer frolics in a pool.

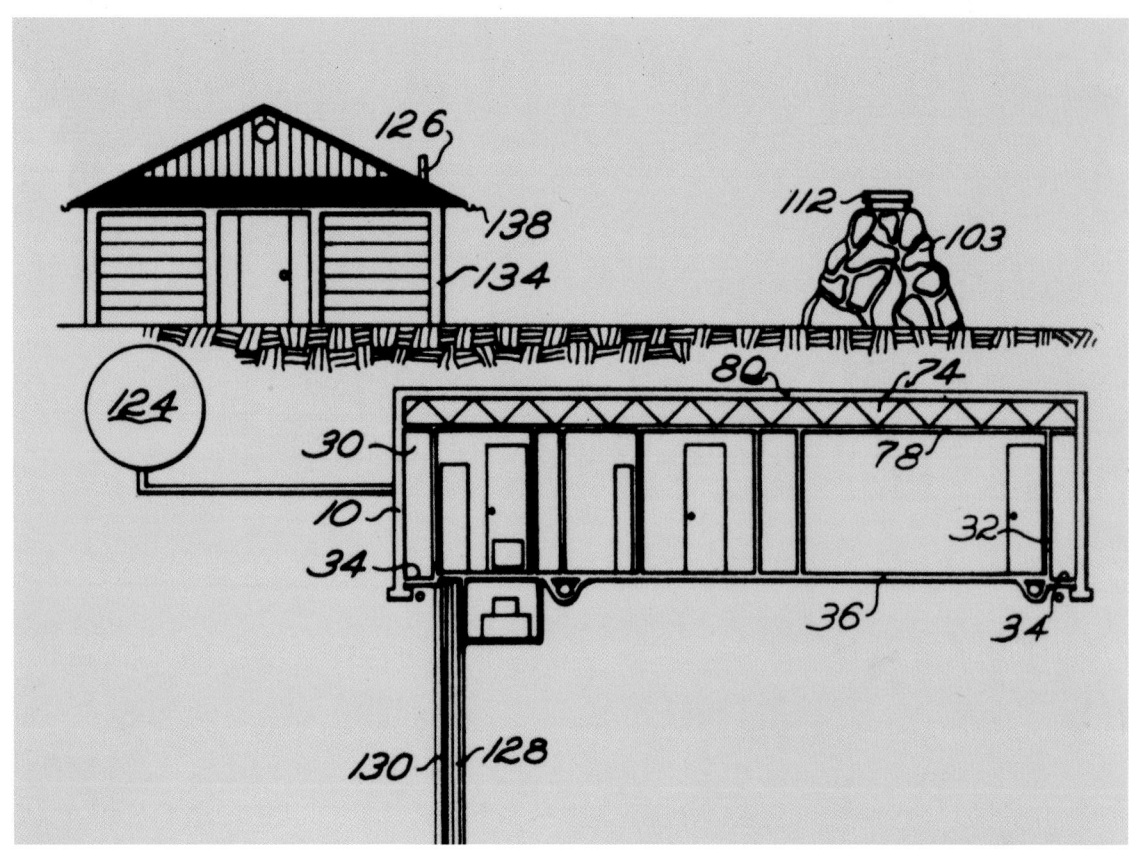

Swayze constructed his first subterranean dwelling in Plainview, Texas, for himself and his family. It was a 10-room, 2,800-square-foot ranch house buried thirteen feet below the surface inside a 3,400-square-foot steel-reinforced concrete shell.

LEFT The belowground location of builder Jay Swayze's four-bedroom home in Plainview, Texas, is revealed in a cross-section drawing.

BELOW LEFT The Swayze house itself was invisible to passersby, who would see only a garage and a stone structure that concealed the exhaust vents for the air ventilation system.

RIGHT A stone wall surrounds the fireplace in the living room of the Texas house. Floor-to-ceiling curtains flank a sliding glass door that led to the "outdoors."

BELOW RIGHT The tiled-floor patio was fully equipped for "outdoor" living, with a table, four chairs, stacking side tables, and a bar trolley.

OVERLEAF Southern California architect Paul Laszlo designed a bomb shelter for his client John D. Hertz, the founder of the Hertz Rent-A-Car agency, shown in this architectural rendering. The shelter, a structure made from a corrugated steel shell with concrete bulkhead walls, was installed in the yard of Hertz's residence in Los Angeles in 1955. The entry was from aboveground, right, via either a circular stairway or an elevator, both of which opened onto a space housing an electrical generator. Beyond, there was a living space, followed by the kitchen. A Chemex coffee maker on the counter provided a domestic touch. An "escape tube" led out from the kitchen, providing a second route to the outside. Laszlo was a fervent advocate of underground living. He designed a utopian community called Atomville, a belowground suburb that could be completely sealed off from the surface in the event of a nuclear attack. It was never built.

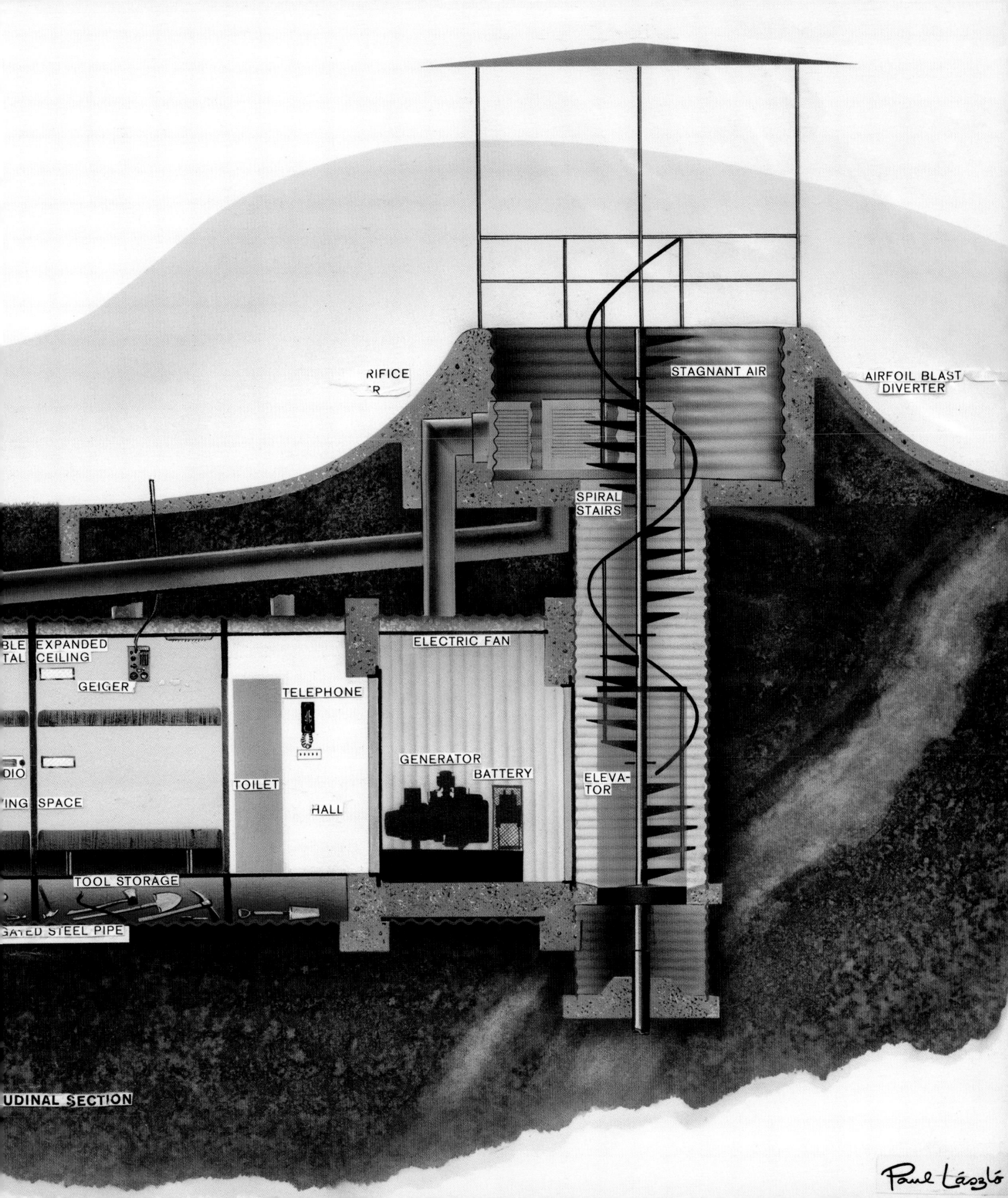

UTILITY SEWING ROOM
FALL-OUT SHELTER

designed by
TOM LEE, A.I.D.
NEW YORK CITY, NEW YO...

In 1959, Civil Defense authorities commissioned interior designers to create fallout shelters that could do double-duty in the hopes of making a home bunker more palatable to Americans.

ABOVE Tom Lee of New York City envisioned a Utility Sewing Room with a black-and-white motif. Striped banquettes would also serve as beds. A sewing machine slides out on its base from a circular built-in cabinet.

RIGHT Dorothy H. Paul of Los Angeles created a Fun Room. To create a feeling of openness in the completely enclosed space, she had a stylized mural painted on one wall depicting leafy trees in a park-like town square complete with a steepled church. "Fun" activities apparently would include editing movies, represented here by the reel-to-reel film-editing machine sitting on the round table on the left.

FUN ROOM
FALL-OUT SHELTER
designed by
DOROTHY H PAUL, A I

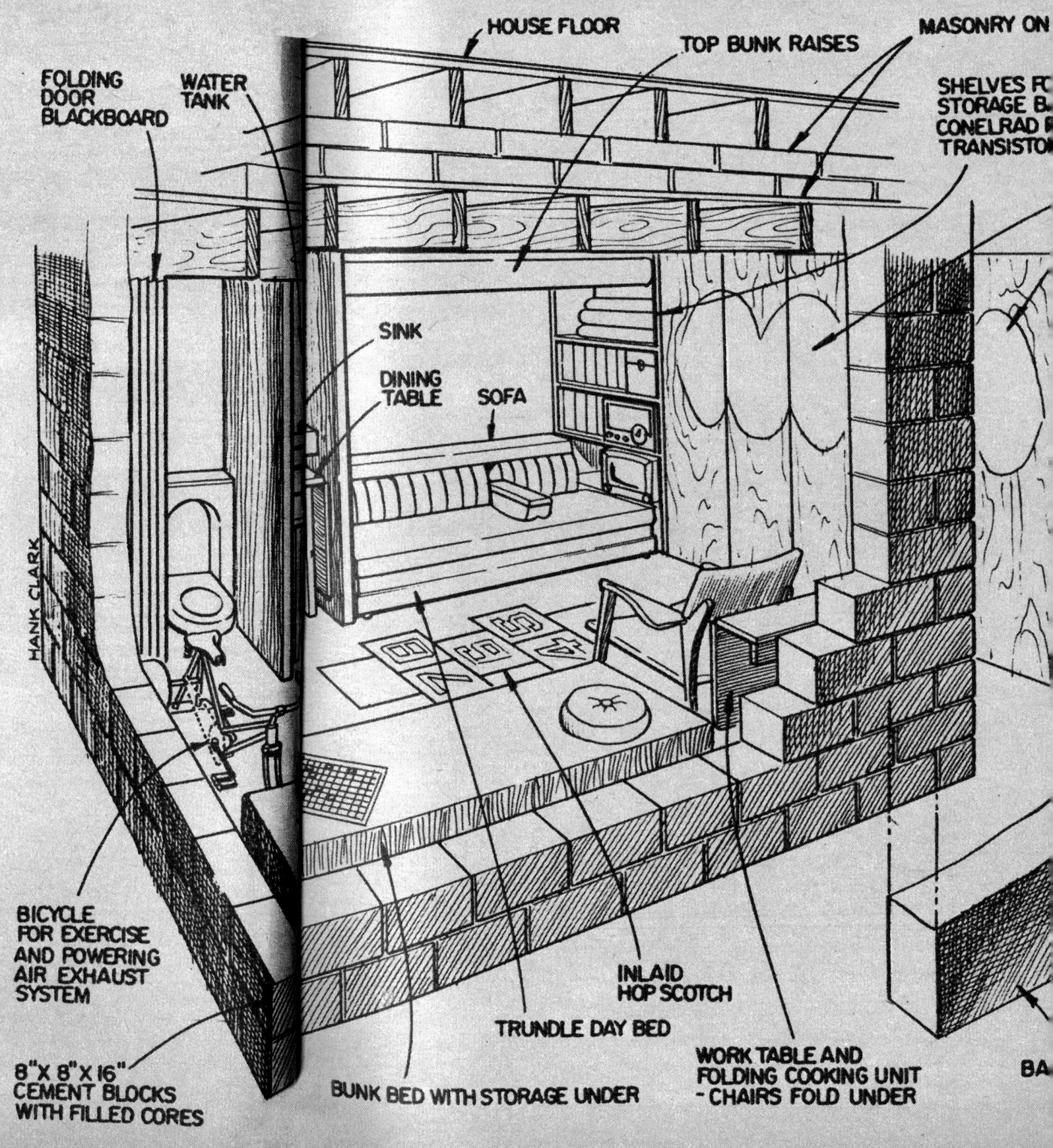

FOLDING DOOR BLACKBOARD

WATER TANK

HOUSE FLOOR

TOP BUNK RAISES

MASONRY ON

SHELVES F
STORAGE B
CONELRAD R
TRANSISTOR

SINK

DINING TABLE

SOFA

HANK CLARK

BICYCLE FOR EXERCISE AND POWERING AIR EXHAUST SYSTEM

8" X 8" X 16" CEMENT BLOCKS WITH FILLED CORES

BUNK BED WITH STORAGE UNDER

INLAID HOP SCOTCH

TRUNDLE DAY BED

WORK TABLE AND FOLDING COOKING UNIT - CHAIRS FOLD UNDER

BA

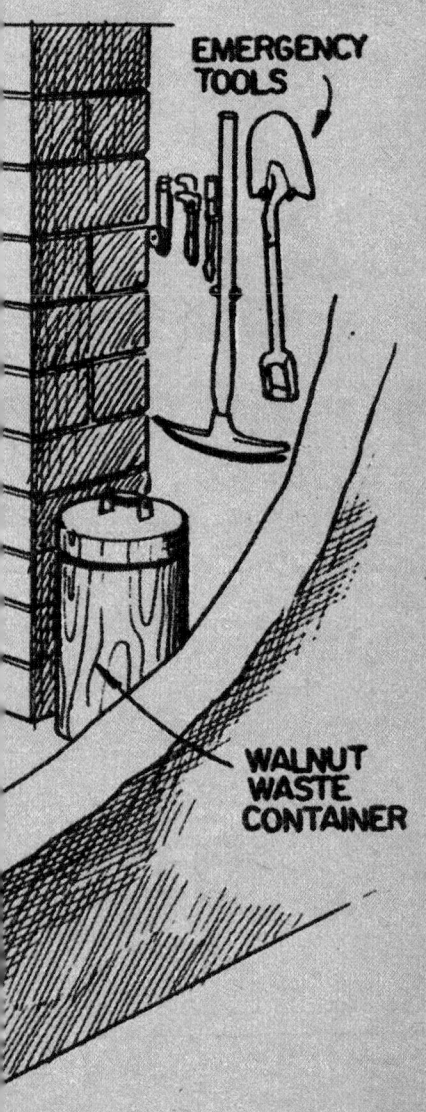

JER ROOF

ST AID
IES

SIMPLIFIED RANALLY
MAP ON FACES OF
REVOLVING DOORS
COVERING CLOSETS

EMERGENCY
TOOLS

WALNUT
WASTE
CONTAINER

WALL

51

LEFT The Family Room of Tomorrow, by interior decorator Marc T. Nielsen of Chicago, Illinois, is shown in a rendering. Civil Defense officials believed that this design had the power to persuade reluctant Americans that a family fallout shelter was more than insurance against disaster and that it could be used, in the meantime, as a family room.

ABOVE Civil Defense authorities had a three-dimensional full-size model of the design constructed for public exhibition. It was an exact reproduction of Nielsen's design, down to the prehistoric Lascaux Caves-like animal mural painted above the banquette. The model made its public debut at the Merchandise Mart in Chicago in January of 1960, where it was on exhibit for three weeks, after which it traveled across the country.

Subterranean living enthusiast Swayze's finest expression of underground living still exists. Designed for his client Girard B. Henderson in Las Vegas, Nevada, the ranch house lies buried beneath a small two-story structure on a large corner lot with tract houses on either side. An exhaust pipe that extends a few feet aboveground is the only clue to the house's twenty-five-foot–belowground existence. As the long distance down makes a stairway entrance impractical, the house is reached by an elevator. When its doors open, a visitor steps onto a walkway and faces a sprawling stone-and-brick ranch house with huge picture windows and sliding glass doors. Murals painted on the interior of the concrete shell provide a "landscape" of places held dear to Henderson—his childhood home in New Jersey, and his sheep farm in New Zealand. The time of day and "weather" of this "outdoor" area is artificially generated: it can be a bright, warm sunny day or a crystal clear night, complete with twinkling stars. Situated in the "yard" is a guesthouse, a barbecue, and a pool (which, Swayze said, never needed cleaning because the ventilation system filtered contaminants out of the air). After Henderson died in 1983, the house was sold. It now sits empty, dark and lifeless, entombed in its decorated concrete shell, a bizarre and little-known relic of the Cold War.

RIGHT A wide terrazzo walkway sweeps up to the double-door front entrance of the house. The brightly illuminated living room is visible through the windows and sliding doors.

PREVIOUS PAGES The landscaped "backyard" features a rock-lined swimming pool and two artificial trees that end at the "sky," which is painted on the interior of the buried steel-reinforced concrete shell that encloses the property. The guesthouse is set in front of a painted backdrop of mountains and a lake, by Jewel Smith, a Texas-based artist. At right is part of the "exterior" of the main ranch-style house.

LEFT The "outdoor" barbecue grill is camouflaged inside a large fake boulder. Smoke would rise through the imitation tree behind it.

BELOW LEFT "Outdoor" chaise lounges with cushions upholstered in a cheery bright floral print are lined up against the wall of the guesthouse. Beyond the arch, which is festooned with artificial flowers, is a putting green. A golf club can be seen to the left of the arch leaning against the stone wall.

OPPOSITE A crystal chandelier, reinforcing the surrealistic "indoor-outdoor" feeling, hangs above an ornate furniture set on the patio adjacent to the main house. At the rear on the right is a tree fully decorated for Christmas.

PREVIOUS PAGES Family portraits are lined up on a console in the carpeted living room that has been eclectically furnished, juxtaposing upholstered French Provincial chairs with a square-arm three-cushion sofa sitting behind a glass coffee table. Silk wallpaper covers the ceiling and the walls.

LEFT AND BELOW LEFT The up-to-the-minute brightly lit pastel-hued kitchen featured wall ovens, a central island with electric burners, and a dishwasher.

OPPOSITE The formal dining room with its huge Venetian chrystal chandelier was entirely upholstered in a floral fabric. Eight people could be seated at the table surrounded with tall wing-backed chairs.

ABOVE A sunken bathtub, illuminated from below in pink light, is the focus of the luxuriously appointed master bathroom with wall-to-wall carpeting and luxurious floor-to-ceiling sheers on the windows.

ABOVE Twin beds furnish the all-pink master
bedroom. The chandelier, fringed draperies
and sheer curtains, candle sconces, delicate
matching bedside tables, and sculpted
carpeting complete the French Provincial décor.

U.S. FLEET BEGINS CUBA BLOCKADE

Kennedy Says U.S. Will Attack Soviet if Island Fires Missiles

BY ROBERT THOMPSON
Los Angeles Times News Service

WASHINGTON — President Kennedy ordered a blockade of Cuba Monday night to halt the buildup of Soviet-made missiles that could inflict mass destruction on every nation in the Americas.

The President announced that the United States will turn back ships hauling offensive weapons to the Communist-ruled island. He also pledged full retaliation against the Soviet Union if a single nuclear missile is fired from Cuba against any nation in the Western Hemisphere.

The United States will not shrink from the threat of nuclear war to preserve the peace and freedom of the hemisphere, Mr. Kennedy said over nationwide radio and television.

He directed the armed forces to "prepare for any eventualities" if Russia does not cease shipping offensive military equipment to Fidel Castro's "imprisoned island."

U.S. ships and planes immediately moved into position in the Caribbean to enforce the blockade. They had orders to shoot if necessary.

The Navy announced at San Juan, Pue~

~?,000 men ~~~

MESSAGE ON CUBA- -President Kennedy delivers radio and television address in which he told the nation that Cuba is being placed under naval blockade.

6

SHELTER SKELTER

The Cold War turned hot during the summer of 1961. The incendiary spark was at its front line—the border that separated the Soviet-controlled East Berlin from the United States-controlled West Berlin. In June, Soviet Premier Nikita Khrushchev threatened the military takeover of free West Berlin. In a televised speech on July 25th, President John F. Kennedy told the nation he had ordered a massive military buildup of troops and weaponry and said the United States would defend West Berlin by any means necessary. In an age of nuclear weaponry, this had terrifying implications. The President's speech, along with the graphic descriptions in the media of the potential scope of nuclear destruction, frightened the nation and triggered fallout-shelter frenzy.

An industry that had been languishing only a year earlier—"Fallout Shelter Market Sagging: Contractors Push Sales, but Find

OPPOSITE The front page of the *Washington Post* on October 23, 1962, delivered terrifying news during the Cuban Missile Crisis.

Public Mostly Apathetic to New Program," the *Los Angeles Times* had reported—suddenly found itself booming.

The race was on. Builders, remodelers, and swimming pool contractors rushed into the business. As one pool maker explained, "a fallout shelter is just a swimming pool, upside down." Marketers trumpeted their sales pitches. In Los Angeles, Carl-Ray General Building promoted its easy financing, with no down payment and low-interest loans. The KCS Corporation threw in a bonus of "2 weeks' supply of condensed food" with its shelters. Fox Hole Shelter, Inc., emphasized speed, promising that its "fully-equipped" reinforced Gunite backyard shelter could be installed in one day. As business boomed, so did swindles and scams. "Reports of shelter gyps are coming in from every state in the union," Frank Norton, the interim president of the newly formed National Shelter Association industry group, told *House + Home*. In Denver, "hucksters with a long record of troubles with the Better Business Bureau" had leapt into the fray. In Kansas City, a company was

advertising a shelter for six that was in fact nothing more than a steel tube too short to stand in. "The company just digs a hole, drops it in the ground and says, 'There it is,'" a Better Business Bureau official said.

The relatively high cost of shelters meant they were often seen as the exclusive domain of the well to do. An article titled "Man Builds Luxurious Shelter to Guard Family, Dogs from Bomb" described a Southern California businessman who spent $175,000 in today's dollars to build a steel-and-concrete shelter to protect his family, four servants, and three pets. Many Americans found the idea that one's ability to survive a nuclear war was directly related to their financial status morally repugnant, as was the "every man for himself" nature of a family shelter. In an essay titled "Let's Stop the Fallout Shelter Folly!" published in *Good Housekeeping* magazine, historian William L. Shirer expressed this revulsion. "Our legislators have passed the buck to the individual citizen. They have said in effect: every American family for itself and the devil take the hindmost. What kind of an

American society is this? What kind of a Christian civilization?"

Shelters pitted neighbor against neighbor. Should a homeowner equip his shelter with a firearm? And, if so, was it morally defensible for him to shoot if a neighbor shows up when the bomb drops, begging for entry? This dilemma became known as the "gun thy neighbor" debate, and it raged in the popular press. Some homeowners built shelters in secret out of shame and fear of ridicule. When curious neighbors asked him about his construction project, Edward Yanis of Delaware Township, New Jersey, told them he was putting in a basement, or building a wine cellar. Others kept the news of their shelters to themselves so that, if the worst did happen, they'd be able to avoid the "gun thy neighbor" dilemma altogether because their neighbors wouldn't know the shelter was there.

The satirical *MAD* magazine neatly captured the anxiety surrounding shelters in a cartoon called "Nuclear Jitters." In it, a panicky homeowner decides to build a shelter. He digs a hole, mixes cement, lays concrete bricks, hammers on a roof, buries the shelter with dirt, and nails a "No trespassing" sign above the door. A newsman comes to photograph it. The frazzled homeowner is startled by the camera's flash and…drops dead. Clearly, emotion management wasn't working.

More than 100 prominent architects came out against shelters in an editorial published in the *Journal of the AIA,* the professional publication of the American Institute of Architects. Among the luminaries were some of the most important modern architects of the twentieth century: German émigré Walter Gropius, who headed the Bauhaus, Morris Lapidus, the creator of Miami Beach's flamboyant, neo-baroque Fontainebleau and Eden Roc hotels in Florida, and Austrian émigré Victor Gruen, inventor of the suburban shopping mall. They were united in the belief that architects should play no role in designing shelters: "The technical aspects of the architectural problem become impossible assumptions, and the question of how to design a fallout shelter is one with no real answer."

If Americans were scared during the Berlin Crisis, they were flat-out terrified during the Cuban Missile Crisis. On the evening of October 22, 1962, in a nationally televised address, President John F. Kennedy told Americans the U.S.S.R. had secretly installed missiles in Cuba "capable of striking Washington, D.C., the Panama Canal, Cape Canaveral, Mexico City, or any other city in the Southeastern part of the United States, in Central America, or in the Caribbean area." What's more, the President said, the U.S.S.R. was making preparations for an installation for missiles "capable of striking most of the major cities in the Western hemisphere." He implored Soviet Premier Nikita Khrushchev to "eliminate this clandestine, reckless and provocative threat to world peace" and remove the weapons. President Kennedy ordered a naval blockade be thrown around Cuba. All ships bound for Cuba would be examined for weapons. If weapons were found, the ships would be turned back. The question was: Would Russian ships defy the blockade, triggering a conflict between the Superpowers that could result in a nuclear war? For four long days, Americans wondered if they were on the brink of nuclear war. The crisis was resolved on October 26, after Premier Khrushchev agreed to remove the weapons in exchange for a guarantee from the United States that it would not invade Cuba. (In fact, the real reason the crisis ended was that the United States made a secret agreement to remove nuclear missiles aimed at the U.S.S.R. from Turkey.)

Even before the crisis, the groundswell of opposition to family fallout shelters made selling the idea a losing battle for the Kennedy administration. Polls showed that Americans rejected home fallout shelters for a number of reasons. They didn't believe they could get to a home shelter in time if there were an attack. They had no faith that a shelter would protect them. There was no consensus among authorities that a shelter would work. Plus, shelters were too expensive. Many people adopted a fatalistic attitude. One poll respondent said, "Why should we do anything? If that bomb is dropped, we'll all be blown to bits anyway."

The Kennedy administration quietly abandoned its endorsement of the family fallout shelter. Instead, it shifted its attention to its National Fallout Shelter Survey. After determining it was impossible to build enough shelters to house every American, the government decided to find existing structures that could provide post-attack protection. The Department of Defense dispatched an army of architects and engineers to travel across the country and locate buildings with spaces large enough to house at least fifty people for two weeks. The sites were stocked with water, food (crackers and wafers), emergency medical supplies, radiation-measuring instruments, and "sanitation kits"—large brown fiber barrels which, when lined with plastic bags and topped with commode seats, would serve as toilets. These buildings were emblazoned with the now-iconic sign featuring three yellow triangles set inside a black circle on a yellow background and the words "Fallout Shelter." Now, fifty years later, these signs remain, rusted and faded legacies of the Cold War.

OPPOSITE In the 1964 Cold War black comedy *Dr. Strangelove, or, How I Learned to Stop Worrying and Love the Bomb,* directed by Stanley Kubrick, an insane U.S. Air Force general gives orders that an atom bomb be dropped on the Soviet Union. The President and the Joint Chiefs of Staff frantically try to cancel the nuclear attack, but to no avail.

L 1728

IF THE BOMB FALLS

HI-FI **TOPS**

A Recorded Guide To Survival

OCDM Gives TOPS Full Co-operation

Hear what to do in case of nuclear attack

Free Government Survival Pamphlets are enclosed

The Office of Civil and Defense Mobilization has gone all out in its co-operation with Tops Records. This record and the enclosed suggestions, charts, guides and highly researched protective measures will give you the basic plan for survival.

In the interest of the safety of our nation and its people, we must all do our part by being informed and being prepared to meet any emergency that threatens our homes and families.

Plans for practical food stocks, clothing etc., is incorporated in this well planned program.

Give these records to your friends; you may save their lives.

Office of Civil and Defense Mobilization Director In All Out Effort To Alert America

Frank B. Ellis has extended all out support in an effort to prepare the American public in the event of an atomic war. Details of preparation, step by step suggestions for public action after the attack warning signals, building up food reserves and first aid are stressed by Mr. Ellis.

Literature in this field is specific and educational. Being prepared will be an all important factor in surviving, is his firm warning.

Can You Survive A Hydrogen War?

If the bomb falls—and you are near it—nothing will save you. If the bomb falls—and you are not near it—only protection against fallout may save you. But such protection requires prior preparation: the nuclear bomb has a far-reaching, long-lasting killing power. It is for this reason that our agencies of Civil Defense have been trying to impress upon us the urgency of being prepared for this dreadful possibility.

Free government publications on survival are available to the public. They give instruction in First Aid, explain the function of Conelrad, describe protective measures against fallout, show building plans for shelters, and give information on living in a shelter.

If the bomb falls...be prepared. It's a matter of life or death!

J.F.K. URGES PREPARATION

"...Common prudence demands that we take all necessary measures to protect our homes, our institutions, and our way of life so that they can survive should an enemy thrust war upon us... For unless Americans plan to protect their own families, the most ambitious and carefully organized activities of government will prove inadequate... Therefore, I ask you to support civil emergency planning in your local communities ...I express my appreciation for your active response to the obligations of citizenship in a free country."

Protect Your Family

The best protection is to plan and prepare in advance. To protect your family, be sure that they understand what to do in case of a hydrogen bomb explosion.

PRINTED IN U.S.A.

OPPOSITE This is the cardboard cover of "If the Bomb Falls," a vinyl LP record produced in the early 1960s by Precision Radiation Instruments of Los Angeles. With a sober narration by David Wiley, Side One addresses: "What to Do in Case of Nuclear Attack." Side Two covers: "Supplies Needed for Survival."

RIGHT The September 15, 1961, issue of *Life* featured a photograph of a man wearing a glowing red transparent plastic suit below the words, "How You Can Survive Fallout." The photograph was shot using red lighting to illuminate the scene, probably to represent radioactive fallout. Inside, the magazine devoted 14 pages to family fallout shelters and included detailed building plans for three different types. President John F. Kennedy introduced the section, with a letter that urged people to "read and seriously consider the contents of this issue of *Life*."

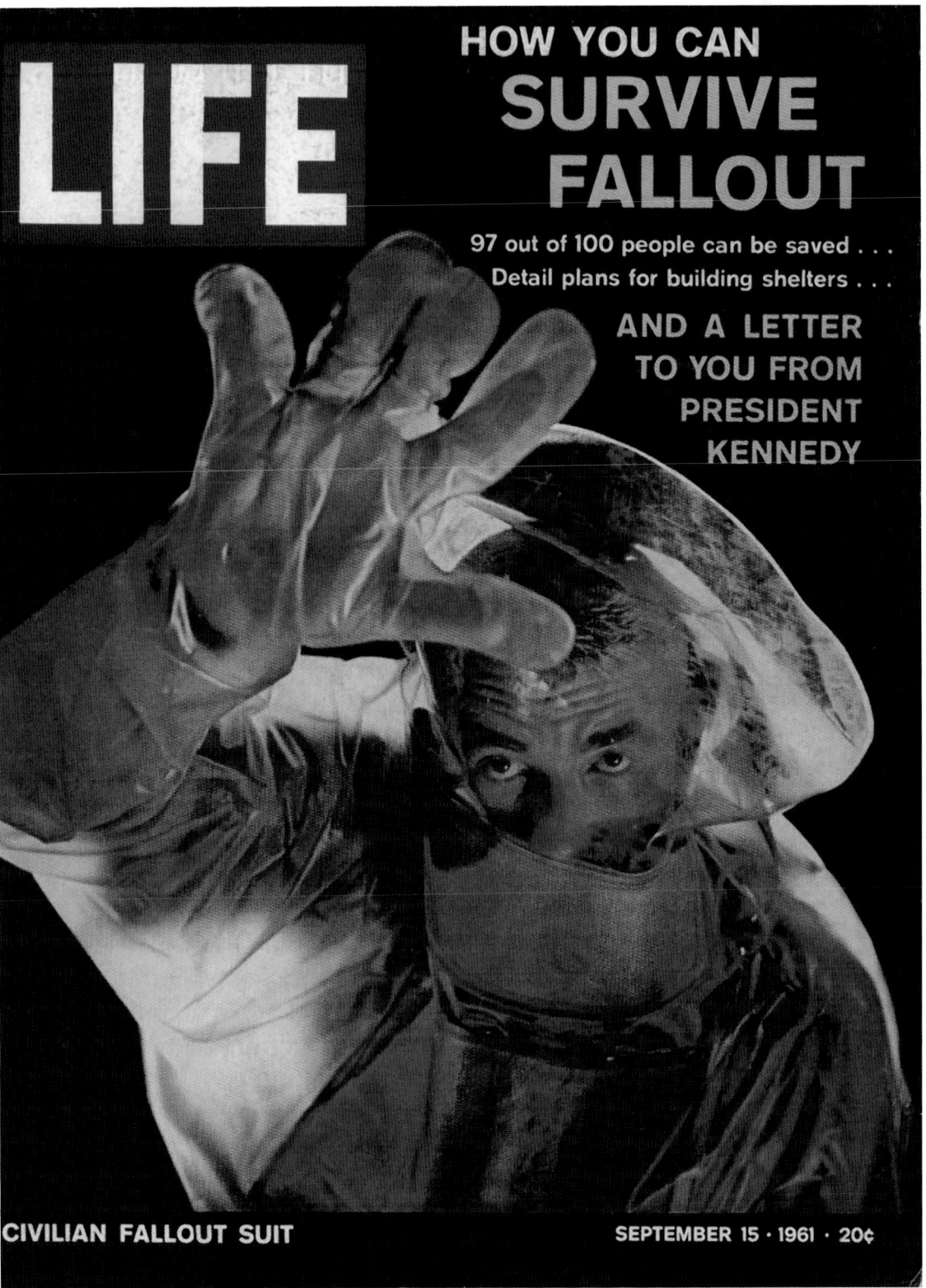

LIFE

HOW YOU CAN
SURVIVE
FALLOUT

97 out of 100 people can be saved . . .
Detail plans for building shelters . . .

AND A LETTER
TO YOU FROM
PRESIDENT
KENNEDY

CIVILIAN FALLOUT SUIT   SEPTEMBER 15 · 1961 · 20¢

NOVEMBER 6, 1961 25c

Newsweek

SHELTERS OR SURVIVAL?

LEFT Red arrows represent a rain of fallout pouring down from the mushroom cloud of a nuclear blast on the cover of the November 6, 1961, issue of *Newsweek*, which asked the question: "Shelters for Survival?" Judging from the illustration of a family safely ensconced in their Concrete Block Shelter, the answer would clearly seem to be "yes."

RIGHT The cover of the November, 1962, issue of *Esquire* depicted a fallout shelter as a modern-day Noah's Ark. It was designed by the magazine's creative director George Lois and photographed by Harold Krieger.

OVERLEAF Newspaper advertisements for fallout shelters published in 1961 and 1962 capitalized on Americans' terror of impending nuclear annihilation. Though the typography, layout, and text of the advertisements varied, their sales pitch was the same: Buy our shelter, and you and your family can survive a nuclear attack.

NOVEMBER, 1962
PRICE 60c

Esquire

THE MAGAZINE FOR MEN

NOAH'S ARK/1962: FOR PEACE MOVEMENTS IN A MORE HOPEFUL MOOD, SEE PAGE 103

SHELTER

GEORGE LOIS / HAROLD KRIEGER

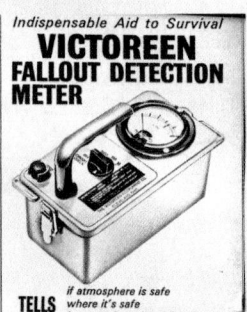
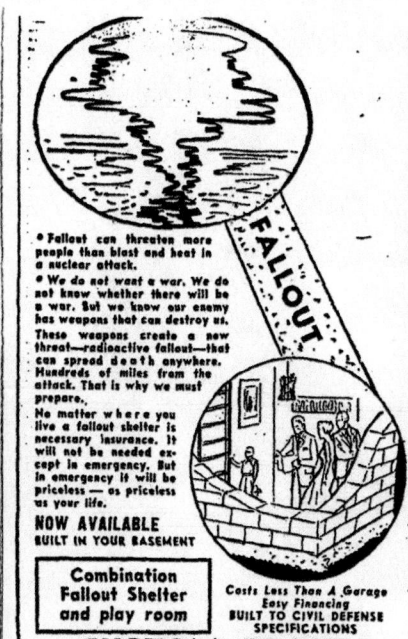
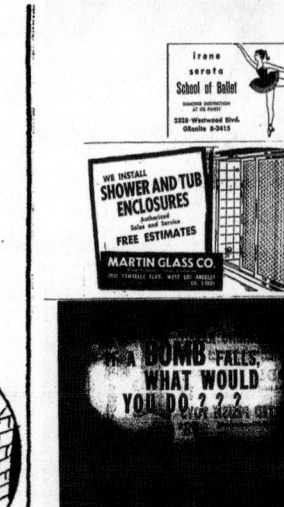
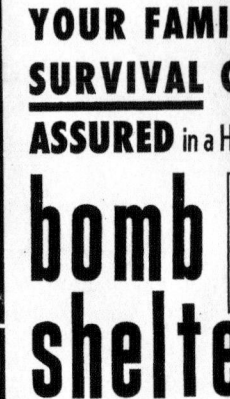
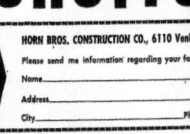

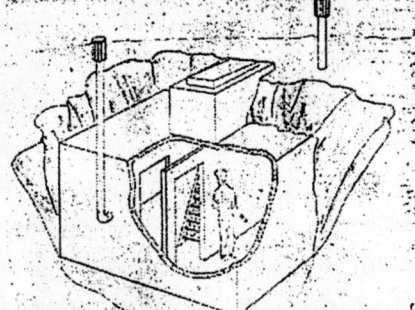

U.S. GOVERNMENT APPROVED!

$1.00

1962 OFFICIAL FALLOUT SHELTER PLANS

FOR HOME & FAMILY

what to do about...

Emergency Shelter
Shelter in Apartment Buildings
Foods • Sanitation
First Aid • Child Care
Bedding • Ventilation
Tools • Radio Reception
Cooking & Heating Equipment

Everything you need to know to survive!

11 Complete Plans

for

BASEMENT, PATIO, OUTSIDE SHELTERS

All Plans Approved by the United States Government Department of Defense

OPPOSITE Publishers capitalized on the crisis by repackaging the free public Civil Defense fallout shelter plans into publications like the *1962 Official Fallout Shelter Plans for Home & Family* from the McNiles Press in Chicago, Illinois, and selling them for profit.

ABOVE In his 1962 book *Run, Dig or Stay?*, author Dean Brelis sought a personal answer to the shelter question that was sweeping the nation: To build or not to build? He ultimately decided against it: "This country, this land, these hopes of America as I see them, are no good down there in the ground."

ABOVE A ghostly skeleton is silhouetted against an abstracted image of a nuclear firestorm on the cover of the 1962 book *No Place to Hide: Fallout Shelters—Fact and Fiction*, edited by Seymour Melman, Professor of Industrial and Management Engineering at Columbia University, in New York. It is a collection of essays debating the value of shelters. Melman opposed them, saying, "the United States deserves and can have more effective ways of coping with international problems than civil defense systems of questionable merit."

ABOVE Men use a battering ram to try to break into their neighbor's fallout shelter after hearing a warning of atomic attack in an episode of the television series "The Twilight Zone" that aired in September 1961. In this drama, a town's respected physician builds a basement shelter and his neighbors ridicule him for his folly. But when an air-raid signal sounds the attack warning, his once-skeptical neighbors rush to his house, first asking—and then begging—for entry. He repeatedly refuses, explaining that he has only enough supplies for himself and his family, so the neighbors agree to destroy the door to gain entry. It turns out that the signal was a false alarm, and everyone finds himself at a loss as to how to behave in the aftermath of this breakdown of civilized behavior. Rod Serling, "Twilight Zone's" creator and the writer of this episode, said he deliberately left the ending ambiguous, endorsing

neither the behavior of the shelter owners nor that of the neighbors. "I was up in the air about it, morally and ethically," Serling said in a radio interview. "I didn't know what position philosophically I could take." Personally, he and his wife weren't building a shelter. "If we survive, what do we survive for? What kind of a world do we go into? If it's rubble, and there is poisoned water and inedible food and my kids have to live like wild beasts, I'm not sure I want to survive."

OPPOSITE An alarmed man races to build a fallout shelter in this cartoon by Joe Orlando, published in *Mad* in April 1962. The comic strip satirizes the atomic anxiety that pervaded the nation during the heightened Cold War tensions between the United States and the Soviet Union.

NUCLEAR JITTERS

ARTIST: JOE ORLANDO

48

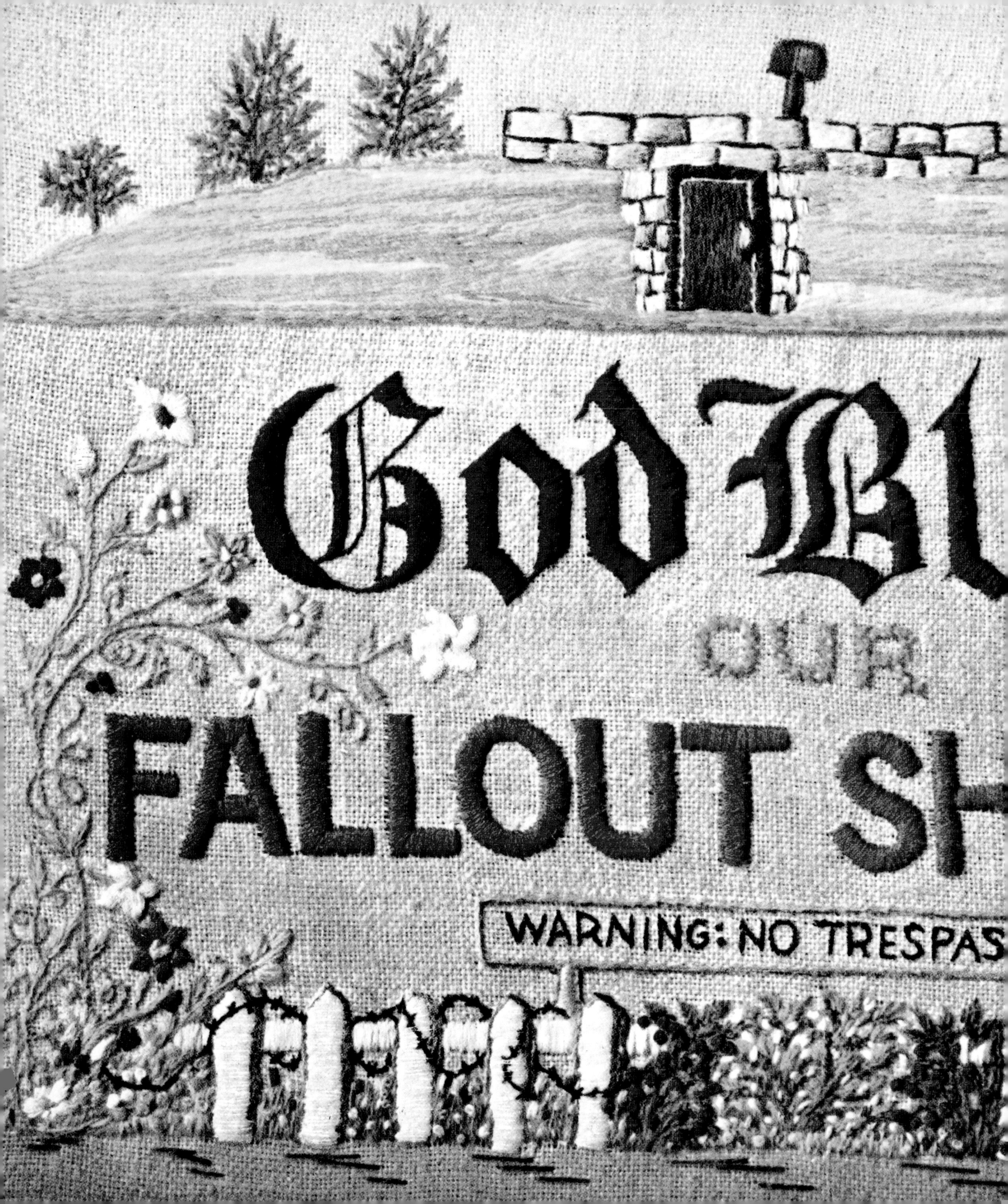
God Bl
OUR
FALLOUT SH
WARNING: NO TRESPAS

LEFT Domesticity embraces the backyard bunker on this sampler, embroidered by Margaret Szep, that was published on the back cover of *Mad* in April 1962. Flowers and vines enliven the scene. A sign warns "No trespassing," and, to emphasize that message, the picket fence is festooned with barbed wire.

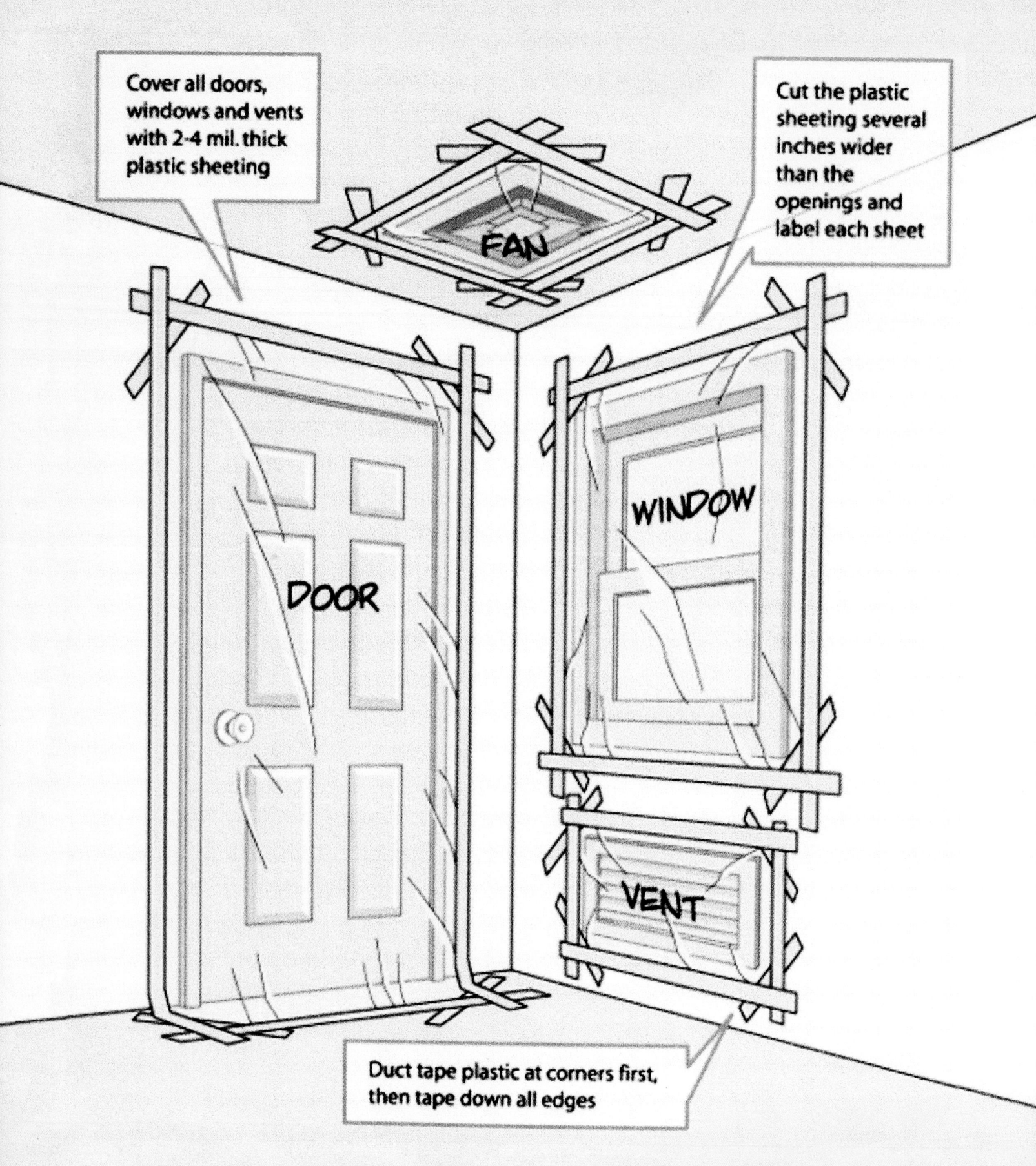

PLASTIC SHEETING & DUCT TAPE

The Cold War officially came to an end on Christmas Day, 1991, when Soviet President Mikhail Gorbachev signed the decree that brought the existence of the U.S.S.R. to an end. The war between the Superpowers was over.

Now, twenty years later, we continue to live with the fearsome legacy of that conflict: the nuclear bomb. The Ploughshares Fund, a foundation whose goal is the elimination of all nuclear weapons, estimated last year that the United States has 9,600 nuclear weapons and Russia has 12,000, and that 2,200 of these weapons in both countries are on "high alert"—ready for use at short notice.

We are living with another legacy of the Cold War: the government policy of "emotion management." After the Sept. 11, 2001, Al Qaeda terrorist attack that killed nearly 3,000 people, Americans were bewildered, confused, upset, uncertain, and frightened—just as they were in the early years of the Cold War, after the U.S.S.R. developed its atomic bomb.

In an attempt to calm the fears of Americans, the George W. Bush administration delivered messages straight out of the 1950s Civil Defense playbook. It acknowledged the threat and the possibility of an attack, just like the 1950 Civil Defense film, *Survival Under Atomic Attack*. Then, it told citizens to "be prepared" by

OPPOSITE This illustration of a "shelter-in-place" came from the Federal Emergency Management Agency (FEMA) website, www.ready.gov. When warned of a nuclear, biological, or chemical attack, a citizen is directed to go inside one room of his residence and cover all vents, windows, and doors with plastic sheeting and duct tape to seal out contaminants. It is the modern-day equivalent of the family fallout shelter.

assembling a three-day supply of food and water, a battery-powered radio, and a change of clothes.

A few months later the White House introduced a color-coded "terror alert" system to advise Americans about the relative level of threat. The five-level color-coded scale went from "low risk" (green), up to "severe risk" (red). It was every American's job to be aware of the nation's "threat level," but exactly what they were supposed to do was unclear. Critics argued that the alert system was merely a political tool created to scare Americans into supporting the Bush administration's War on Terror, including its controversial invasion of Iraq. On February 7, 2003, citing classified intelligence reports, President Bush raised the terror alert level from "elevated" to "high." A panicked nation sought guidance. What could Americans do to protect themselves?

In the event of a biological, chemical, or "dirty bomb" attack, Homeland Security Secretary Tom Ridge told citizens they should go inside a designated "safe room" in their home, and cover all vents, doors, and windows with plastic sheeting and secure it to the walls with duct tape. Ridge's announcement alarmed Americans and set off a national run on plastic sheeting and duct tape. Stores were sold out within days. His recommendations also provoked outrage and ridicule. New York City Mayor Michael Bloomberg called them "preposterous." Television comedian Jay Leno cracked, "This means the only people who are going to survive an attack are serial killers. Who else has duct tape and plastic sheeting in their car?"

Chastened by the criticism, the administration shifted its tone. On February 19, 2003, Secretary Ridge introduced a Civil

Defense-style preparedness program called the Ready Campaign. "Today, America's families declare: We will not be afraid and we will be ready," Ridge said. "Make a kit! Have a plan! Get informed!"

The Ready Campaign, the terror alert system and the safe room, like the 1950s Civil Defense programs that preceded them, are all examples of "security theater," a phrase coined by security expert Bruce Schneier in 2006 to describe a measure that creates an illusion of security without actually providing any protection. To respond to public demands for increased airport security after 9/11, the federal government created the Transportation Security Administration (TSA), which nationalized airport security functions. Tens of thousands of security screeners were hired and a dizzying panoply of equipment was installed at a cost of billions of dollars a year. Meanwhile, uninspected traffic, cargo and people moved freely through the nation's ports, train stations, and highways.

Suspecting that the TSA was nothing more than a very elaborate form of security theater, in 2008, Jeffrey Goldberg, a writer for the *Atlantic*, decided to test the system. In an article called, "The Things He Carried," Goldberg detailed the prohibited items he brought through TSA checkpoints, all of which went undetected by screeners, including pocket knives, lengths of rope, bottled water, and a box cutter. He was even able to board a plane using a fake boarding pass, without a photo I.D., while wearing an Osama Bin Laden t-shirt!

So next time you are at the airport, enduring a hands-on "pat-down," or standing barefoot inside a full-body scanner, you might ask yourself: Is this keeping us safe, or are we merely being bomboozled all over again?

BIBLIOGRAPHY

Abella, Alex. *Soldiers of Reason: The Rand Corporation and the Rise of the American Empire.* New York: Harcourt, Inc., 2008.

About Fallout. Wilding Picture Productions, 1955. Prelinger Archives. <*www.archive.org/details/AboutFal1955*>.

Albert Einstein to President Franklin D. Roosevelt. Aug. 2, 1939. FDR Library: http://docs.fdrlibrary.marist.edu/psf/box5/a64a01.html.

Allen, Woody. Untitled monologue about fallout shelters. *That Was the Week That Was.* NBC. 1965. http://www.tvparty.com/movwoody.html.

Allison, David. "Fallout Shelters At Once." *Architectural Forum* 116 (1961): 127-9.

American Iron and Steel Institute. *Steel Shelters for Fallout Protection.* New York: The Institute, n.d.

Amrine, Michael. "How to Build a Family Foxhole." *Popular Science* March 1951: 113-119.

"Anderson shelter." *The Oxford Companion to World War II.* Oxford Reference Online. Oxford University Press. *www.oxfordreference.com/views/ENTRY.html?subview=Main&entry=t129.e60.*

"Angel Food." *Time* Nov. 18, 1946: http://www.time.com/time/magazine/article/0,9171,777288,00.html.

Anne Arundel County Office of Civil Defense. *Boats as Fallout Shelters.* Annapolis: Ann Arundel County Office of Civil Defense, n.d.

Arnold, David. "Blast from the Past." *Boston Globe* Dec. 12, 1999, 14: 1.

Asimov, Isaac. "Visit to the World's Fair of 2014." *The New York Times,* Aug. 16, 1964: SM20.

Associated Universities. *Report of Project East River.* New York: Associated Universities, Inc., 1952.

"Atomic Bomb Hits Japan." *Los Angeles Times* Aug. 7, 1945: 1.

The Atomic Café. Dir. Kevin Rafferty, Jayne Loader and Pierce Rafferty. New Video Group, 1982. DVD.

"Avon Paying." *Time* June 17, 1966: <*www.time.com/time/magazine/article/0,9171,899253,00.html*>.

Barson, Michael and Steven Heller. *Red Scared: The Commie Menace in Propaganda and Popular Culture.* San Francisco: Chronicle Books, 2001.

Bascom, Willard. "Difference Between Victory and Defeat." *Life* Mar. 18, 1957: 146-162.

"Berlin Crisis Stimulates Fallout Shelter Trade." *Chicago Daily Tribune* Aug. 6, 1961: A8.

Bernstein, Jeremy. *Nuclear Weapons: What You Need to Know.* Cambridge: Cambridge University Press, 2008.

"Booklets That Can Save Your Life." *Chicago Daily Tribune* Aug. 19, 1961: S-A8.

Boyer, Paul. *By the Bomb's Early Light: American Thought and Culture at the Dawn of the Atomic Age.* New York: Pantheon, 1985.

___. "Exotic Resonances: Hiroshima in American Memory." *In Hiroshima in History and Memory.* Michael J. Hogan. New York: Cambridge University Press, 1996.

___. *Fallout: A Historian Reflects on America's Half-Century Encounter with Nuclear Weapons.* Columbus: Ohio State University Press, 1998.

"Breath of Fresh Air Welcomed by Family." *Hartford Courant* Aug. 8, 1960: 7.

Brelis, Dean. *Run, Dig or Stay? A Search for an Answer to the Shelter Question.* Boston: Beacon Press, 1962.

Brown, Harrison and James Real. *Community of Fear.* Santa Barbara: Center for the Study of Democratic Institutions, 1960.

"Buildings Can Be Designed to Resist A-Bombs." *Architectural Record* Aug. 1952: 182-6.

Burchard, John Ely. "Architecture in the Atomic Age." *Architectural Record* Dec. 1954: 119-130.

Cahn, Robert. "A is for Atom." *Collier's* June 21, 1952: 15-17.

Caidin, Martin. *Common Sense and Civil Defense.* New York: WNEW Radio, 1961.

Campbell, John W. Jr. "Choice." *Astounding Science Fiction* November 1950: 4-5.

Capp, Al. Mr. Civil Defense Tells About Natural Disasters. New York: Graphic Information Systems, 1956.

Carlson, Peter. *K Blows Top.* New York: Public Affairs, 2009.

"Can a House be Blast-Resistant?" *Architectural Record* Sept. 1955: 236-7, 248.

Champion Blower & Forge Co., Inc. *Fallout Protection Kit.* Ohio: Collection Ohio Historical Society, 1961.

Cirincione, Joseph. *Bomb Scare: The History & Future of Nuclear Weapons.* New York: Columbia University Press, 2008.

Civil Defense Liaison Office, Office of the Secretary of Defense. *Fire Effects of Bombing Attacks.* Washington, DC: GPO, 1950.

Colomina, Beatriz. *Domesticity at War.* Cambridge: MIT Press, 2007.

Colomina, Beatriz, Annmarie Brennan and Jeannie Kim, eds. *Cold War Hothouses.* New York: Princeton Architectural Press, 2004.

Conant, Jennet. *109 East Palace: Robert Oppenheimer and the Secret City of Los Alamos.* New York: Simon & Schuster, 2005.

Coolidge, Matthew. *The Nevada Test Site: A Guide to America's Nuclear Proving Ground.* Culver City, CA: The Center for Land Use Interpretation, 1996.

Corsbie, Robert L., AIA. "Nuclear Effects and Civil Defense." *Journal of the AIA* Nov. 1959: 83-90.

Cotter, Bill and Bill Young. *Images of America: The 1964-1965 New York World's Fair.* Charleston, SC; Chicago; Portsmouth, NH; San Francisco: Arcadia Publishing, 2004.

___. *Images of America: The 1964-1965 New York World's Fair – Creation and Legacy.* Charleston, SC; Chicago; Portsmouth, NH; San Francisco: Arcadia Publishing, 2008.

Cowan, Edward, "Interest in Fallout Shelter Increases Since 'Berlin'." *Washington Post, Times Herald* Aug. 12, 1961: D9.

Cromley, Ray. *Can We Survive An Atomic War?* Washington, DC: GPO, 1960.

Crosby, Gregory. "Tales of Vegas Past: Going Underground." *Las Vegas Mercury* July 24, 2003. http://www.lasvegasmercury.com/2003/MERC-Jul-24-Thu-2003/21776691.html.

Crowley, David and Jane Pavitt, eds. *Cold War Modern: Design 1945-1970.* London: Victoria & Albert Museum, 2008.

Crump, Spencer. "Family Hopes to 'Waste' $2,500." *Los Angeles Times* July 24, 1960: WS3.

Curtis Jr., William. *Modern Architecture Since 1900.* New York: Phaidon Press, 1996.

Daisy, Mike. If You See Something, Say Something. Performed by Daisy at The Public Theater. New York. 2008.

Dallek, Robert and Terry Golway. *Let Every Nation Know: John F. Kennedy in His Own Words.* Naperville, Illinois: Sourcebooks, Inc, n.d.

Dalton, Dudley. "Experiment in Atomic-Age Housing Will Be Exhibited at the World's Fair." *New York Times* March 29, 1964: R1.

Dash, Norman. "Man Builds Luxurious Shelter to Guard Family, Dogs from Bomb." *Los Angeles Times* Sept. 24, 1961: WS1.

Davis, Tracy C. *Stages of Emergency: Cold War Nuclear Civil Defense.* Durham, NC and London: Duke University Press, 2007.

"Defense Exhibits Going on the Road." *New York Times* Oct 12, 1951: 20.

Department of Agriculture. *Family Food Stockpile for Survival.* Washington, DC: GPO, 1962.

___, *Your Family Survival Plan.* Washington, DC: GPO, 1963.

Department of Defense, Office of Civil Defense. *Family Shelter Designs.* Washington, DC: GPO, 1962.

___, *Survival: How to Protect Yourself, Your Family, Your Community.* Marceline, Missouri: Walsworth Brothers, 1956.

Department of Energy National Nuclear Security Administration. Nevada Test Site. www.nv.doe.gov/main.aspx.

Dick, Philip K. "Foster You're Dead." *Second Variety.* New York: Citadel Press, 2002.

___, "The Perfect Sales Pitch: Buy or Die." *Second Variety.* New York: Citadel Press, 2002.

Dobell, I. "A Place to Hide." *The New Yorker* Mar. 1, 1952: 19-20.

Divine, Robert A. *Eisenhower and the Cold War.* Oxford: Oxford University Press, 1981.

Dobbs, Michael. *One Minute to Midnight.* New York: Knopf, 2008.

Dylan, Bob. Chronicles, Volume 1. New York. Simon and Schuster, 2005.

___, "Let Me Die in My Footsteps." *The Freewheelin' Bob Dylan.* Columbia Records, 1963.

Eden, Lynn. *Whole World on Fire: Organizations, Knowledge, & Nuclear Weapons Devastation.* Ithaca: Cornell University Press, 2004.

Editors of Time-Life Books. *Official Guide: New York World's Fair 1964/1965.* New York: Time Inc., 1964.

Ehrlich, Phyllis. "Young React to the Fear of Radiation." *The New York Times* Nov. 6, 1951: 50.

"Emergency Stockpile." *Chicago Sun-Times* Oct. 27, 1962.

Encyclopaedia Britannica Films. *Atomic Alert.* 1951. Prelinger Collection, Internet Archive: <*http://www.archive.org/details/AtomicAl1951*>.

"Fallout Shelter Brings National Comment." *Hartford Courant* Sept. 10, 1961: 15B1.

"Fallout Shelter Fills Dual Role as a Recreation Room." *Chicago Daily Tribune* Dec, 29, 1959: SW_AB.

"Fall-out Shelter With a Dual Life." *Chicago Daily Tribune* Sept. 17, 1960: N29.

"Fallout Shelters." *Life* Sept. 15, 1961: 95-108.

"Fallout Shelters: Bonanza for Builders?" *House & Home* November 1961: 47-8.

"Fallout Shelters: Boom or Bust?" *The Washington Post, Times Herald* Oct. 1, 1961: B11.

"Fallout Shelters Rousing Interest," *Los Angeles Times* Sept. 3, 1961: F5.

Federal Civil Defense Administration. *Atomic Blasts Creates Fire: Are You Prepared?* Washington, DC: GPO, 1951.

___. *Duck and Cover.* Washington, DC: GPO, n.d.

___. *Emergency Action to Save Lives.* Washington, DC: GPO, 1951.

___. *Facts About Fallout.* U.S. National Archives & Records Administration: <*www.archives.gov/education/lessons/fallout-docs*>.

___. *Fire Fighting for Householders.* Washington, DC: GPO, 1951.

___. *Four Wheels to Survival.* Collection Ohio Historical Society, 1955. omp.ohiolink.edu/OMP/NewSearch?fieldname=xml&search=all&searchstring=four+wheels+to+survival&search.x=111&search.y=11&sort=title.

___. *Revised Civil Defense Air Raid Instructions.* Washington, DC: GPO, 1956.

___. *The Warden Service.* Washington, DC: GPO, 1951.

___. *This is Civil Defense.* Washington, DC: GPO, 1951.

___. *What About You and Civil Defense?* Washington, DC: GPO, n.d.

Duck and Cover. Sponsored by Federal Civil Defense Administration. Archer Productions, Inc., 1951. <*http://www.archive.org/details/DuckandC1951*>.

Let's Face It: America's Atomic Bomb Tests. Federal Civil Defense Administration. DVD. Woodland Hills, CA: St. Clair Entertainment, 2007.

Operation Cue. Produced by Federal Civil Defense Administration,1955. <*www.archive.org/details/Operatio1955*>.

Operation Doorstep. Federal Civil Defense Administration and Byron, Inc.. <*http://video.google.com/videoplay?docid=5476562785126796683#*>.

Our Cities Must Fight. Sponsored by Federal Civil Defense Administration. Archer Productions, Inc., 1951. <*www.archive.org/details/OurCitie1951*>.

Federal Civil Defense Administration and Norwood Studios. *Warning Red, 1956. Atomic Testing.* DVD. St. Clair Entertainment Group, 2007.

Fleming, Louis. "Fallout Shelter Market Sagging." *Los Angeles Times* May 22, 1960: F1.

Foley, Michael S. and Brenda P. O'Malley, eds. *Home Fronts: A Wartime American Reader.* New York/London: The New Press, 2008.

Fradkin, Philip L. *Fallout: An American Nuclear Tragedy.* Boulder: Johnson Books, 2004.

Gaddis, John Lewis. *The Cold War: A New History.* New York: Penguin Press, 2005.

___, *We Now Know: Rethinking Cold War History.* Oxford: Oxford University Press, 1997.

Gallup, George. "U.S. Confused Over Shelters." *Los Angeles Times* Oct. 29, 1961: B6.

Garrison, Dee. *Bracing for Armageddon: Why Civil Defense Never Worked.* Oxford: Oxford University Press, 2006.

Geerhart, Bill. "Watch Out Below." *Bulletin of the Atomic Scientists* Jan.-Feb. 2001: 6-7.

George, Alice Louise. "The Cuban Missile Crisis: Americans' Responses to the Threat of Nuclear War." PhD diss. Temple University, 2001.

George, Alice Louise. *Awaiting Armageddon: How Americans Faced the Cuban Missile Crisis.* Chapel Hill and London: The University of North Carolina Press, 2003.

Gewirtz, Marvin Herbert. "An Investigation of Some Personality Determinants of Attitudes Towards Fallout Shelters." PhD diss. Washington University, 1965.

"Gilbert U-238 Atomic Energy Lab." Oak Ridge Asssociated Universities: <*www.orau.org/ptp/collection/atomictoys/GilbertU238Lab.htm*>.

"Gimme Shelter." *Houston Chronicle* Feb. 20, 2000: 8.

Glasstone, Samuel, ed. *The Effects of Nuclear Weapons.* Washington, DC: Department of Defense & Atomic Energy Commission, 1957.

___, ed. *The Effects of Nuclear Weapons.* Washington, DC: Department of Defense & Atomic Energy Commission, reprinted 1964 from 1962 edition.

Goldberg, Jeffrey. "The Things He Carried." *Atlantic* Nov. 2008: <*www.theatlantic.com/magazine/archive/2008/11/the-things-he-carried/7057/*>.

Goldstein, Daniel M., Katherine V. Dillon and J. Michael Wenger. *Rain of Ruin: A Photographic History of Hiroshima and Nagasaki.* Dulles, VA: Brassey's, 1995.

Goldstein, Richard. "Paul W. Tibbets Jr., 92, Dies: Dropped Atomic Bomb on Hiroshima." *New York Times* Nov. 2, 2007: C11.

Gordin, Michael D. *Five Days In August: How World War II Became a Nuclear War.* Princeton: Princeton University Press, 2007.

Gordon, Jane. "Preparing for the Unthinkable." *The New York Times* Feb. 23, 2003: CT 1.

Goshko, John M. "Confusion, Red Tape Stall Shelter Building." *Washington Post* Oct. 8, 1961: A1.

"Grim Picture of Bomb Hit in Loop is Given," *Chicago Tribune* Aug. 23, 1961: 8.

Grosser, George H., Henry Wechsler and Milton Greenblatt. *The Threat of Impending Disaster: Contributions to the Psychology of Stress.* Cambridge: M.I.T. Press, 1964.

Grossman, Andrew. *Neither Dead Nor Red.* New York: Routledge, 2001.

"Gun Thy Neighbor?" *Time* Aug. 18, 1961: N.p. <*www.time.com/time/magazine/article/0,9171,872694,00.html*>.

"H-Bomb Hideaway." *Life* May 23, 1955: 169-170.

Hampson, Rick. "Nuclear Blasts Recall Time of Shelter, Drills." *USA Today* June 8, 1998: N.p.

Hansen, Henry M. "Gourmet Dining in Fallout Shelter." *Chicago Daily News,* March 14, 1962: N.p.

Heinlein, Robert A. *Farnham's Freehold.* Riverdale, NY: Baen Publishing Enterprises, 1992.

___, "The Last Days of the United States." *Expanded Universe.* Riverdale, NY: Baen Publishing Enterprises, 2007.

Henriksen, Margot A. *Dr. Strangelove's America: Society and Culture in the Atomic Age.* Berkeley and Los Angeles: University of California Press, 1997.

"Here is a Double Purpose Fallout Shelter." *Chicago Daily Tribune* Mar. 4, 1961: N.p.

Hine, Thomas. *Populuxe.* New York: Alfred A. Knopf, 1986.

Hodge, Nathan and Sharon Weinberger. *A Nuclear Family Vacation.* New York: Bloomsbury USA/Macmillan, 2008.

Holland, Madeline. "Meals for Two Days in Fallout Shelter." *Chicago Tribune* June 24, 1960: B1.

Holt, Jim. "Shelter from the Storm." *Los Angeles Times* June 18, 2002: E1.

If the Bomb Falls. Tops Label, Precision Radiation Instruments, Inc.. Los Angeles, CA, 1961.

"Interest Up in Fallout Shelters." *Washington Post* Sept. 2, 1961: B6.

"It's Time to Take Another Look at Fallout Shelters." *House & Home* July 1962: 215-7.

Kaganovich, Gar. "Family of 5 Spends 4 Days in a Shelter." *The Washington Post* Aug. 16, 1959: B12.

Kahn, Herman. *On Thermonuclear War.* New Brunswick, N.J.: Transaction Publishers-Rutgers, 2007.

Kaplan, Fred. *The Wizards of Armageddon.* Stanford: Stanford University Press, 1983.

Keeney, L. Douglas. *The Doomsday Scenario.* St. Paul, MN: MBI Publishing Company, 2002.

Kelsey-Hayes Co. *You Can Protect Your Family Against Fallout.* N.p.: Kelsey-Hayes Co., n.d.

Kennedy, John F. "Letter to the Chairmen of the Senate and House Appropriations Committees on Civil Defense." Letter. Aug. 3, 1962: <americanpresidency.org>.

___. "Radio-TV Address of the President to the Nation from the White House." July 25, 1961. www.jfklibrary.org/Asset+Tree/Asset+Viewers/Audio+Video+Asset+Viewer.htm?guid={2C529501-7B4E-4E12-8C1D-78F9C53F2BDC}&type=Audio.

___. "Radio-TV Address of the President to the Nation from the White House." Oct. 22, 1962." http://www.presidency.ucsb.edu/ws/index.php?pid=8986&st=&st1=.

Kennedy, Robert F. *Thirteen Days: A Memoir of the Cuban Missile Crisis.* W.W. Norton & Co.: New York, 1971.

Kihss, Peter. "Governor Builds 4 Bomb Shelters." *New York Times* July 23, 1961: 40.

Kinsman, Simon. "Fallout Dosage and Monitoring." *California Medicine* Aug. 1960: 72-8. <*http://www.ncbi.nlm.nih.gov/sites/entrez*>.

Knebel, Fletcher. "The Great Fall-Out Shelter Panic." *Look* Dec. 5, 1961: 21-5.

Kornfeld, Howard, M.D. "Nuclear Weapons and Civil Defense: The Influence of the Medical Profession in 1955 and 1983." *California Medicine* Feb. 1983: 207-12. <*http://www.ncbi.nlm.nih.gov/sites/entrez*>.

Krugler, David F. *This is Only a Test: How Washington, D.C. Prepared for Nuclear War.* New York: Palgrave Macmillan, 2006.

Kubo, Michael, Irene Hwang, Jaime Salazar, eds. *Desert America: Territory of Paradox.* Barcelona: Actar, 2006.

Kuran, Peter. *How to Photograph an Atomic Bomb.* Santa Clarita, CA: VCE, Inc., 2006.

BIBLIOGRAPHY

Lamont, Lansing. *Day of Trinity*. New York: Atheneum, 1965.

Larsen, Gordon Lee. "The Fallout Shelter Syndrome." PhD diss. University of Georgia, 1964.

Lear, John, "Hiroshima U.S.A.: Can Anything Be Done About It." *Colliers* August 5, 1950: Cover, 11-16, 64-9.

Lee, Chris Paul. "An Exercise in Utility: Civil Defense from Hiroshima to the Cuban Missile Crisis." PhD diss. Saint Louis University, 2001.

Lichtman, Sarah A. "Do-it-Yourself Security: Safety, Gender, and the Home Fallout Shelter in Cold War America." *Journal of Design History* Vol. 19. No. 1 (2006): 39-55.

Lichtblau, Eric. "Bush Heights U.S. Terror Alert." *New York Times* Feb. 8, 2003: A1.

Luce, Clayton S., and George P. Woodward. "Portable A-Bomb Shelter." U.S. Patent 2,827,004. Mar. 18, 1958.

Lustick, Ian S. *Trapped in the War on Terror*. Philadelphia: University of Pennsylvania Press, 2006.

McFeatters, Ann. "This Time, Ridge Says Be Ready, Not Scared." *Pittsburgh Post-Gazette* Feb. 20, 2003: A1.

McNamara, Robert S. *In Retrospect: The Tragedy and Lessons of Vietnam*. New York: Vintage Books, 1996.

McPhee, John. *The Curve of Binding Energy*. New York: Farrar, Straus and Giroux, 1974.

Malcolm David. "Notes and Comment." *New Yorker* July 18, 1964: 10.

Malcolm, Donald. "Comment." *New Yorker* March 5, 1960: 29.

Maloney, Russell, "Forearmed." *New Yorker* Oct. 24, 1942: 14.

"Man Builds Luxurious Shelter to Guard Family, Dogs from Bomb." *Los Angeles Times* Sept. 24, 1961: WS1.

Mann, Martin. "Plain Facts About Fallout Shelters." *Popular Science* December 1961: 56-60.

Mariner, Rosey B. and G. Kurt Piehler, eds. *The Atomic Bomb and American Society: New Perspectives*. Knoxville: University of Tennessee Press, 2009.

Masters, Dexter and Katharine Way, eds. *One World or None*. New York: New Press, 2007.

Mayer, Albert. "A New-Town Program." *Journal of the AIA* January 1951: 5-10.

Meier, David. "Fallout Shelters' 'Lived-In' Look." *Science News Letter* Oct. 14, 1961: 258-9.

Melman, Seymour, ed. *No Place to Hide: Fact and Fiction about Fallout Shelters*. New York: Grove Press, 1962.

Morland, Howard. *The Secret That Exploded*. New York: Random House, 1981.

Monteyne, David Patrick. "Shelter from the Elements: Architecture and Civil Defense During the Early Cold War." PhD diss. University of Minnesota, 2005.

Morrison, Charles A., ed *Seattle Civil Defense Manual*. Peoria, IL: American Radio Publications, Inc., 1951.

National Concrete Masonry Association and the Office of Civil and Defense Mobilization. *Walt Builds a Family Fallout Shelter*. Washington, DC: 1961.

National Security Resources Board, Executive Office of the President, Civil Defense Office. *Survival Under Atomic Attack*. Washington, DC: GPO, 1950.

The House in the Middle. National Paint, Varnish and Lacquer Association, 1954: <www.archive.org/details/Houseint1954>.

New York State Civil Defense Commission. *You and the Atomic Bomb*. New York: Time, Inc., n.d.

New York State Department of Health. *Assisting at the Birth of a Baby after Enemy Attack if No Doctor is Available*. Albany: New York State Civil Defense Commission, 1962.

1962 Official Fallout Shelter Plans for Home & Family. Chicago: McNiles Press, 1961.

"Noah's Ark." *Esquire* November 1962: Cover.

Norman, Lloyd. "Atomic Blast to Test Family Bomb Shelters." *Chicago Tribune* March 15, 1953: 26.

Oakes, Guy. *The Imaginary War: Civil Defense and American Cold War Culture*. New York: Oxford University Press, 1994.

O'Brien, Robert F., and Kenneth A. Milette. "Method and Means for Operating a Toilet in a Fallout Shelter." US Patent 3,183,525. May 18, 1965.

Office of Civil and Defense Mobilization. *Between You and Disaster: A Civil Defense Home Food Storage Program*. Washington, DC: GPO, 1958.

___. *Clay Masonry Family Fallout Shelters*. Washington, DC: GPO, Feb. 1960.

___. *Continuity of State and Local Government*. Washington, DC: GPO, 1958.

___. *Facts about Fallout Protection*. Washington, DC: GPO, April 1958.

___. "Family Shelters for Protection Against Radioactive Fallout." *Civil Defense Technical Bulletin*. Washington, DC: GPO, 1958.

___. *Handbook for Emergencies*. Washington, DC: GPO, 1958.

___. *Home Protection Exercises: A Family Action Program*. Washington, DC: GPO, 1959.

___. *Individual and Family Preparedness*. Washington, DC: GPO, 1960.

___. *Fallout Protection: What to Know and Do About Nuclear Attack*. Washington, DC: GPO, 1961.

___. *The Family Fallout Shelter*. Washington, DC: GPO, 1959.

___. *Family Fallout Shelters of Wood*. Washington, DC: GPO, 1960.

___. *Family Shelter Designs*. Washington, DC: GPO, 1962.

___. *Personal and Family Survival: Civil Defense Adult Education Course Student Manual*. GPO: Washington, D.C., April 1963.

___. *Reducing the Vulnerability of Houses: Interim Edition*. Washington, DC: GPO, 1963.

___. *Ten for Survival: Survive Nuclear Attack*. Washington, DC: GPO, 1960.

___. *What to do NOW about Emergency Sanitation at Home*. Washington, DC: GPO, 1958.

___. *What You Should Know about the National Plan for Civil Defense and Defense Mobilization*. Washington, DC: GPO, 1958.

Survival Under Atomic Attack. U.S. Office of Civil Defense, 1951. <http://www.archive.org/details/Survival1951>.

Office of the Historian Joint Task Force One. *Operation Crossroads: The Official Pictorial Record*. New York: William H. Wise & Co., 1946.

Office of the President, National Security Resources Board. *United States Civil Defense*. Washington, DC: GPO, 1950.

"120 Shelter Permits issued in 3 Weeks." *Los Angeles Times* Sept. 21, 1961.

O'Neill, Dick. "What You Need to Know to Design and Build Shelters Against Radioactive Fallout." *House & Home* Oct. 1959: 206-8.

"Operation Doorway." *Time* July 5, 1953: <www.time.com/time/magazine/article/0,9171,822856,00.html>.

Orlando, Joe. "Nuclear Jitters." *MAD* April 1962: 48.

Orwell, George. *1984*. New York: Penguin, 1983.

Page, Max. *The City's End*. New Haven & London: Yale University Press, 2008.

Panter-Downes, Mollie. "Letter from London." *New Yorker* Nov. 25, 1961: 207-13.

Previti, Marte. "Combination Swimming Pool and Fallout Shelter." US Patent 3,074,080. Jan. 22, 1963.

"Reader Builds a Bomb Shelter." *House and Garden* March 1942: 20-1.

"Red Alert!" *Los Angeles Times* March 12, 1961: I1

Reppert, Ralph, "The Safest Place in Baltimore." *The Baltimore Sun Sunday Magazine* March 21, 1954: Cover, 16-17.

Rhodes, Richard. *Arsenals of Folly: The Making of the Nuclear Arms Race*. New York: Vintage Books, 2008.

___. *The Making of the Atomic Bomb*. New York: Simon & Schuster, 1986.

Rice, William Maxwell, A.I.A. "Architecture and the Nuclear Age." *Journal of the AIA* July 1958: 61-4.

"Rocky's Fight on Fallout." *Life* April 11, 1960: 81-2.

"Rod Serling Talks about Fallout Shelters with Bob Crane." KNX Radio, Los Angeles, 1961. http://www.youtube.com/watch?v=TghYXxm3wq8&feature=related.

Roeder, Jr., George H. *The Censored War: American Visual Experience During World War Two*. New Haven: Yale University Press, 1993.

Rose, Kenneth. *One Nation Underground: The Fallout Shelter in American Culture*. New York University Press: New York, 2001.

Ross, Richard. *Waiting for the End of the World*. New York: Princeton Architectural Press, 2004.

Rowan, Jan C. "The Shelter Program." *Journal of the AIA* Dec. 1962: 68-9.

Scanlan, Francis V. "CD Chief Urges Early Plans to Preserve Home in Attack." *Hartford Courant* June 14, 1959: 1B.

Scheibach, Michael. *Atomic Narratives and American Youth*. Jefferson, NC and London: McFarland & Company, 2003.

Scheibach, Michael. *In Case Atom Bombs Fall: An Anthology of Governmental Explanations, Instructions and Warnings from the 1940s to the 1960s*. Jefferson, NC and London: McFarland & Company, 2009.

Schlesinger, Arthur M. Jr. *Journals: 1952-2000*. New York: Penguin Press, 2007.

Schneier, Bruce. *Beyond Fear: Thinking Sensibly about Security in an Uncertain World*. New York: Copernicus Books/Springer Science & Business Media, 2006.

Schwartz, Stephen I. *Atomic Audit: The Costs and Consequences of U.S. Nuclear Weapons since 1940*. Washington, DC: Brookings Institution Press, 1998.

Science Service. *Atomic Bombing: How to Protect Yourself*. New York: Wm. H. Wise & Co., Inc., 1950.

"Scientists Warn of World Suicide." *Los Angeles Times* Feb. 27, 1950: 1.

"Sees 2 Million Fallout Shelters in U.S. in 1961." *Chicago Daily Tribune* Dec. 3, 1960: 8.

Schwieder, Elmer William, Jr. "Social Psychological Factors Related to Adoption of Public Fallout Shelters." PhD diss. Iowa State University, 1966.

Serber, Robert. *The Los Alamos Primer: The First Lectures on How to Build an Atomic Bomb*. Berkeley: University of California Press, 1992.

Severud, Fred N. and Anthony F. Merrill. *The Bomb, Survival and You*. New York: Reinhold, 1954.

"The Shelter." Episode 68. *The Twilight Zone*. Sept. 29, 1961.<www.Hulu.com/search?query=twilight+zone+shelter&st=0>.

"Shelter in McLean." *Washington Post* April 14, 1962: A6.

"The Sheltered Life." *Time* Oct. 20, 1961: <www.time.com/time/magazine/article/0,9171,872787,00.html>.

"Shelters for Survival?" *Newsweek* Nov. 6, 1961.

Sherman, Gene. "GIs Four Miles from Biggest A-Bomb Blast." *Los Angeles Times* April 23, 1952: 1.

Sherwood, Robert E., Hanson W. Baldwin, Lowell Thomas, et. al. "Preview of the War We Do Not Want." *Collier's* Oct. 27, 1951: 17-33, 68-129.

Shirer, William L. "Let's Stop the Fall-Out Shelter Folly!" *Good Housekeeping* February 1962: 56-7, 151-2.

"Spare Room Fallout Shelter." *Life* Jan. 25, 1960: 46.

Stein, Justin J., M.D. and Stafford L. Warren, M.D. "Civil Defense: The Medical Aspects of Atomic and Thermonuclear Warfare." *California Medicine* Oct. 1955: 271-281.

Steiner, Barry H. *Bernard Brodie and the Foundations of American Nuclear Strategy*. Lawrence, KN: University Press of Kansas, 1991.

Stimson, Henry L. "The Decision to Use the Atomic Bomb." *Harper's* Feb. 1947: <http://harpers.org/archive/1947/02/0032863>.

Stimson, Thomas E. Jr. "A House to Make Life Easy." *Popular Mechanics* Vol. 97, No. 6: 65-9, 228-30.

Strom, Stephanie. "Behind Duct Tape and Sheeting, an Unlikely Proponent." *New York Times* Feb. 23, 2003: 15.

"Subterranean Atomic Suburbia." *Interiors* February 1953: 70-1.

"Suede Shoe Gyps Pose Growing Threat to Legitimate Fallout Shelter market." *House & Home* Nov. 1961: 47-8.

"Survival: Are Shelters the Answer?" *Newsweek* Nov. 6, 1961: 19-23.

Swayze, Jay. *Underground Homes and Gardens*. Hereford, TX: Geobuilding Systems, Inc., 1980.

Swayze, Kenneth & Jay, Firm. "Henderson Underground House." Architecture Studies Library, University of Nevada, Las Vegas Libraries: <www.library.unlv.edu/arch/archdb2/index.php/projects/view/1083>.

Szep, Margaret. "God Bless Our Fallout Shelter." *Mad* April 1962: Back cover.

Tannenwald, Nina. *The Nuclear Taboo*. New York: Cambridge University Press, 2007.

"Texan Builds a Dreamhouse Underground." *Life* April 24, 1964: 53, 56.

Thomas, Sherry. "Gimme Shelter." *Houston Chronicle* Feb. 20, 2000: TM8.

"Tilley Heaters." Advertisement. *New York Times* Oct. 15, 1961: S19.

"Total Survival for Your Family: BRINC Fallout Shelters." Austin TX: BRINC Fallout Shelters, Inc., n.d.

Truman, Harry S. "Annual Message to the Congress on the State of the Union." Jan. 7, 1953: http://www.presidency.ucsb.edu/ws/index.php?pid=14379.

"Underground Shelter Held Best Protection Against Atom Bomb." *Chicago Daily Tribune* March 18, 1948: A6.

Vanderbilt, Tom. "Buried Alive." *Nest* Spring 2003: 112-27.

___. *Survival City: Adventures Among the Ruins of Atomic America*. New York: Princeton Architectural Press, 2002.

VorHees, Walker, Smith, Smith & Haines. *Shelter Designs For Protection Against Radioactive Fallout*. Albany: New York State Civil Defense Commission, 1960.

"War Can Come: Will We Be Ready?" *Life* Feb. 27, 1950: 19-40.

West, Chuck. *The Fallout Shelter Handbook*. Greenwich, CT: Fawcett Publications, 1962.

"West Coast Gets Ready." *Life* March 12, 1951: 64, 67-68.

Whitfield, Stephen J. *The Culture of the Cold War*. Baltimore/London: Johns Hopkins University Press, 1996.

Whitmore, Benette. *Shelter*. New York: Walker & Co., 2006.

Williams, Robert Moore. *Doomsday Eve*. New York: Ace Books, 1956.

Wills, Gary. *Bomb Power: The Modern Presidency and the National Security State*. New York: Penguin Press, 2010.

Winkler, Allan M. *Life Under a Cloud: American Anxiety about the Atom*. Urbana and Chicago: University of Illinois Press, 1999.

Withey, Stephen B. *4th Survey of Public Knowledge and Attitudes Concerning Civil Defense: A Report of a National Study in March, 1954*. Survey Research Center, University of Michigan: Ann Arbor, 1955.

Wittner, Lawrence S. *Confronting the Bomb*. Stanford: Stanford University Press, 2009.

Wylie, Philip. *The Smuggled Atom Bomb*. New York: Avon Publications, 1951.

X (George Kennan). "The Sources of Soviet Conduct." *Foreign Affairs* 25 No. 4. 1947: 566-82. <http://www.jstor.org/stable/20030065>.

Zeman, Scott C. and Michael A. Amundson. *Atomic Culture*. Boulder: University Press of Colorado, 2004.

Zitner, Aaron. "Ad Drive Targets Terror Threat." *Los Angeles Times* Feb. 20, 2003: A21.

Zuckerman, Edward. *The Day After World War III*. New York: Viking Press, 1984.

Zullo, Joseph. "Fallout Shelter Fills Dual Role as a Recreation Room." *Chicago Daily Tribune* Dec. 27, 1959.

COLLECTIONS

Department of Energy (DOE) OpenNet. www.osti.gov/opennet/

National Archives and Records Administration (NARA), College Park, MD
  Still Picture Reference
    RG 304-NT. Records of the Office of Civil and Defense Mobilization (OCDM)
    RG 311-D, 311-M. Records of the Federal Emergency Management Agency (FEMA)
    RG 397-S. Records of the Defense Civil Preparedness Agency (DCPA)
  Motion Picture, Sound and Video Records Section, Special Media Archives Services Division
    RG 311 FEMA
    RG 263 Central Intelligence Agency (CIA)

Nevada Site Office, U.S. Department of Energy (DOE), National Nuclear Security Administration, http://www.nv.doe.gov/main.aspx
  DOE Digital Photo Archive
    Atmospheric Testing: Doorstop, Ivy, Teapot

New York Public Library, Manuscripts and Archive Division
  New York World's Fair Corporation (1964-1965)

Prelinger Archives. www.archive.org/details/prelinger

University of California at Santa Barbara, Architecture & Design Collection (ADC)
  Paul Laszlo Archive

ENDNOTES

4: "The nuclear paranoia...radiation detector.": "H-Bomb Hideaway," Life, May 23, 1955, 169-170.

PREFACE

10: "During...dangerous." Dylan, 270-272.

CHAPTER 1: ATOMIC ANXIETY

12–15: "On August 2...same.'": FDR Library

"I am become death...worlds.": Rhodes, Making of the Atomic Bomb,1986, 676.

"Now with the release...complete.": Stimson, Harper's, 1947.

"Gene Sherman...deadly mushroom.": Sherman, Los Angeles Times, April 23, 1952.

"In his final...generations.'": Truman, "State of the Union," Jan. 7, 1953.

"In 1951...flames.": Collier's, Oct 27, 1951.

"In its...knockout.": Life, Feb. 27, 1950, 19-40.

"The New York...bomb!": New York Times, Nov. 6, 1951, 50.

"On July 20...Could!'": Rose, 57-64.

CHAPTER 2: YOU CAN SURVIVE!

28–31: "In search of a solution...survive": Associated Universities, Information and Training for Civil Defense, Part IX of the Report of Project East River, 2.

"The report...the bomb.": Oakes, 46-51. See also Grossman, 59-62.

32: "Civil Defense trumpeted...shelters work!": Federal Civil Defense Administration, Operation Doorstep, 1953.

32: "Time magazine pointed out...insidious force.": "Operation Doorway," Time, July 6, 1953.

32–36: Descriptions of 1953 and 1955 tests: Glasstone, Effects of Nuclear Weapons, 1957, 123-140, also "Civil Effects Tests," DOE Nevada Test site website www.nv.doe.gov/nts/default.htm

35: "The time from...less than three seconds.": Eden, 169.

40: "An efficient...public.": Office of the President, U.S. Civil Defense, 1950, 85.

46: "Four-year-old...1955." Caption, UPI Telephoto, April 23, 1955.

50: "Rebecca Fowler...techniques.": Caption, United Press Photo, August 2, 1952.

60: "In 1946...the Washington Post.": "Angel Food," Time, Nov. 18, 1946. "On May 24....Miss Atomic Blast." Miss Atomic Bomb, http://www.nv.doe.gov/main.aspx

CHAPTER 3: BETTER HOMES & BUNKERS

"War is...Doublethink.'": Orwell, 1984, 3, 189-93.

"No one knows...considered doing so.": At the annual meeting of the Governor's Conference in 1961, officials of forty states estimated that more than 60,000 shelters had been built, as reported by Kihss, "Governor Builds," New York Times, July 23, 1961. In a Dec. 30, 1960 letter from President Dwight D. Eisenhower accepting the resignation of Leo A. Hoegh as Director, Office of Civil and Defense Mobilization, the President stated that since 1950 more than one million family fallout shelters had been built.

"The national fallout shelter policy....premises.": National Security Council paper quoted in McEnany, Civil Defense Begins at Home, 59.

"We do not want...priceless as your life.": Office of Civil and Defense Mobilization, The Family Fallout Shelter, 1961, 19.

"Millions saw...bank in 1960.": "Rocky's Fight on Fallout," Life, April 11, 1960, 81-2.

"Protection of...home and a fortress.": Individual and Family Preparedness, 1961, 10.

66: "West Coast Gets Ready," Life, March 12, 1951, 64.

68: Shelter names from Family Shelter Designs, 1962.

74–75: Office of Civil Defense, The Family Fallout Shelter, 1961.

77: Kelsey-Hayes Co., You Can Protect Your Family Against Fallout, n.d.

80: From captions on archival photos, RG 311-D-15, Shelter Construction, Still Pictures Branch, National Archives and Records Administration.

83: West, Fallout Shelter Handbook, 20-26.

83: "Shelter in McLean," Washington Post, April 14, 1962, A6.

84: Bascom, Life, Mar. 18, 1957, 146-162.

86: "Fallout Shelters," Life, Sept. 15, 1961, 100-101.

88: Luce and Woodward, U.S. Patent application. Severud and Merrill, The Bomb, Survival and You, 110-111.

CHAPTER 4: NUCLEAR FAMILY VALUES

"To promote family...90 degrees." Geerhart, "Watch Out Below," 2001.

"Harold Peters...fresh air.": "Breath of Fresh Air," Hartford Courant, Aug. 8, 1960.

"A Houston family...we could find.": "Gimme Shelter," Houston Chronicle, Feb. 20, 2000.

"Thomas A. Powner...to their children.": Kaganovich, "Family of 5," Washington Post and Times Herald, Aug. 16, 1959.

"We entered...if you want to.": , Author's transcription, Allen, That Was the Week That Was, www.tvparty.com/movwoody.html

"Emergency Stockpile," Chicago Sun-Times, Oct. 27, 1962.

99: "Fallout Shelter," Life, Sept. 15, 1961, 104-5.

104: Knoxville News Sentinel website: http://www.knoxnews.com/photos/galleries/2009/aug/07/photos-fallout-shelters/

120: O'Brien and Millette, U.S. Patent application, 1961.

CHAPTER 5: DROP DEAD GORGEOUS

122–125: "Millions saw photographs...today's dollars.": "A Spare Room Fallout Shelter," Life, Jan. 25, 1960, 46.

Descriptions of Swayze and his homes from Swayze, Underground Homes and Gardens, 1980, and Dudley, "Experiment in Atomic-Age Housing," New York Times, March 29, 1964, R1.

"This structure....not suit ours." Malcolm, "Notes and Comment," New Yorker, July 18, 1964, 19.

"You were greeted...affixed to her derrière.": New York World's Fair Contract Compliance Report, May 29, 1965, Box 305, P1.501 Underground House. New York World's Fair 1964-1965 Corporation Records, New York Public Library.

135: Paul Laszlo archive, File: P. Laszlo: Hertz, John, Bomb Shelter; Hertz House, Architecture and Design Collection, University of California Santa Barbara.

142: Description of Las Vegas home is drawn from Vanderbilt, "Buried Alive," Nest, Spring 2003, 112-27 and Swayze, Underground Home.

CHAPTER 6: ON THE BRINK

"An industry....booming.": Fleming, "Fallout Shelter Market Sagging," Los Angeles Times, May 22, 1960, F1.

"As one pool maker...upside down.": "Fallout Shelters," House + Home, Nov. 1961, 47-48.

"In Los Angeles...low-interest loans.": Carl-Ray General Building Contractors advertisement, Los Angeles Times, Aug 20, 1961, 126.

"KCS...with its shelters.": KCS Corporation advertisement, Los Angeles Times, Aug. 31, 1961, A16.

"Fox Hole...one day.": Fox Hole Fallout Shelter advertisement, Los Angeles Times, July 30, 1961, N37.

"An article titled...canines.": Dash, "Man Builds," Los Angeles Times, Sept. 24, 1961, WS1. 2010 dollar value calculated on U.S. Department of Labor website: http://data.bls.gov/cgi-bin/cpicalc.pl

"In an essay...civilization?": Shirer, "Let's Stop," Good Housekeeping, February 1962, 56-57, 151-152.

"Edward Janis...wine cellar.": "Fallout Shelter Brings National Comment," Hartford Courant, Sept. 10, 1961, 15B1.

"The satirical Mad...drops dead.": "Nuclear Jitters, Mad, April 1962, 48.

"More than 100...no real answer.'": Rowan, Journal of the AIA, December 1962, 68.

"On the evening of...Caribbean area.": Kennedy, Radio-TV Address of the President to the Nation from the White House. July 25, 1961. www.jfklibrary.org

"Polls showed...blown to bits anyway.": Gallup, "U.S. Confused Over Shelters," Los Angeles Times, Oct. 29, 1961, B6.

"Let me die...under the ground.": Dylan, "Let Me Die in My Footsteps, 1963 www.bobdylan.com/songs/footsteps.html.

166: "Men use...behavior": "The Shelter," Episode 68, The Twilight Zone, airdate Sept. 29, 1961, www.hulu.com/search?query=twilight+zone+shelter&st=0.

166: "Rod Serling...survive.": "Bob Crane Talks," 1961, KNX Radio, Los Angeles, http://www.youtube.com/watch?v=2UZfuCo0tJG, accessed May 21, 2009.

EPILOGUE

"The Ploughshares Fund...notice.": Ploughshares Fund, www.ploughshares.org accessed Sept. 8, 2010.

"On February 7...duct tape.": Lichtblau, "Bush Heightens," New York Times, Feb. 8, 2003, A1.

"Experts...away." Zitner, "Ad Drive Targets," Los Angeles Times, Feb. 20, 2003, A21.

"Ridge's announcement...in their car?": Strom, "Threats and Responses," New York Times, Feb. 23, 2003, 15.

"On Feb. 19...informed!'": McFeatters, "This Time, Ridge," Pittsburgh Post-Gazette, Feb. 20, 2003, A1.

"To prove that...t-shirt.": Goldberg, "The Things He Carried," Atlantic, Nov. 2008.

RESOURCES

WEBSITES

www.conelrad.com. The authoritative site covering Cold War atomic popular culture, edited by Bill Geerhart.

atomictourist.com. A detailed compilation of bomb-related destinations for the atomic tourist.

civildefensemuseum. Eric Green, a longtime collector of Civil Defense memorabilia, shares his wide-ranging collection on this website.

ATOMIC HOTSPOTS

Atomic Testing Museum, Las Vegas, Nevada.
History of the Nevada Test Site. In the Ground Zero theater, a replica of a bunker, visitors "experience" a multi-sensory nuclear explosion. http://www.atomictestingmuseum.org/

Bradbury Science Museum, Los Alamos, New Mexico.
History of the Manhattan Project and the invention of the atomic bomb; replica of "Fat Man," the world's second atomic bomb used in war when it was dropped on Nagasaki in August 1945. http://www.lanl.gov/museum/

Greenbrier, White Sulphur Springs, West Virginia.
A huge underground bunker built to shelter members of Congress during an atomic attack. The existence of this secret installation, completed in 1962, wasn't revealed to the public until 1992, when the Washington Post published an expose. Public tours are offered. http://www.thegreenbrier.com/site/bunker.aspx

National Museum of Nuclear Science and History, Albuquerque, New Mexico. Highlights: a walk-through exhibit of a re-created family fallout shelter; examples of pop culture items based on the bomb. http://www.nuclearmuseum.org

Nevada National Security Site, formerly known as the Nevada Test Site, 65 miles northwest of Las Vegas, Nevada.
The "ground zero" for nuclear bomb testing in the United States. Access is limited to once-a-month guided tours that must be booked in advance. http://www.nv.doe.gov/outreach/tours.aspx

Smithsonian Museum of American History, Washington, D.C.
An actual family fallout shelter, donated by a woman who had it dug out of her front yard, is displayed in the Science of American Life exhibit. http://americanhistory.si.edu/

Smithsonian National Air & Space Museum, Steve. F. Udvar-Hazy Center, near Dulles Airport in Washington, D.C.
The Enola Gay, the B-29 Superfortress plane that dropped the atomic bomb on Hiroshima, is on display. www.nasm.si.edu/udvarhazy

Titan Missile Museum, Sahuarita, Arizona.
A deactivated nuclear missile silo that is open to the public. It offers overnight stays four times a year. titanmissilemuseum.org

White Sands Missile Range, central New Mexico.
The site of the detonation of the world's first atomic bomb on July 16, 1945, known as Trinity, is open to the public twice a year. http://www.atomicarchive.com/History/trinity/landmark.shtml

ATOMIC MOVIES

Invasion, USA (1952)
The Communists invade the U.S.A. and New York City is hit with an atomic bomb...but did it really happen?

Them! (1954)
Radioactivity from bomb tests in New Mexico transform common ants into giant killing machines.

The Incredible Shrinking Man (1957)
After passing through a cloud of radioactive fallout from an atomic bomb test, a man slowly, but surely, grows smaller and smaller and medical science is unable to help him.

On the Beach (1959)
The last survivors of a worldwide nuclear war await the inevitable arrival of the atmospheric fallout that will kill them.

Panic in Year Zero (1962)
Los Angeles is destroyed by an atomic bomb, and a family heads for the hills in search of survival.

Dr. Strangelove (1964)
A deranged general orders an atomic attack on the U.S.S.R. and the President, politicians and the military desperately try to prevent it from happening.

Fail-Safe (1964)
A series of technical and human errors results in a squadron of U.S. military aircraft being ordered to bomb Moscow. Unable to stop the mission, the President negotiates with the head of the U.S.S.R. to achieve an ultimately horrific solution.

Desert Bloom (1986)
A coming-of-age film set against the backdrop of the atomic bomb tests outside Las Vegas in the 1950s.

Little Boy and Fat Man (1989)
The story of the creation of the atomic bomb by the Manhattan Project in Los Alamos, New Mexico.

Matinee (1993).
Set in Key West during the Cuban Missile Crisis, this film satirizes the atomic exploitation films of the 1950s.

Blast from the Past (1999)
During the first day of the Cuban Missile Crisis, believing the atomic apocalypse was at hand, a paranoid scientist and his pregnant wife move into their underground fallout shelter and shut the door behind them. She gives birth to a boy and thirty-five years later, he emerges to discover the world outside.

Thirteen Days (2000)
A somewhat fictionalized dramatization of the President and his advisors during the Cuban Missile Crisis in 1962.

Indiana Jones and the Kingdom of the Crystal Skull (2008)
Set against the backdrop of the Cold War, it is notable for scenes inspired by the mannequin-equipped houses built at for atomic tests at the Nevada Test Site in 1953 and 1955.

DOCUMENTARIES

The Day After Trinity (1981)
A documentary about the dawn of the nuclear age and the invention of the atomic bomb, with a particular focus on J. Robert Oppenheimer, head of the Manhattan Project. It includes interviews with many of the participants and footage of the bombings of Hiroshima and Nagasaki.

The Atomic Café (1982)
An artful compilation of government Civil Defense propaganda films from the 1950s and 1960s.

The Fog of War: Eleven Lessons from the Life of Robert McNamara (2003)
At the age of 85, Robert McNamara, Secretary of Defense during the Kennedy administration, reflects on war, killing, atomic weapons, and much, much more.

Nuclear Tipping Point (2010)
Four Cold Warriors – William Perry, former Secretary of Defense; George Shultz and Henry Kissinger, former Secretaries of State; and Sam Nunn, former Senator from Georgia and Chairman of the Armed Services Committee—argue for the international reduction of nuclear arms with the eventual goal of total elimination.

Countdown to Zero (2010)
A chilling documentary about the history of atomic weapons and the dangers posed by the possibility of terrorists getting their hands on nuclear materials. It seeks to inspire a worldwide movement to eliminate all nuclear weapons.

U.S. Civil Defense films – Duck & Cover, Survival Under Atomic Attack, Operation Cue, Atomic Alert, Operation Crossroads, A is for Atom, The House in the Middle, Our Cities Must Fight and About Fallout—can be viewed and downloaded from Prelinger Archives: http://www.archive.org/details/prelinger

PHOTOGRAPH CREDITS

Every effort has been made to locate holders of copyright; any omissions will be corrected in future printings.

6: Walter Sanders/Time & Life Pictures/Getty Images; 8-9: Courtesy National Archives (428-NPC-18813); 10: Copyright © 1963, 1965 by Warner Bros. Inc.; renewed 1991, 1993 by Special Rider Music. All rights reserved. International copyright secured. Reprinted by permission; 11: Arts & Architecture Magazine, December 1946 issue. www.artsandarchitecture.com; 12: Used with permission of The Associated Press Copyright © 2010. All rights reserved; 16: Reproduced courtesy of Bonestell LLC; 18–19: Reproduced courtesy of Bonestell LLC; 20: From Chicago Daily Tribune © August 23, 1961. All rights reserved. Used by permission and protected by the Copyright Laws of the United States; 22: Reproduced courtesy of Avon Books/HarperCollins; 25: Courtesy of The Everett Collection; 28: From Chicago Daily Tribune © March 15, 1953. All rights reserved. Used by permission and protected by the Copyright Laws of the United States; 30: Permission granted by Popular Science® Bonnier Corporation. Copyright 2010. All rights reserved; 33–37: Photo courtesy of National Nuclear Security Administration/Nevada Site Office; 44: Courtesy National Archives (311-M-23-22); 51: Courtesy of the Baltimore Sun Company, Inc., All rights reserved; 60: Stock Montage/Archive Photos/Getty Images; 61: Las Vegas News Bureau; 62: From Los Angeles Times © July 24, 1960. All rights reserved. Used by permission and protected by the Copyright Laws of the United States; 64: Shel Hershorn/Contributor/Hulton Archive/Getty Images; 66–67: Loomis Dean/Time & Life Pictures/Getty Images; 68–69: Courtesy National Archives (311-M-09-38); 76: Courtesy National Archives (311-D-14-1); 78–79: Courtesy National Archives (311-M-23-05) 80–81: Courtesy National Archives (311-D-15-6; 311-D-15-7; 311-D-15-8; 311-D-15-4; 311-D-15-5; 311-D-15-2; 311-D-15-3); 83: Keystone/Hulton Archive/Getty Images; 84: Courtesy National Archives (311-M-23-13); 85: Pictorial Parade/Staff/Getty Images; 90:Courtesy Los Angeles Times, from Hartford Courant © June 14, 1959. All rights reserved. Used by permission and protected by the Copyright Laws of the United States; 98-99: Dmitri Kessel/Time & Life Pictures/Getty Images; 101: From Chicago Daily Tribune © August 23, 1961. All rights reserved. Used by permission and protected by the Copyright Laws of the United States; 108: Oak Ridge Associated Universities; 109: Courtesy of Sears Holdings Historical Archives; 112: Courtesy of the Ohio Historical Society; 120: From Chicago Daily Tribune ©December 27, 1959. All rights reserved. Used by permission and protected by the Copyright Laws of the United States; 122: Courtesy National Archives (311-D-16-4); 127: From New York Times © March 29, 1964. All rights reserved. Used by permission and protected by the Copyright Laws of the United States; 134–135: Architecture & Design Collection, University Art Museum, University of California, Santa Barbara; 136–37: Courtesy National Archives (311-D-16-3; 311-D-16-2); 140–151: Robert Polidori; 152: From Washington Post © October 23, 1962. All rights reserved. Used by permission and protected by the Copyright Laws of the United States; 154: Courtesy of The Everett Collection; 157: Photo by Ralph Morse/Life Magazine, Copyright Time Inc./Time & Life Pictures/Getty Images; 158: Howard Koslow, artist/illustrator; From Newsweek Magazine © November 6, 1961; 163: Cover image from: Run, Dig or Stay reprinted by permission of Beacon Press. Cover image from: No Place to Hide, copyright © 1962 by Grove Press, Inc. Used by permission of Grove/Atlantic, Inc; 164: 165–167: From MAD # 70 © 1962 E.C. Publications, Inc. All Rights Reserved. Used with Permission; 176: Author photograph by Michael Steinberg.

INDEX

ACKNOWLEDGMENTS

One summer day, I found myself standing in the middle of a grassy park in Flushing, New York, wishing I had a backhoe. I had come to see the site of the Underground Home exhibition at the 1964–1965 New York World's Fair, a traditional home with a difference: it was buried underground so that its residents could survive a nuclear war. It was the ultimate expression of the tangled knot of insanity, absurdity, paranoia, and terror that gripped the emotions of Americans during the early years of the Cold War.

The family fallout shelter was the subject of my master's thesis in architectural history at Columbia University. The ink on the thesis was barely dry when Joan Kron read it, told me it could be a book, created the title—*Bomboozled*—and passed it along to her friend Suzanne Slesin, publisher of Pointed Leaf Press. She shared Joan's enthusiasm and you are holding the result in your hands.

I thank Joan for her encouragement, counsel, and wisdom. I thank Suzy for her care, patience, attention, interest, enthusiasm, support, and sense of humor. I thank art director Stafford Cliff for combing through more than 800 images of widely disparate materials—bookcovers, magazines, Civil Defense films, radiation meters, and much more—and not only making sense of it all, but figuring out how to use them to create a beautiful book. And I thank him for his helpful comments on the manuscript.

I am very grateful to Columbia University for its unusual policy of permitting members of the public to audit classes. In 2003, through the School of Continuing Education, I audited an introductory architecture course taught by Hilary Ballon, who later generously sponsored my application for the graduate program in architectural history at Columbia's Graduate School of Arts and Sciences. I also thank Barry Bergdoll, my thesis advisor.

More thanks: My agent Will Lippincott; Holly Reed and Teresa Roy, Still Picture

Reference, National Archives and Records Administration; Jennifer Whitlock, Architecture and Design Collection, University of California Santa Barbara; and Martha DeMarre, Department of Energy.

I thank everyone at PLP: the unflappable Regan Toews, Jonathan Lazzara, Dominick Santise Jr., Nyasha Gutsa, and Deanna Kawitzky.

My heartfelt gratitude goes to my friends who encouraged and supported me through school and through this project: Kate Jennings, Nancy F. Smith, Catherine Winters, Carol Wallace, and Sioux Oliva, Ph.D., Geoffrey and Kathryn Precourt, Carol Klyman, Janet Junod, and Rick Moranis.

And to my husband, Randall Rothenberg, for his support and for always being there.
—SUSAN ROY New York, November 2010

Susan Roy is a writer and editor on architecture, design, and cultural history. The founding managing editor of *Allure,* she has also held senior editorial positions at *This Old House, SELF, Good Housekeeping,* and *Avenue.* She has a master's degree in architectural history from Columbia University and *Bomboozled* is loosely based on the subject of her thesis, "The Family Fallout Shelter During the Cold War."

ABOVE An illustrated timeline by Robert Osborn satirically depicted man's architectural progress in the *New Republic* of January 15, 1962.

FRONT ENDPAPERS The *Fallout Shelter Handbook* depicted the Concrete Block Shelter interior in a mid-century modernist style.

BACK COVER A crystal chandelier, reinforcing the surrealistic "indoor-outdoor" feeling, hangs above the patio furniture of an underground house.

Pointed Leaf Press would especially like to thank Joan Kron for all her help and support; and photographer Robert Polidori (along with Marianna Coleman and Brittany Lee Sanders of his studio.) Also Beacon Press, Arthur Gallego, Pawel Kaminski, Justin King, the Las Vegas News Bureau, Stan Lovenworth, Roger Ma, Oak Ridge Associated Universities, Penguin Group USA, Michael Steinberg, and David Travers.

POINTED LEAF PRESS, LLC.
136 Baxter Street, New York, NY 10013
www.pointedleafpress.com

Pointed Leaf Press is pleased to offer special discounts for our publications. We also create special edition copies and can provide signed copies upon request.
Please contact info@pointedleafpress.com for details or visit our website at www.pointedleafpress.com.

Printed in China by Globalink

First edition
10 9 8 7 6 5 4 3 2 1
Library of Congress Control Number: 2010939730
ISBN: 978-0-9823585-7-3

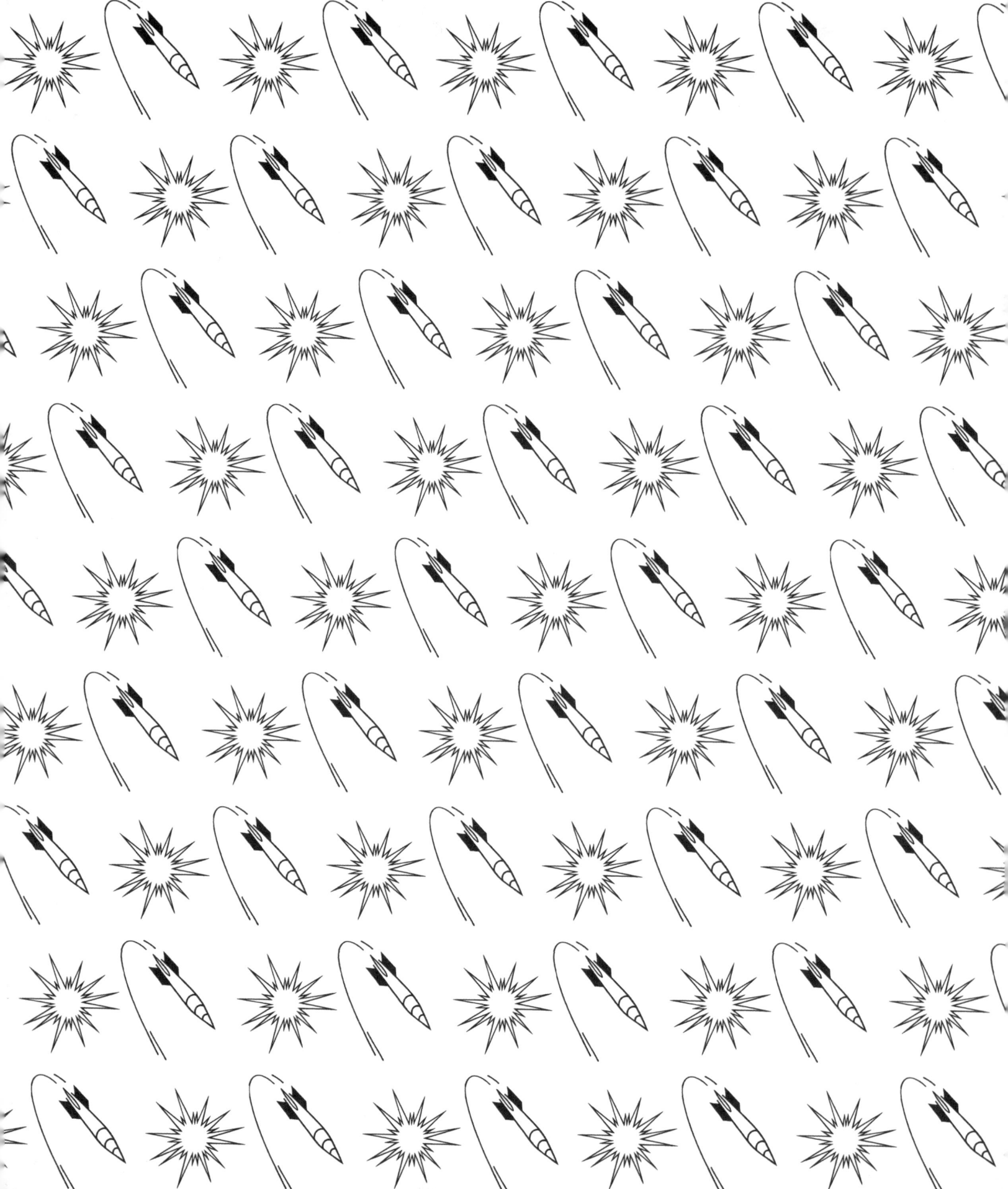